What They're Saying a

*"It's an extraordinary adve~~~~~~~~~~~~~~~~~~
tion of the goodness of man . . . a book jor anyone* ~~~
*wondering why we are all going through the amazing explosive
changes on planet Earth at this time."*

Anne Price, R.N., Healer
Seattle, WA

*"If Bashar doesn't take the reader on a metaphysical joyride, he/she
should read it again. This is far more than a book; it is a brilliant
gateway to the future."*

Theodore Hall, Ph.D.
New Haven, CT

*"After reading hundreds of what I call 'Better World' books, a few
stand out . . . and this volume is easily in the top five per cent.
How about a few adjectives: clarity, reaffirmation, empowering
joyride— I think you get the idea. . . . It's all very energizing and
reassuringly believable. It's also one of the most powerful recom-
mendations for having some serious fun here on planet Earth."*

Michael Honsa
The Open Line
Spokane, WA

*"Be advised, the ETs are here, and their intentions are far more
electrifying than we could ever have dreamed. Their purpose is
neither to conquer nor to save, but to establish foreign relations
with us, and in Bashar's own words, 'to be of assistance in reflecting back to you what you already know about the power you
have to create the lives you want. . . .' This may well be the most
important book you will ever read."*

Joan A. Bishop, Editor,
Dolphin Dreams Newsletter,
Ferndale, WA

*"An Rx for doubts, fears and uncertainties . . . very inspiring
. . . the future looks brighter than ever."*

Dr. Peggy Horne,
Stress Management
Lake Arrowhead, CA

More . . .

"Bashar takes us into a whole new world, expanding our understanding of extraterrestrial civilizations and their interaction with our Earth. Definitely well worth reading."

Daved Rubien
MUFON State Director
Cranston, RI

"Bashar is not some strange alien with whom we cannot relate, but instead the ultimate in sanity and reason. He gives us information about what is going on in both the extraterrestrial realm and on our Earth, imparting solid basic truths that align perfectly with our great Earth masters, such as Buddha and Christ. This alignment is what fascinated me the most. Highly recommended reading for a clear look at basic philosophical and spiritual truths."

Thea Greenberg, Director
Holistic Center for Higher Awareness
Altadena, CA

"This 'future voice' provides one of the clearest, in-depth insights yet on how we create our experiences on this physical plane of existence, and how we can change these experiences for the better. It offers some simple working tools for achieving higher levels of love, joy and fulfillment. For anyone who desires to enhance his understanding of life, and discover how he can evolve in ways he desires, I highly recommend the book."

Mark Jones, former Editor,
Free Spirit Magazine,
Los Angeles, CA

"This book is a great gift for Earth civilization at this time. Thanks to the joint efforts of dedicated souls such as Darryl Anka, Bashar, Luana Ewing and those of us Earth people interested in remembering Who We Are and in Being Willing to Reclaim Our Power, we can see a peaceful future ahead for this troubled planet. Thank you for this magnificent gift. We are grateful."

Dorothy Compinsky,
Violinist/Teacher
Santa Monica, CA

BASHAR:

Blueprint
for Change

BASHAR:

Blueprint
for Change
A Message from Our Future

*Material Channeled
from an Extraterrestrial*
by DARRYL ANKA

Compiled, Edited and Arranged
by LUANA EWING

New Solutions Publishing
4838 50th Avenue S.W.
Seattle, Washington 98116
(206) 935-7689

Publisher's Cataloging in Publication
(Prepared by Quality Books Inc.)

Bashar.
    Bashar, blueprint for change : a message from our future / channeled
material from an extraterrestrial by Darryl Anka [channel]; compiled
and edited by Luana Ewing.—
    p. cm.
    ISBN 1-56284-113-0

    1. Channeling (Spiritualism)   2. Man.   3. Civilization.   4. Life on
other planets.   I. Anka, Darryl, 1951–   II. Ewing, Luana, 1934–
III. Title.

BF 1301   133.93
                                                       QBI90-340

First Printing: October 1990
Second Printing: August 1991

Published in the United States of America

Contents

Cover photo by Debbie Andersen

Acknowledgments

First and foremost I thank Darryl—for his years of bringing Bashar to us, and for his giving me permission to create and publish this book. It has been a great joy for me to do so.

In January 1987, while listening to an excellent session that had been recorded very poorly, I suddenly wanted to transcribe the session, getting it down on paper for easier enjoyment by others. Then followed more than three years of transcribing session after session, giving them to Darryl's agent Steve Muro for him to sell. Now, while it had been immensely satisfying for those years to transcribe over 100 taped sessions, I would ask myself now and then, 'Why do I continue donating my time to these transcripts?"—having rapidly moved to doing them full time. And another question, "Why was I continuing in a typesetting job for so long after wanting to move on to something else?"

In February 1990, with a nudge from Ted Hall, the answer became crystal clear: do a book! That's why all the transcribing. That's what the typesetting/editing training was for: to compile, edit, typeset and publish a Bashar book myself! . . . Thank you, Ted—first for the initial inspiration, and then for your expert and valued proofing and advice.

Next I want to thank Anne Clarke and Debbie Andersen, both of whom provided the most loving support imaginable, besides offering suggestions and helping with the proofreading. Extra thanks to Anne for helping put together the Index, and more thanks also to Debbie for her search for just the right sunrise/sunset.

Craig Jones deserves a hefty pat on the back for his conscientious, professional touch on the paste-up, letting me hound him into giving up much week-end time to do so. And thanks to all my reviewer friends for their support and good words about the book. Also to Andrew Bayuk for a very special private session with Bashar. (Andrew channels him also, as do several other people around the world.)

Above all, my deepest thanks and loving gratitude go to Bashar for helping this project "fall together" so magically, quickly and well. For as he said to me in that private session (when the book was finished), "Don't you understand we've been coming through you all along?". . . And so the strong feeling that I had been getting help in compiling and arranging the book was confirmed. No wonder it had come together relatively easily—and so joyfully!

Equally as much I would like to thank *me*, for finally allowing myself to follow *my* excitement also, no longer enviously watching others follow theirs. I wouldn't have missed this trip for the world.

Luana Ewing
July, 1991

Foreword

One of the most amazing things about this book is its timeliness. It comes to us at the perfect stage of the New Age transformation. As more and more people become aware of the inherent power within them, any aid to the handling, management and channeling of that power falls within perfect timing.

In addition, a most distinguishing feature of this material is its applicability. So many books and sources sound so good to most of us, but do not seem so achievable in practice. This material is workable within the parameters of each of our particular lives. Generally speaking, when we are creating upsets, our sense of reason seems to alter. We don't see things as clearly as usual. Most of our "educated" thinking falls by the wayside, and instead of acting, we are more likely to *react*.

The information you will read within these pages is obtainable and usable when *in* this reactive frame of mind. It literally allows you to transform these situations into useful components of your life. The mechanics for creating your life according to your preferences are outlined in this book. By applying it you will enable yourself to live the life you choose, doing what you have always most wanted to do. It will enable you to live on a planet where people can actually respect one another's viewpoint, regardless of whether they agree with that viewpoint or not. It will also enable you to live a life of harmony, abundance, fulfillment and joy.

Lastly it can reempower you to have FUN. The very implementation of this type of thinking is, in and of itself, FUN. If this sounds at all appealing, read on.

Andrew D. Bayuk, D.C.

About the Channel

Darryl Anka is an illustrator and designer and has a partnership in a special effects miniatures company. His company has for some time been working on a futuristic theme resort, a dynamic simulation of our future world—which will demonstrate the possibilities of what can be done.

Late in 1983, in a channeling class, Bashar and Anima began coming through Darryl. By mid-1984 he was channeling both entities once a week to more and more people.

Then over the next 2½ years Darryl's channeling sessions expanded to several nights a week. By now he was almost solely doing Bashar, as word spread and Bashar's popularity grew. Early in 1987 a necessary larger space in Encino was found to accommodate the crowds, these crowds quickly growing to average over 200 people at the regular Thursday evening sessions. Meanwhile Darryl was also channeling for other groups as well, while giving private sessions on request, and traveling throughout the United States and Japan doing public sessions and workshops.

Now that Darryl's excitement, and thus his main focus, is on his futuristic theme park, **Andromeda**, he has been only occasionally available for channeling since early 1989. This is by mutual agreement with Bashar, who is excited for Darryl and his theme park also, and is sending much energy to Darryl's project.

Darryl is at present residing in Woodland Hills, California.

Introduction

Darryl on Channeling

My basic understanding of most channelings is that they are usually the product of an arrangement, an agreement that is made on some conscious, unconscious or subconscious level between the person you are and another facet of yourself. Or it is an aspect of another consciousness somewhere else in time or space on a different plane. Your life contains whatever circumstances are necessary to get you to remember making such an agreement, and to give you whatever tools and abilities you need to fulfill that agreement, if you still have a mind to.

Each of you will have a different life style. Therefore, how you arrive at that recognition will be different according to the different person you are. One person might take a long time to realize that such a thing is possible for him. Another individual will one day be walking down the street and be hit with a recognition that something has changed within his consciousness, something representative of a new direction that would be beneficial for him to go in—not only for himself, but perhaps for others as well. So how everyone gets there is different.

How I got there began about 17 years ago. On two occasions within the same week, with four friends present the first time, and two friends present the second time, we had very close broad daylight physical sightings of Bashar's craft over Los Angeles. The first time it was about 150 feet distant, and the second time about 70 feet distant. On both occasions the craft was approximately an equilateral triangle, about 40 feet on a side, roughly about eight feet thick, of a very dark gray metallic substance.

After we all got excited about seeing this, we began to double-check our stories with each other, to make sure we had seen what we thought we had seen. All of us agreed it wasn't a plane or helicopter, but was something unusual, and very obviously so, since we had about a 30 to 40-second opportunity to view this thing in broad daylight.

What I didn't understand at that time —aside from having seen a so-called UFO— and what I have come to understand since then through research and through the various events that have happened in my life, is that those sightings were Bashar's way of tapping me in the subconscious memory to get me to remember that I made this agreement, and to get me to start learning the things I needed to learn to fulfill that agreement with him. It turns out that a lot of preparation was necessary, in terms of my mental patterns, my thought patterns, my emotional patterns, that needed changing in order to make some sort of a link possible between our respective mentalities.

Now, Bashar does present himself as a member of an extraterrestrial community. Most channelings involve connections with disembodied forms of consciousness, and on that level there are probably about three types that have been classified—or at least informally so. The first type has to do with your own consciousness. Channeling, as Bashar has said, is really only that process of allowing more than your typical day-to-day personality to come through in a free-flowing stream of consciousness in a very creative way.

Any artistic endeavor at all, under the fundamental definition of channeling, is a manifestation of channeling. So all aspects of channeling, all levels, all types, always involve a portion of your own consciousness at least. You are always involved in the process, since it's coming through you. Your own consciousness may be all that is involved, but it does manifest itself in a number of ways that seem to present other personalities, aside from the one we normally believe ourselves to be. Therefore other categories have been set aside to more or less describe these different levels of channeling.

The second level is basically what is called mediumship, involving disembodied spirits communicating—people who have died who have been physically alive at one time or another. These now exist as non-corporeal consciousness, and somehow have the ability to communicate through mental processes with people who are still alive. This is probably the most commonly known, the most familiar.

The other type would be dealing with levels of consciousness in other dimensional planes that have never experienced at all the physical reality with which we are familiar. These have never taken any kind of physical form, as we would describe physicality; they are disembodied as their natural state.

The fourth type, which is this type —not to imply that one is more powerful or better than any other— is what is called the extraterrestrial connection. Basically what this means is that a mental connection is made, a channeling is done with and between another entity who, for lack of a better term, is also discrete as a personality like we are. Bashar has explained that his "people" have physical beingness; they are not disembodied spirits, but rather a literal race of beings. They do have existence in another dimensional plane, as he describes it—in a slightly different frequency from our dimension. And so unless a shift or adjustment is made in their frequency, they are invisible to us, and we are invisible to them.

However, as they are somewhat humanoid, and do have a form that is not too dissimilar from ours, Bashar has often described that form in these sessions. Being in a physical existence, I feel he can relate perhaps a little more strongly to our human lives than can a disembodied consciousness.

But the most important thing I want to say about these interactions between you and Bashar is as follows, and this to me is the most critical thing I could say: I have my own validation for Bashar being who he says he is—because of my sightings, because of my experiences, because of unsolicited validations that have come from many different sources. These reinforce that what I'm experiencing is real, at least in my world—real enough to allow it to continue to occur, because the information that comes through seems to be valid for many people. It allows them to make the changes in their lives they want to make.

The thing I want to stress most importantly is that there is absolutely nothing about this interaction that in any way insists you must believe Bashar is who he says he is. I cannot prove this to you at this time anyway. You must each decide for yourselves whether the data is something you want to use. If you find it works for you, then by all means utilize it. If you find it doesn't work for you, don't worry about it. You will get what you need somewhere else.

None of this is impressed on you to force you to believe that he is who he says he is. Whether he is a separate being or not is not really ultimately what's important. The idea is that whatever is going on here, it represents the idea that all people have an ability to lock into certain states of consciousness within us, and to access information that can be applied in positive ways in our lives. Just as equally anything can be applied in negative ways also—and it's up to us which one we choose.

A word about what transpires for me in this channeling process. I allow myself to go into what most people call a trance state. This is somewhat of a misnomer. I'm in an altered state of consciousness, and I know there is an interaction going on, but I go into a type of altered state where it's very much like a daydream for me, like an energetic daydream. I feel the energy; I feel the emotions; I feel the basic concepts of the interactions. But I don't really hear the words. This is the same as if you were daydreaming very strongly about something when someone walked into the room and called your name, and you didn't hear them because you were not paying attention, not being focused in that way.

The experience is more like listening to music than like listening to a conversation. It moves me, and I know something is being communicated; the raw essence of the idea is instilled within me, but only in a way that I can apply it in my life. I don't have a recollection of how he discussed the idea with you specifically. That just passes right by me, words in this state being secondary.

As Bashar has described it, and as I understand the process, my consciousness becomes diffused, or softened and expanded, which allows the frequency of his consciousness to impress itself upon my energy. When that occurs, a telepathic link is formed between us and I become susceptible to his frame of reference. So what is actually happening here is as follows: he is not coming down and possessing me; he's not inhabiting my body. As far as I understand, that is not literally what is happening anywhere in any channeling, and never has at any time. Our definition of that circumstance makes it seem as if that is so. What I understand is happening is that my energy, the energy I always have as myself, is being transformed into a model, or a pattern of his energy, so that what you are getting is a representative mirror of his personality, of his thoughts, made out of the energy that exists right here and right now—which is my energy.

As such, when he speaks to you, he is not literally speaking English. I am "programmed" with English, and functioning like a translation box for him. Whatever concepts he sends with his thoughts are automatically translated by my subconscious into whatever language I am comfortable and familiar with. It's an automatic process. If there are words coming through I don't comprehend, it causes a fuzziness or static in the translation going the other way. He can discuss most concepts with you, but now and then there may be a confusion in terminology because of the way he looks at things, and because of the way we look at things.

Bashar's point of view is relatively expanded—relative to the way we generally perceive things. Therefore, his point of view gets us to think in new ways, and that's the biggest benefit he usually has on people. Therefore I urge you to go ahead and take advantage of that expanded point of view, and may your lives be the better for it.

Dedicated to Margo Chandley and Steve Muro,
for receiving Darryl and Bashar into their
homes in the early years.

PART I

Transforming Earth

CHAPTER ONE

Masters of Limitation

What is your purpose in coming here, Bashar?

First of all, let me say that even though you seemingly perceive a single identity, I represent hundreds of thousands, even millions of consciousnesses that make up the Association of Worlds. In their own manner they have—telempathically, you could say— "plugged into" my consciousness for each of the interactions we have with you. So understand that while there may be a gathering of individuals on your side for these channelings, there is a gathering of individuals on our side as well.

We have interacted with many other civilizations that are going through transformations such as yours, civilizations that are in stages of development where they have not yet allowed themselves to realize they could interact with other worlds in an open way. Those of us assisting in your transformation do so in an unobtrusive way that allows you to know *you* are responsible for that transformation, and not us.

Be aware, however, that we have a non-interference directive totally in effect. This is the idea that any new civilization is left alone if it is in an evolutionary stage where it does not necessarily express an absolute conscious recognition that there are other civilizations with which it could communicate. The idea of our existence is not forced upon any world until such time as that world exhibits the willingness to communicate in positive, loving ways.

Using this format we thus stay one step removed for that and many other reasons. First of all, we recognize that you usually have a penchant upon your planet—at least in the past have had a

3

penchant—for following the messenger, and not listening to the message. Therefore, since the information is more important than who we are, for now we remain removed, allowing the information to have a paramount place in your minds. For if we were to appear and utter these phrases ourselves in physical form, people would be bowing left and right. Rather than your continuing to hold us above yourselves in some sort of awe, we wish to assist you in returning your power to yourselves, helping you to wake up and take back responsibility for the creation of your lives.

Why are you here at this time in our history?

We have always interacted with every civilization knowing beyond the shadow of a doubt that they are in every way equal to any civilization of which we are aware. If you, however, label other civilizations more advanced than your civilization, know that this is not just a matter of labeling; it is also a matter of perspective. But this may now afford you an opportunity to realize your civilization is changing and expanding, perhaps in ways similar to how our civilization has expanded. We recognize that your world is exploring ideas and levels of consciousness we have already explored, ones which have worked for us. As you create that exploration in your consciousness, we note that you radiate a particular frequency. We have picked up on this frequency and accepted it as an invitation, in a sense, to interact with you.

We communicate in order to reflect to you some of the ways these ideas you are exploring have worked for us, so that if you wish to, you can adapt and adopt some of them into your own reality—IF you find they work for you. This method always works best, because it allows you to decide for yourselves what the information is and whether it works for you or not.

We are in this interaction to put ourselves out of a job. Our dearest desire is to have there come a day on your planet when you do not need us at all. And then on that day we will be able to interact with you on an equal level. However, for that level of interaction you must open the door for us. It's your planet. The way you open that door is not by *wishing* for us to interact with you; not by the desire alone, but by expressing more of a desire for *you* to interact with *yourselves* as equals. Only when you do that among yourselves do you create the vibration that makes it possible for us to be able to come through into your dimension and see you face to face.

Very Low Frequency

For you see, there is an energy reason keeping us at bay. You have created your society to be one full of people who hide things from themselves, and this has created gaps in your energy field. These gaps create the illusion that you are vibrating at a very low and slow frequency. We are being of assistance to you so as to give you an opportunity to recognize that you can change your frequency and go through your transformation with an absolute minimum amount of negativity, in terms of the manifestations as they occur on your planet . . . in the great changes which will take place during the next few years.

We do not mean this to sound egotistical or derogatory to you in any way, but when you encounter beings who are willing to be their full selves, these beings operate at a higher frequency. We could use the analogy of a faster spinning gear and a slower turning gear. When you bring a slow gear and a fast gear together without allowing them to match frequencies, and jam them into physical interaction, there will only be a disruption, a psychotic breaking. Because the idea is that our frequency physiologically in a sense would force your vibration to accelerate at a higher level by being in proximity to our frequency. That would allow all the things many of you have kept buried within you to rise to the surface, forcing you to face them. This can cause psychotic shock to certain individuals.

Therefore, being of a different vibratory field than you, we cannot interact with you in a physiological way unless there is some meeting of the minds, or some pre-arranged purpose fitting the timing that best serves all those who are concerned. When the timing allows it; when it serves the purpose that has been agreed upon by you, we shall meet face to face. If we have not done so, then I will ask you to trust that the timing is not appropriate. And to know that when it *is* appropriate, nothing will keep us away!

Bashar, how can you prove to us you are who you say you are?

First and foremost, the main purpose of this interaction is not for the validation of *my* existence; it is for the validation of *yours.* We are not here to prove anything to you, nor can we force you to believe we are who we say we are. If your world insists it does not want to know we exist, we must respect that. The governmental structures you have created on your planet at this point are still insisting we do not exist, and therefore we cannot violate that chosen belief system. You have created your governments, and that is who you all *are.* When you make changes within the structure you have said represents you, then they will represent what you say is the popular will. At this point, they do not.

Do understand that your government is very well aware of our existence—*very* well aware. But because you have created your society in layers that can hide information from other layers, many of your members do not have that data—although many of the mainstream members within your governments do. Quite a number of civilizations have already interacted with your world —among them individuals from our world, Essassani, and from Arcturus and Sirius. And there are the Pleiadians and the Zeta Reticuli. There have been actual physical interactions between members of our society and your government.

A lot of us would like you to land your ships now, Bashar.

Before we physically land on your planet, we would suggest you take a good look around your world. We then would ask you this: *Would you want to land in the middle of a war zone?* For without meaning to be derogatory in any way, your entire world is a war zone. . . . We therefore make whatever contacts can be made individually when the opportunities arise, and we do so quietly—allowing the information to filter in, and soothing the raging fires of your world. Then by the time the fires are banked, we may land on Earth and openly communicate with you.

As we have often indicated to you, this time is approaching; within the next two to three decades this can be a relatively common thing. But right now, by many of your own admissions, in the general cross-section of your society you do not want such widespread interaction. Your society is not structured to handle it. It would cause—in our estimation of your energy in general—a destructurization of a negative sort, where there would still be fear and panic, where there would still be self-doubt and the belief that your reality is not in your hands. We do not want you believing we might be something greater than you, for far too many of you would be too willing to give over your power to us. We do not want it, thank you. We have enough of our own—all that we need to live the lives we have chosen to live.

Our methodology is to use what you would call the tried and true method. It is the reflection to you of your own power so that each of you, individually and collectively, can make the decision as to whether or not you want to interact with us as a society. That is completely up to you. Should you decide *no*, we will be on our way. It is our perception, however, that you are deciding *yes*, and so we "hang around."

Do understand: in all the interactions we have shared with you we have been more than willing, and quite ecstatic, to experience and express the interchange of love, and to be of assistance in reflecting back to you what you already know about the power you have to create the lives you want to create. But it is not really our mission to provide this information. The idea is to establish relations, and that is what has been done. In communicating this way, and establishing "foreign relations" with you, we are accomplishing our primary goal.

As we have suggested before, the idea is that we choose to remain obscure so that we are not looked upon as your saviors. We are not here to save you; *you do not need saving!* We are not here to run things, to live your lives for you. We have our own lives, and are very busy, thank-you-very-much! We have no time to take responsibility for living your lives as well. But we do love you; we do desire that your world and our worlds shall one day soon explore together all that exists in the Infinite Creation, as we already do with many other civilizations. And when you determine *as a group* that we can interact as equals, we will then do just that.

Could you give us an estimation of how soon that will be, Bashar?

You are not so very far away. It is our perception that within the next 30 to 50 of your years at the outside the changes that are taking place upon your planet will make it conducive for your world to be fully involved with our civilizations. That is indeed all the time it will take. Rather than the segregation and separation you have been exploring for thousands of years, once you begin to explore integration, it doesn't take that much time, by the definition of integration, to get to highly accelerated places very quickly.

You are all beginning to suspect there is more to you than just the physical form, and that consciousness truly expands and extends beyond what you have believed for many thousands of your years. Your beliefs were that the physical world is all there is; that the physical universe simply exists with or without you, and you have really nothing much to say about it. You may be in it for a while, and you are told that you may be able to affect your immediate surroundings to some degree. But lo and behold: in the ultimate story you have been given on your planet, nothing you do has any real effect on the overall realities.

But now you are beginning to discover this is not so. Even your own scientists, your own physicists are beginning to realize that your thoughts themselves are the actual driving and creative force behind the physical reality, behind the physical experiences each and every one of you have.

You see, you have been created with free will. If you choose to buy into negative beliefs; if you choose to buy into the idea that you can only do just so much, and it is beyond your capability to do more, the universe supports you exactly that far and no further. Because the universe never gives you more than you say you are ready to handle.

How many of you truly believe you are ready to handle absolute infinite unending ecstasy? A great many of you, because of your training, fear ecstasy quite a bit. . . . Quite a bit. Or you at least contain belief systems that are self-regulating, in the sense that when you finally do create something that seems to be going the right way, you say, "Well, this is jolly! How long can this last?"

You always cut yourselves off. As soon as you impose that restriction on yourselves through your belief systems, the universe says, "All right, if that's the way you want it, *cut!*" . . . instantly. Instantly. Instantly! You are that powerful. You have always gotten everything you believed you could get—or perhaps even more importantly for many of you, everything you believed you *deserved* to get. For deservability is a big issue with most individuals in your civilization: "I deserve the negativity" or "I *don't* deserve the positivity."

Introducing Guilt

One of the key ideas engendered upon your planet long ago is the idea of guilt. Not that other civilizations do not experience it, but you have delved so very deeply and so very strongly into it that your civilization, among the many civilizations we have encountered, has an expertise that is matched by none. Not that this makes you any less. In fact, the idea of your willingness to even experience such limitation in many ways actually makes you strong, and is, in and of itself, an indication of how strong you know you are—to be able to subject yourselves to such degrees of limitation. This allows you to create many wondrous occasions of self-incrimination, self-invalidation, self-limitation, segregation and separation in your lives. And many times it is the primary ingredient, the primary symbol, to allow you to prevent yourselves from creating in your lives what you prefer, what you desire, and what you know deep within you is what you deserve to experience in your lives.

Guilt is what will always perpetuate limitation, always perpetuate separation; it keeps you from recognizing your own self-empowerment and your own connection to the Infinite Creation. For recognize that, fundamentally speaking, while many of you for a long period of time have assumed that hate is the opposite of love, guilt is the true opposite of love. Hate may be the diametric, dynamic polarity *expression* of love, but guilt is the true mechanical opposite. For love is complete and utter self-worthiness and creativity, while guilt is the belief in lack of self-worth; it stifles creativity. Hate involves the concept that you deserve *something*, whereas guilt is completely devoid of the sense of deservability. In fact, **guilt is the denial of your very existence!**

Therefore, the belief in your lack of self-deservability allows you to be able to create a scenario in which you actually keep at bay all of the things in life that are yours by birthright—such as happiness, ecstasy and creativity. Guilt is the bitter pill that was injected into your society—by your society—to keep you in the status quo of lack of self-empowerment. Because when you truly believe you are not connected to All That Is, or God, the Infinite Creation; when you truly believe you must control by force in order to get anything at all in life, then do you further the continuation of limitation, further the continuation of guilt.

This scenario has become the very ethic of your society. When you do not believe you are connected, you thus do not believe you can create things you desire in your lives with great ease and effortlessness, and things become worthless to you if you don't create suffering in order to get them. "No pain, no gain," as you say. When you are told a story in your world, and that story contains pain and conflict, struggle and strife, you say, "Oh my! Very realistic story!" When you are told a story where it says, "And they lived happily ever after," you say, "Huh! Fairy tale! That's not real life."

There is absolutely nothing within the creation of the universe that insists that the story containing the conflict is any more real than one that does not. It is your choice, out of your habits, to believe that pain is more real than joy. So as we said, this has become the ethic of your entire civilization—that you cannot have anything in your lives that is worthwhile unless you have *suffered*, unless you have, as you say, *earned* it. But do recognize that you do not have to earn it; *you already own it!*

Your Birthright

You were created from ecstasy; you were created out of love and light. It is your birthright. Everything you do can be an act of love, done with an effortless ease of creativity. You are made in the image of the Infinite Creator; and that means, quite simply, that you are infinite creators, and multi-dimensional ones as well. This is the natural you. If you will allow yourselves to realize that you no longer need the tool of guilt, you will then give yourselves the expansiveness of your birthright.

You will allow yourselves the expressiveness of your vitality, and you will then be able, with all clear consciousness, to create and attract into your lives the things you know you deserve. You will find that when you remove guilt from your tool box, what is left will be this recognition and realization: *NOTHING is too simple or too good to be true.* Nothing! . . . "Any exceptions, Bashar?" . . . No, not one.

Nothing is too simple or too good to be true, and nothing is too wondrous or too ecstatic to be yours—nothing. You deserve *all* you can conceive of—because you exist! And if you exist, then obviously All That Is, the Infinite Creator, believes you deserve to exist. If you exist with the desire for creating peace, harmony, joy and ecstasy in your lives, then know you are not created with that desire without also having been created with the ability to attract that into your lives. Your awareness of that idea, in and of itself, is sufficient to bring it to you. Creation holds nothing back from you, and it never has—*never!* In all circumstances in your lives each and every one of you has always been supported 100% by the universe. *You are not ever given a desire without also being given the ability to accomplish that desire!*

The universe, and Infinite Creation, does not do extraneous and pointless things. Therefore, since you did not have to do anything special in order to deserve existence; since obviously All That Is believes you deserve to exist, give yourselves the same benefit of the doubt; treat yourselves with the same unconditional love and respect. Grant yourselves permission and grant yourselves the right to create life as you desire it to be, for you have the ability to create it that way. All you need do is remind yourselves that your ability to *conceive* of that idea is, in and of itself, the indication of your ability to *create* that idea. Again, you are multi-dimensional creators; and as you think, as you feel, and as you believe, so you experience the creation of the physical reality around you—*always!* No exceptions.

Your physical reality is always the product of what each of you believes it can be—OR fears it will be. For to fear that something will happen in your lives is the same thing as saying you believe that the fearful scenario is the strongest possible reality likely to come into your lives. Your physical reality is always the product of what you believe it can or will be.

Situations do not happen in your lives to show you that you are stuck in them; situations do not happen in your lives to show you that you have failed at creating better ones. Situations come into your lives to show you what beliefs you have been taught, what beliefs you have bought into—and if you don't prefer them, to change them. You always have a self-regulating mechanism to allow you to know what beliefs may be buried in your unconscious minds. The self-regulating mechanism that allows you to know precisely how to bring those beliefs to the surface of your conscious minds—so you can change them if you don't like them and reinforce them if you do—is the experience of physical reality.

If you see that you are involved in situations you don't prefer, then simply recognize that the only way it could be in your lives is for you to have the belief *allowing* it into your lives. Therefore, now that a situation has shown you what the belief is you have been operating on, you are free. You have the opportunity to say, "Aha! Now I have the definition of the belief that has created this; it has been buried within me. It has now come to the surface, because here it is all around me. Therefore, if I don't prefer it, I can understand what the definition was and I can thus change that definition to what I do prefer."

Then use 100% of the trust—the same trust used to create the negative scenario—to now know that once you have changed the definition to a positive definition, reality will reflect that definitional belief just as strongly as it reflected the other definitional belief which you did not prefer. You have your own self-guidance system, your own built-in guidance system. And this is why when we interact with you, what you will always sense from us is that whether *you* choose to believe in yourselves or not; whether *you* choose to believe you have the capability of creating the reality you desire or not, we believe in you! We will always reflect to you that you have that capability, for we *know* you do. We do not *believe* you have it; we *know* you have it—beyond any doubt whatsoever. We know all beings in creation have the ability to create the reality they experience.

Again I remind you: all of you are born on your Earth with a total facility for living your lives in absolute joy; but because of the way you have created your society to be, that joy is drummed out of most of you by the time you are three years of age. Yes, that young! And you begin to buy into the belief systems that your society says are the belief systems you must buy into in order to survive in this world . . . *kid!*

Highly Focused

There are many, many clever ways you are constantly creating restrictions upon yourselves. This stems from the fact that a long time ago you chose as a group consciousness to be highly focused into physical materiality. What came with that choice was the ability to forget that you were the creators of all your physical reality to begin with. You have played the game of forgetting for thousands of years. Now you are remembering; you are waking up, blinking your eyes and saying, "Oh, there is something more; I am now remembering that I began this game. I began this cycle a long time ago; now I'm at the end of it. Time to go on to a new cycle of joy and remembrance and creativity." That choice on your part, that recognition, is why I, and others like myself, are now able to begin to communicate with your civilization.

While we were observing your society for thousands of years, we knew we would have to wait until you had played out the negativity you have been exploring for so long; and now you have played it out. This life now is representative of the transformational age. *This life now is the one you have been waiting for for hundreds of thousands of years. This IS the transformational life!* It has been going on now in accelerated fashion upon your planet for approximately 40 or 50 of your years; it will continue in an accelerated fashion for approximately 40 or 50 years more. You are smack in the middle of the transformational age: the half-way point (1987). In fact you are right on the edge of transforming into a very strong, peaceful and creative planet.

We would like you to understand that even though your world seems to be going through much turmoil at present, you may keep this in mind: *transformation is not the product of mediocrity!* As strong as you have been on the negative side, that is an indication of how strong it can be on the positive side. Let us assume that you have taken a rubber band and stretched it far, far back into the depths of limitation and negativity, as far as you can possibly stretch it. Now you are on the verge of considering exploring the positive side. What do you think is going to happen when you let go of that rubber band? It's going to snap back very rapidly and very far onto the side of positivity.

This is the threshold on which you are standing as a civilization at this point in time on your planet. That is why many of you may be incredulous to understand: "Well, what do you mean 40 years? That's all it's going to take? We're going to be a unified planet in only 40 years? But we've spent thousands of years getting to this point!"

Looking at a general average cross section of the combined rates at which you are all progressing individually, most of you will actually take only about 20 to 25 years. From our point of view, the energy as it now stands reads thus: *every single day* of your time brings with it as many connections to different levels of your consciousness as it took one to three years to make ten years ago. That is the rate at which you are accelerating.

This speeding up— is that one of the reasons some of us have been very spaced out lately?

Yes! The limbo state is in full force. The transition, the shifting of gears is taking place. That is why many of you now find you are coasting along with your clutches out. . . . You are not engaged.

Bashar, are we the least-advanced planet you've ever come across?

Rest at ease that your civilization is not the least-advanced in the universe. There are many civilizations going through their own transformation; by no means are you at the bottom of the totem pole. However, you are one of the most highly focused and accelerated civilizations we have ever encountered. Which means you have experienced a much greater degree of limitation in a more rapid way than almost any other civilization with which we are familiar. You have, in other words, done it all. There is almost no other way you could explore the idea of the limitations you began several thousand years ago.

Once you have the understanding that integration is that much more geometrically progressive and unified, you will understand that all it requires is, as you say, the blink of an eye to accomplish anything you want to accomplish—when you really put your minds to it, and when you rearrange your priorities. So at this time let us share with you a little nickname many of us have for you. Understand that in no way, shape or form is this name meant to be derogatory . . . honest! But the idea is that we, and many of the other civilizations that know about you, have called you the **MASTERS OF LIMITATION.**

Now, recognize that the cycle of limitation begun by your human culture so long ago brought with it an unexpected effect. This unexpected effect was the ability—once you had locked yourselves into materiality from a certain point of view—the ability to *forget* that you did it to begin with, and that you *could* extract yourselves from it any time you chose. This is under the category of what you might call a "catch-22" in your language. The idea is that a certain degree of experience of limitation, a certain focus of limitation, automatically brings with it an ability to forget you created it to begin with. So once you had locked yourselves into that cycle of limitation and focus as physical beings, you then had to play out the natural result of the momentum you generated long ago.

How Could You Forget?

Once there was a time when we encountered a civilization that had come into contact with The Association. Eventually in sharing information back and forth, it came time to describe and define your existence, and what we are doing in our interactions with you. Well, do you realize that one of the closest approaches to an argument we have ever had with anyone—not exactly in the same way: no negativity, no real violent emotionality—but the closest we have ever come to an argument was when they simply could not believe there could exist any expression of individuality anywhere within the physical universe that could not be aware of its own power, that could actually forget it creates its own reality. It took quite some convincing, as it was simply beyond their conception.

This is not to say they are any better than you, but to show you how many different ways there are to perceive reality, and to point out that there are civilizations who have created themselves to not even be able to inherently *conceive* of the ability to forget we are a part of Infinite Creation. Recognize, therefore, that it was quite astonishing to them to realize that you were actually able to funnel your great power in such a manner as to use that power in creating within yourselves the ability to forget you even *had* the power you were using.

They learned something new about themselves that day, and something new about the universe. You taught them, to their very great amazement, that that was one way All That Is can express itself; and now they have a much broader understanding of the variety of ways Infinite Creation can manifest. You taught them something by your willingness to experience such a high degree of limitation in focus. They in turn began experimenting to some degree with the idea . . . not that they created exactly the same degree of forgetfulness.

But you see, the idea in their civilization became a source of enjoyment. They found, as you also found to some degree, that the ability to impose the illusion of forgetting upon themselves, however momentarily, allows them to experience things as if they are experiencing them for the first time. They were able to realize that that was not an experience they had ever had. Thus they were able to generate for themselves a whole new understanding of creativity simply from the altering of the perspective, the altering of the point of view—of creating the scenario of not remembering that you are connected to the experiences you are creating your reality to be.

Therefore be aware that even though you have created such a seemingly negative past, other individuals in the universe have benefited greatly from your unique willingness to create such a reality, one which can be shared in different ways as a learning tool by many individuals in the universe. You have also assisted us in assisting other worlds, because our thought patterns would otherwise be highly alien to you, and yours to us. Without the use of the model of this physical channel; without experiencing Earth life through the connection with him—in a life you would consider a past life of mine—we would not have the model to draw from, the experiences to draw from, to be able to assist you now, or to even speak with you in the same terminology.

And so in using your high degree of focus in limitation, we have been able to know that if our model works on your world, it works marvelously on many other worlds that do not have such a high degree of limited focus. Because you are then the master lock for almost any other civilization experiencing limitation to any degree. And so we thank you for the high focus you have created, because then in dipping into your well, we have most of the tools necessary to deal with almost anyone else. We thank you for forging the type of steel that allows us to cut through many bonds of illusion which we find exist in many other societies beside yours.

Begin to Unify

It will not take very long for your world to transform into a unified state. The idea, in and of itself, of the exploration of limitation means that things are broken down in complex ways; they create a lot of complexity and detail. You have to experience them a step at a time, one after the other. Now that you have begun to unify things back together, and to awaken into your integrity— your integral state—things can speed up and be very accelerated. It will be a very accelerated state, because the sooner you open up to the positive ideas, the sooner you begin to accelerate geometrically. When you begin to integrate, consolidate and unify, everything is within you; you live in the moment spontaneously. *You literally create less time.* So everything is accelerated, things happening more quickly. Your whole world ignites in an ecstatic explosion of ecstasy and coincidence and synchronicity—everything tying into everything else, being interconnected and interrelated; always in the right place at the right time, interacting with exactly the individuals you need to interact with. No accidents. There *are* no accidents. Never have been, are not now, and never will be. Co-incidence is simply that: co-incidents.

*   *   *

We wish to extend to you at this time our deepest appreciation in allowing us to experience the gift of your consciousness. We thank you for choosing to function as representatives and ambassadors of your world, for that is what each and every one of you are right now. We thank you for allowing me to function as an ambassador for all that are listening in on this side. Bit by bit, day by day, through these interactions we shall come closer and closer to the time in only a few of your years hence when we may interact with you openly and joyously.

CHAPTER TWO

Peace in Our Time

January, 1987: *Bashar, are the people of Earth now choosing to destroy their world? Are we going to blow ourselves up?*

No! Even though it may not be apparent on the surface of your world yet, our perception is that about seven of your years ago you all made a general collective unconscious agreement that you will *not* annihilate yourselves through nuclear means. What you perceive to be an acceleration of violence on your planet is the last vestiges of these ideas now being brought to the surface. You are getting it out of your system, so to speak, now that you know unconsciously it's safe to do so—because all of this is not going to lead to your annihilation.

You are bringing what was formerly hidden and covert out into the open, so that you can all look around and say, "Wait a minute. Look what's going on; look what we're doing. Is this the way we want our world to really be? If not, let's change it." You now know it is safe to bring up all of that, examine it, and create it to be the way you wish it to be. We can tell you this at this time because you have made that decision yourselves.

Because you have made that decision, we can also tell you the following: that you never would have been allowed to annihilate yourselves through nuclear means anyway. It is your world; you can do with it what you will . . . *as long as what you do remains in your own back yard!* Nuclear annihilation would have torn through the dimensional fabric of other space/time continuums, and affected other civilizations that have nothing to do with you. That is not allowed.

19

Recognize that your government is very well aware, and has been aware for a long time, that your devices simply would not have worked had they been activated. They have been given blatant demonstrations that this is the case by many of the space craft of The Association. These have centered themselves directly over your missile silos, and deactivated —dampened electromagnetically— all of the launch mechanisms. Your government and your military have been given many demonstrations of this. The idea of the so-called nuclear tension that exists between your super powers from that point forward has been mostly for show. They do not wish to lose their standing in your eyes.

Bit by bit much of this information will begin to leak into your society. The more you open channels of communication and blend yourselves together with the idea of what you have created your government to be; and the more you *allow* them to *serve* you rather than *rule* you, the more they will be able to share with you the information they have kept from you about our existence. They have been doing this basically to protect you in the way they *thought* you wanted to be protected.

So when government heads get together for summit meetings, are they not actually talking about what they say they are?

Not always.

Is it that they are friendly with each other and they're allowing each other to stay in power?

Whether they are friendly literally or not, they both know what the game is they are truly playing.

And the game is that there is never the idea of nuclear destruction—and it is then perhaps mostly a monetary game?

In a sense, yes. It is the idea of maintaining what they fear they will lose—power over you . . . not recognizing that the equalization of the entire world will actually be the gaining of their own self-empowerment along with everyone else.

Do the Russians have the same sort of knowledge we received 40 years ago, when the first space ship crashed here?

Different. But enough information has crossed the lines now that both of your "sides" know just about enough.

This information about advanced space flight: is that known at the governmental level?

Some. Do understand that many of your governments actually have in their possession some extraterrestrial space craft. They have been able to derive some theory and technology from these craft in order to make their own, but not fluently. For they are missing out on several concepts about consciousness as part of the equation in understanding the technology. And also some of the materials are a little bit beyond their capability to penetrate. They have applied parts of this technology to some degree now and then; and in a sense, even before they had possession, they were working on some of these understandings. They do understand some of the basic principles.

Governing Government

However, as long as they choose to utilize them for the idea of self-empowerment and gain, they will find that some of the principles will not work—because these are based on an integrative point of view. Your governments are beginning to learn; but because of what you have created them to be, they act like they are getting it slower than the mainstream of society.

The more you interact with them *not* in an accusatory manner, *not* in an angry manner, but in a loving manner, in a sharing manner, in an unconditionally loving manner, and express to them that you believe in peace; that you know there are other ways that are simpler; that there are other ways more indicative of using the reality that exists rather than attempting to ram your way through walls— then perhaps they will begin to shift their programs toward the types which will allow them to share the information with you, rather than thinking that by doing so they will lose their power.

Much of this data is now being brought out in the open, thus forcing them to face the different portions of themselves that are not working fluidly. And so there is no need for judgment, no need for negative feelings from this point forward. The situation has aligned you; now you know how you can serve: by suggesting alternatives to your government and allowing them to hear the words all of you are saying: "We believe in peace; let's do it this way, shall we—together?"

Is there anyone in our government, any people who represent us who seem to have a clearer vision of this?

Yes, there are a few. You can find them by simply being that vibration. They will be the only ones you will attract—the ones who can get things done, the ones who are equal to you. But first you must be equal to them. So be bold; interact in a loving way— very blatantly and very practically. You *are* your governments, as we have said before. There is no reason why you should not feel just as at home in government buildings as anywhere else. But you will never know unless you initiate some form of communication, some form of action, some form of equalization between you and what you have for so long thought to be the different levels of your society—those levels to which you have given over the responsibility of taking care of your lives for you.

Take back that responsibility. Interact; participate. It is all one world. If you really believe you wish it to be one world, act as if it *is* one world. If it really were one world in the same way our world is one, there would be absolutely no place barred to you. Simply know that if you radiate that frequency, you will find that there are absolutely no barriers to any so-called level of government on your planet—not anywhere at any time. You will find yourselves being invited, or you will find that the opportunities will automatically present themselves to you. You will flow into areas where you can drop a little hint here, have a little conversation there, over tea, and get to know one another.

The idea is that something you absolutely strongly believe in you will act upon. The two are not segregated. Actions and beliefs are tied together; they are one thing: you act as you believe, and as you believe, you will act. Recognize that the more you are willing to allow yourselves this freedom of action, the less you will create for yourselves the opportunities to sit around and complain about the way things are.

But how can I, as only one individual, make a difference?

Recognize that *you have chosen your purpose in being in this society at this time on your planet. Know that if you were not going to make a difference, you would not be here.* As you begin to see the idea of the connection of everything in your society as it relates to you, and as you relate to it, you will begin to understand that each and every individual makes a difference within the society as a whole.

This understanding will allow the society to recognize within each individual the ability of the society to relate to each one specifically, and the ability of each individual to recognize within him or herself the totality of the society. Thus is formed the first bridge and link and connection from the individual self, from the personality to the mass consciousness, allowing you to know that because you are connected to everything else, every move you undertake, every move you support, every move you create will always act as a lever for everything else, subtly shifting ideas in one direction or another.

You will know you are connected in various ways through the mental fields you create on your planet, through the physiological fields you create through manipulation of the energy fields of the planet itself. All ideas that you call your civilization —physiological and mental, emotional and spiritual— all are diversifications out of the same primal homogenous energy field, the primal consciousness. All are diversifications out of that. And all are, as we have often said, the different shelves, or layers, of the idea of the onion on your world. Many different layers have been created by you out of the homogenous oneness of the energy field, that which is the underlying primal foundation of all creation you know as physical.

As you diversify these layers, recognize that because you are creating the diversification, you are still connected to every single layer. You are connected and pass through all layers from without and from within. All layers are within you, and so every move you make within yourself is a move made in the outer physical awareness—because the outer physical reality is only a reflection of every idea you are exploring within the self. To travel, to move through the physical reality —no matter what the mode of your motion: whether walking, running, riding in your automobiles or airplanes, or even in space craft— any idea of motion through space is the idea of movement within, exemplified and reflected back to you as a symbol.

Recognize, therefore, the idea that every one of you has an effect on the society as a whole with every small subtle movement you make. For every movement —every movement— is significant to every other movement. All movements are equal, and go into the totality of the creation of your society as you perceive it. So now that you are beginning to recognize that there is no longer any separation between yourselves as individuals and the society, you can begin to recognize that as you move, the society moves as a whole. You are immersed in the fluid.

Every other being, every other individual, every other self-created perspective within that fluid, will always feel the eddies and the currents as you make your move around in the fluid. They will always be able to sense the directions of your flow, the directions of your movement, the strength you give and the energy you impart to the fluid. All of you, whether you know it consciously or not, are sensitive to this activity, sensitive to your willingness to be exactly who and what you are, what you chose to be in this life.

Toxicity/Radioactivity

I am very concerned about toxic waste on our planet at this time, Bashar, and would like us to find appropriate ways by which we could either neutralize or clean up this waste safely.

Many of you already recognize that certain forms of energy exist upon your planet, specifically with regard to the electro-magnetic field of your planet—energies which can be tapped in non-polluting methods to supply all the power you need for every endeavor you could possibly imagine. Since you have already decided to create certain technologies that have detrimental by-products, there are a few ideas which might be used to alleviate some of that concern.

One we have discussed before. You will find that some individuals, as we perceive the energy of your consciousness now on your planet, are beginning to investigate and discover certain polymer materials, plastic materials that will actually have the ability to molecularly bond with the residue given off by the toxic waste. These will be able to form some sort of containment, some sort of absorption containment process, so that the toxicity —and we are talking about radioactivity specifically— will no longer pass beyond that barrier. These polymers may exist in your society within the next twelve to fourteen of your years, as we read the energy now of your technological evolution.

Of course you can also create electromagnetic bubbles around such substances to isolate them. Certain types of electromagnetic bubbles are capable of actually changing some of the molecular composition of that material, rendering it at least neutral, if not actually usable. However, when the vibrational rate, or frequency of each and every individual upon your planet accelerates to a higher state, then some of the substances you have created at your lower frequency will also simply no longer have an effect upon your corporeal forms. They will be of another reality level, another frequency level, and will not be able to create an effect in a physical reality that no longer relates to —or shall we say is no longer synchronized with— the former reality in which those substances were created.

You can truly create a separation of universes, so that the old substances will no longer affect you physically, because you will be operating on a different plane entirely. However, you will no longer, as we have said, need to create such substances anymore when your society allows itself to realize that all the power you need, all the technology you can invent, can be based upon electromagnetic or gravitic principles. Then that will be sufficient for any endeavor you would wish to create. From that point on you will no longer create any toxic or radioactive by-products.

Now, many individuals have been exploring and experimenting with this idea of electromagnetic utilization for quite some time. But because of the way you have structured your society's interests, some of that experimentation has been suppressed. This is because it does not serve the interests of the individuals who control your technology at this time. Once those barriers have been lifted, many individuals will then come to understand that certain methodologies have existed —some for decades of your time— that would alleviate all of your power problems.

Could you tell us how to produce those electromagnetic bubbles, and what frequency it is?

You do not have the technology at this time. We can perhaps be of a little more assistance with the idea of the polymers, pointing you in certain directions—but only pointing. We cannot give you the entire idea— a) Because some of your technology has not yet been decided on; therefore we can not predict such a thing with absolute certainty. Your future is still in flux about what it is you will discover. b) Because some of these things you *must* be allowed to discover yourselves. We cannot necessarily remove the process of discovery from you.

However, it is our perception that individuals who are exploring and experimenting with certain types of molecular arrangements in polymers that simulate certain biochemical processes in the body, certain biochemical arrangements in your human bodies within the DNA and RNA structures, will be closest to the mark. In a sense, what we are saying is that these polymers, to use that term very loosely, will be almost bio-organic in nature, and will to some degree contain an affinity to certain heavier elements. And in absorbing those heavier elements into their structure, they will set up a matrix, a certain type of magnetic matrix, that will actually create a type of polarized effect for the particles being absorbed by the polymer.

In other words, the particle will strike the polymer— let's say a radioactive polymer particle will be absorbed on one side of the barrier. So something will be released on the other side of the barrier, but it will be polarized in a way you have not seen polarization yet. The new polarized particle will be harmless to your species, yet it will still exist. In a sense it will be pollution of another type, but one that is not harmful to you. All we can do at this time is describe this basic mechanism to you. The knowledge is not now available to us to understand more specifically exactly how this mechanism will be created in terms of the technology on your planet.

Well then, do you see us killing our planet, Bashar?

Right now, yes; but not ultimately. It is our perception at this moment that you are basically forcing yourselves into a corner, and this will finally cause you to face the idea that there are more beneficial and efficient ways to go about things. It is our perception that within the next twenty or so of your years as a society, in full recognition of that fact you will then find these ways and transform your world very rapidly. For once the recognition is made, then the changes can occur, historically speaking, almost overnight.

The Middle East

Bashar, there is so much conflict all over the world; one area in particular is always at war. For some reason it just never seems to initiate any of the positive changes we see happening in the rest of the world.

Your Middle East.

That's the place. Can you give us any information as to why that is the situation?

Because in many ways that area was the reception site and the reception point for very early infusion, in an incarnational sense, of some of the very strongest of negative energies upon your planet. A very, very strong Orion incarnation was the historical individual you call Sargon of Akkad. This individual is recognized in your history as being responsible for the creation of the Arabic Empire, using the sword to conquer that whole area. Therefore, it was founded on many Orion principles. Individuals in that area are struggling because they believe —as the Orions did in those times— that to struggle was the only way to express and understand the self, that it must be done through the idea of conflict. Thus, basically you will find that much of their energy, in many past incarnations, has been put toward the idea of warfare.

Never having learned about unconditional love being the ultimate power in creation, they sought to dominate and domineer, this being the only way they could understand their relationship to Creation. They are jostling to understand themselves as different expressions, learning that they can express the power and the energy with which they feel so naturally connected in terms of your Earth. And now it can be expressed in more positive ways.

They can begin to recognize an immensely important idea: that *every individual is as powerful as he needs to be to have anything he desires in life without having to hurt anyone else, or himself, in order to get it.* They are beginning to assimilate into many other cultures, which gives them the opportunity to recognize they can blend and balance that energy in a positive way, that it does not have to be a struggle or a conflict of ideologies. For the blending of all ideologies is what will, paradoxically, allow them to express their own ideology the easiest.

That area of your world has indeed represented a high degree of limitation and focus and the playing out of that very energetic negative state. So in that sense, they are the crucible around which all other realities and cultures on your planet rotate and revolve. They are playing out much of the negativity of the remainder of your planet through that small area, that small theater representing some of the very highest concentrations of the old belief systems on your world.

In a sense, this can be looked at as a circumstance which allows the rest of you to make the changes you are making, since they are willing to function as the repository of the majority of the negativity on your planet, thus releasing the rest of you to change in the ways you desire to change. Once the rest of you have stabilized yourselves, then can the greatest and most rapid changes potentially occur within that area, as they will no longer have to hold the symbolic torch for the rest of you.

Negativity Personified

February, 1987: *And in my country of Iran, Bashar, what about that madman who killed so many people?*

Understand that that individual was only acting as a collective reflection for the belief systems —the combined belief systems in negativity collected down through your centuries— in that particular country, and in your whole civilization at this time. Other individuals have served in this way, and more will do so also. These individuals do not know they are strong enough to not have to reflect that degree of negativity.

So at this time that whole area, the energy of that area through many lifetimes, has built up this volatility, this understanding, this particular point of view, and allowed certain individuals to embody all the fears, all the negativities, all the disconnections from Creation that culture has felt.

Every culture at this time upon your planet is going through its own transformation in its own way. At this time in each culture there are those individuals who have been brought up to believe they are weak; and those weak individuals will take upon themselves what they perceive to be the idea of power and strength, which is to dominate and harm other individuals.

But that is a sign of powerlessness. These individuals are only thrashing about in their own self-created nightmares, and they are taking as many individuals with them as they can—because they feel themselves to be dying inside. That culture is going to go through many rapid changes within the next decade; there will, in fact, be an utter complete transformation of that entire area on your planet.

The Sword of Sargon

There will be a spark, and the spark will be ignited. That spark that is ignited will touch off what you might call an emotional chain reaction in the people of that area—over a wide expanse. From your year 1997 through your year 2000 —and with ramifications proceeding up to 2011— that entire area will undergo a change as it has never known in your recent history.

That spark will be the recognition that the barriers and the definitions and the creeds that have kept everyone separate—*that* is what you are actually fighting against, and not truly an individual. That individual has only taken it upon himself to represent all of the symbols that keep your people separate—all of the ideas and beliefs; all of the creeds and the old ways; all of the habits and rituals; the old ideas of the inequalities of the races, of the castes, of the levels in society.

The spark will unite and bind that entire area, and there can be a burst of light that will transform many throughout that entire Mediterranean area, spreading out as a shock wave . . . a shock wave of light. As we perceive your energy now, approximately in 1997 there will be a tumultuous interaction, concerning their social, political and religious understanding, that will allow them to reexamine all they believe in. However, at the same time it will form a crucible that will allow certain souls to shine very brightly, very hotly.

Our perception is that within a very short period of time— before your year of 2001— there will be such a major transformation in that area that a new line, a new understanding, a new model or template for how your entire world could develop a government will issue from that area. This laying down of the foundation of a world government subsequently will be accomplished by your years of 2011 to 2013.

Now, we do perceive that the situation in your Middle East will come to a head. Great degrees of accelerated polarities will be created, similar to the polarities the rest of your world is exploring now. The various stages that it has taken you decades to pass through, they will pass through in a very short period of time. There may be still much escalation of violence; many ideas may be torn down physiologically. But yet, violent though it is —and it does not have to be— out of that will still come a way to make room for a new understanding.

One way or another that society must free itself of the shackles it has wrapped around itself. And in a sense, even if it must break down its entire social structure to do so, it will. Again, not that it has to. But out of that deep, deep suffering— out of that will come a momentous transformation in that land . . . *and the sword of Sargon will now reflect the light!*

A New Triumvirate

This transformation you are talking about: do you mean they will become a Communist country?

No. We are talking about your entire planet beginning to recognize that all borders are confining; that all labels and all ideologies are simply different points of view; and that there are many things in every culture that each culture can blend, assimilate and benefit from. It will not be any label you now possess on your planet; it will simply be the unification of your planet— as a planet.

You will soon allow yourselves to form a triumvirate association of your three major powers: the United States, the Soviet Union, the Peoples Republic of China. And together, as the triumvirate, they will set the stage as a leading example for the proposal upon which the rest of your civilization can form its own world peace, its own world government. From that moment on the idea of national boundaries will begin to dissolve over a period of the following 100 years.

Is there anything we can do to help out and further along the transition in that Middle Eastern area?

You can send your love, each of you acting according to what you believe is the thing that represents the light and love of your truth, thus being a shining example to that nucleus, to that core around which you rotate. You could then be mirrors, 360 degrees all around, to reflect back to them their potential for change in a positive direction.

Do recognize that they have limited themselves by refusing to acknowledge other points of view, doing so in order to remain within that limited focus which allows them to get the job done, as you say. The more willing you are, as an outer world around them, to change and do the things that represent your love and light, the stronger the reflection of that love and light will shine back to them. And there will be a time when the momentum and the weight of the love and light you are sending will be something they can no longer resist.

You can interact with them along whatever avenues and conduits may open up to represent your ability to be of service. Not that you must go into interacting with them appearing as if you're out to change them, making it seem as if you believe they should change, and you are doing it in a judgmental fashion. That is not what we are referring to. But you could allow yourselves to just avail yourselves of whatever opportunities you find to slide into and share of who you are. And then they will see around themselves more reflections of that willingness to balance the idea of positivity with all that ancient negativity.

War-Like Planets

What about a planet with a life system that has developed with a war-like mentality, one that can enter this part of our galaxy with intentions of conquering? Will that likely happen, Bashar?

Understand that individuals with that intention do not really get very far. The idea is also that your energy as a world now has changed sufficiently so that even if there should be another civilization close at hand with intentions of conquering and dominating, they would be hard pressed to even find you now. For your vibration is a little bit too different from any society that might actually wish to push themselves into space with war-like intentions of coming here to take over.

Now, the idea is also that traveling in space is actually traveling within. And true, space travel is not the idea of what your technology is right now, where in a sense you are sliding around on the *surface* of space. When you understand how to breach the barriers of space and time itself, you will discover it requires a very highly integrated attitude, and a highly integrated attitude makes it very unlikely you will ever be of a war-like nature, and in fact you would not get very far if you were. For even if you were to make the attempt, you would most likely find yourselves dispersed at the other end. . . .

The idea of war-like planets in conquering modes can and have happened, but they are usually relegated to certain levels of dimensionality. Many times that means they actually have to be in physical proximity to each other, and in our perception, not on any level is there a race of such a nature within hundreds of light years of your world. For the idea is this: now that your vibration is changing into a modality they would not even begin to be able to understand, they probably would not find you even if they looked. So in a sense, that makes *you* the most war-like planet around . . . and *we* have no fear of you. Therefore, in actual fact, if there were going to be any concern at all, it would probably be from our end, not yours.

But aren't there wars between other planets?

If we might draw an analogy to what many of you have assumed *must* exist elsewhere in the universe, simply because it exists upon your planet. . . .

In a sense, there are other places, and have been interactions throughout the different galaxies, that might loosely amount to what you call warfare. There have been many variations of this theme on many different worlds from time to time. You are not unique in that. But the idea many of you have perceived, which has to do with alien consciousness that may have negative intentions toward other worlds: this particular negative intention does not always manifest itself in the absolute format you would recognize as warfare.

For recognize, in many ways warfare is quite improbable in terms of galactic and stellar distances. There is rarely any need for such an idea, since there is always more than enough room for expansion, and therefore more than enough room for different ideologies. Every civilization is a different reality in many ways, and generally speaking one reality is usually experienced only by one civilization until they make agreements to share common frequencies, common wave lengths between different worlds—which then allows them to interact in various ways.

But if they do not make that agreement, then chances are they will rarely even encounter other civilizations if they are not of a mind to interact with those other civilizations in mutually beneficial ways . . . unless they wish to lure themselves to civilizations that as a whole are choosing to function as victims, and draw to themselves —out of their fears, out of their doubts— the idea of a conquering civilization. However, even this notion is usually not able to be played out in your typical fashion of warfare and domination. For, as we said earlier, the stellar distances make this very improbable.

Do recognize also that although it may seem symbolically like planets are being conquered, none can be conquered if they do not vibrate to the idea that they *can* be. And thus you will find that the so-called best safeguard to that idea is to simply know you are not of that vibration, that idea. And they, not being of the same reality, will never find you. If they should come to what represents —to them— your planet, it will not —to them— seem to be at all inhabited.

So the idea, more often than not, of what could be considered a conquering race, and a conquered race —to use those terms loosely— would be simply the willingness of the conquered to give up their power completely to the conqueror, to allow their lives to be run by someone else, and to have all their power removed and all the responsibility for the creation of their lives taken from them. But not taken without their consent, for it cannot happen without that consent.

Thus the type of warfare that has occurred in this sense has simply been one of a people succumbing to an idea and allowing themselves to fall in line, to fall under the domination and the auspices of another civilization successfully using the idea of seduction to lure that other civilization under their banner. The "conquering" civilization then is able to increase its numbers and increase its strength very literally by talking the other civilization into allowing them to be dominated. They can do this by taking responsibility for their needs, by pretending they will take care of those needs, and by removing from them in the process all of their ability to know and believe they can create their own lives as they choose them to be.

This is the type of warfare that is more common. It is a mental idea, a psychic idea, in that sense. But even that, in our experience, is a relatively uncommon thing. For not *that* many civilizations we have encountered are that willing to forget who and what they are to the degree where they would attract such a liaison with another civilization that would even *want* that type of dominion over other worlds. Both of these ideas are relatively rare in our experience.

Star Wars

All the ideas of what you now represent to be war-like projections into space are, for the most part, in your long distant past. Do understand something: though we are not saying the scenario that has been painted in literal terms is actually literal, the idea of your science fiction stories —particularly the one you call *Star Wars*— did carry with it one of the strongest insights of all, and that is that you were told it was a long time ago. For indeed it no longer has anything really to do with your present. At least not, as you say, in your neck of the woods! It is a representation of the old cycle of negativity, and a connection to many other star systems through which you have come. It was simply applied to a future format.

Well then, how do we stop wars and have a peaceful planet?

Please understand that if you believe in peace, then you do not have to hate war. ***You do not get peace by hating war; you get peace by loving peace.*** Hate only reinforces the things you say you do not prefer, because that's what you are focusing on. *Be* peace; *live* peace. *Breathe* peace; *share* peace. Love, unconditional love, will transform your entire world in the twinkling of an eye. *UNCONDITIONAL* love for all.

The Peace Clock

At this time (December, 1987) we would like to suggest to you a project we have called the Peace Clock. A very simple idea, but very impactful. It goes as follows:

Step one: every single day of your time, at noon in your time zone —for one full minute at noon time— meditate on world peace in any way that is comfortable for you. See your world enjoying the idea of peace and harmony, in any way you wish to imagine, or visualize. What you will be creating is a motion, a momentum, an electromagnetic thrust around your planet—for we recognize you have many different time zones on your world.

If at midday in your time zone that entire slice, one-twenty-fourth of your planet, is focused for one minute in meditation on world peace —and then the next slice, and the next slice, all the way around your planet, around and around and around, day after day— you will actually generate an electromagnetic momentum that will almost literally spin you, before you know it, into fourth density, into synchronicity all around you.

Allow yourselves to truly feel the strength of your power, for you *are* empowered. If you know that *every single individual has a profound impact upon your entire planet,* you will change your world in ways you have not yet imagined—very rapidly. You will be accelerating your world at such a pace that if this is accomplished by your year 2000, then beginning from that year many things will happen you will perhaps hardly even believe.

Now, step two: take that information —that idea of the one-minute meditation at noon— and share it with as many as you possibly can. Involve individuals, cities and whole communities, states and nations; all levels of your society. Involve your radio and your television media, so that at 12 noon every day they will also allow the one minute of silent meditation. Remind everyone with a tone, if you wish, or with a comment. All participating.

The basic goal is to have every individual —yes, every *single* individual— on your planet doing that one-minute meditation by January 1, 2000. You will find such a high degree of accelerated energy focused on world peace around your world that you will be able to have the foundations laid down for one world between 1990 and the year 2000. No later than 2013, 2011. . . .

And there will indeed be peace in our time.

PEACE IN OUR LIFETIME
PEACE CLOCK

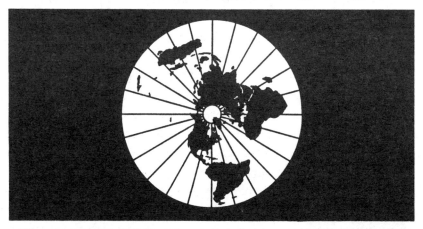

A WORLDWIDE EVENT

STARTING NOW: Wherever you are, perform a silent meditation for world peace
EVERY DAY AT NOON FOR ONE FULL MINUTE.

THE GOAL: To have EVERY PERSON ON EARTH performing this event
by the year 2000.

SYNCHRONIZED INTENTION IS THE KEY

- With an alarm, a bell, a note or any other method that works for you, remind yourself when it is noon in your time zone.
- Acquire the active participation of your company, your school, community, city, state and nation.
- Involve radio and television. Have them broadcast the PEACE CLOCK name, slogan and logo, accompanied by one minute of silence every day.
- Above all: approach all interactions with others in peaceful, constructive and creative ways.
- Copy and share this information with as many people as you can.
- Report your participation, or write for further information to: PEACE CLOCK, P. O. Box 8307, Calabasas, CA 91302.

NOTE: Peace Clock flyers and cardboard master copies are available in 12 languages (8½ x 11), as are 5 x 7 post cards. Write to: Dorothy Compinsky, 2717 Arizona Ave., #5, Santa Monica, CA 90404, U.S.A.

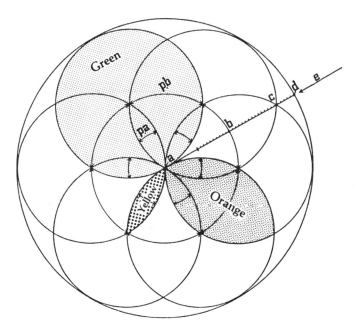

Harmonic Wave Template

This Template is used to predict general trends within groups or societies. The radius of the central circle is based on the number of years representing a repeating "completion" cycle for the society being observed. In this case 40 years shows a major shift in social, economic, political and philosophical trends in human affairs. The points at which the outwardly radiating circles overlap indicate approximate years in which other types of events will likely occur in that society.

a = *Harmonic Initiation,* beginning in 1947 and marking the recovery of a crashed alien saucer in New Mexico, proving the existence of aliens. b = *Harmonic Convergence,* a conjunction of energy in 1987 representing greater global awareness and Earth's relation to other worlds. c = *Harmonic Identification,* and will occur around the year 2027. This conjunction should represent a unified Earth, balanced ecological management and open interaction with and participation in the Association of Worlds.

The areas in the Template where the circle arcs are farthest apart portray an effect called "Polarity Resonance Manifestation," where a society manifests a creative form representing the process of growing global awareness and approaching interaction with extraterrestrial beings. This was embodied in the creation of the space drama, *Star Trek.*

pa represents the year 1967, the year *Star Trek* was introduced, and *pb* is 1987, when a new edition of *Star Trek (The Next Generation)* came into being— more accurately reflecting the Earth's growing knowledge of space and the possibility of alien life. The segmented line, *(a to d),* is the number of years represented by the Template, each increment being two years.

The Template is drawn in this manner because only six circles can circumnavigate a central, seventh circle while passing only through each circle's mid point. This creates the most stable geometric wave function that can represent a repeating cycle.

CHAPTER THREE

Harmonic Wave

August, 1987

We wish to discuss a tool, a perspective we will refer to as the harmonic wave —what you have labeled the Harmonic Convergence— in order to begin to recognize what the meaning of this idea was about. From our point of view in our interactions with you, from the perspective of extraterrestrial societies as they are beginning to interact with your terrestrial society, the explanation in mechanical terms of the Harmonic Convergence is as follows.

As suggested earlier, many of you have begun to instinctively recognize that great changes are taking place on your planet, that these changes are indicative of levels of awareness you have created within yourselves that have heretofore not been experienced on your planet for quite some time—hundreds of thousands of your years. The idea of this recognition of the Harmonic Convergence was basically an observation of the overlapping of many different frequencies of energy, frequencies of consciousness.

You have put many different kinds of labels upon the idea, none of which are wrong, but many of which may be attributable to the idea of the labels you are accustomed to using in your society to refer to ideas and events, to allow you to understand them through the symbology you have been used to for all these thousands of years. While this does not make those labels incorrect, it may be that some of those labels are limiting, or perhaps in some senses a little bit misdirecting—in terms of what the actual mechanical event was all about: an energy event, an overlapping number of vibratory frequencies of the primal energy of creation.

Everything moves in cycles; this most of you already understand. The Harmonic Convergence was simply representative of a nodal point, if you will, an overlapping of many different cycles coming into reinforcement play, one unto another—reinforcing each other and opening up a gateway, a doorway. That is, in one sense reinforcing each other and in another sense cancelling each other out. Forming a vacuum, so to speak, a limbo state, a state of disorientation and floating, in which you found yourselves able to perceive all the different variations, all the different probable realities that can exist, and thus in that floating state you could choose which reality you prefer to create on your planet.

The 40-Year Cycle

Different societies at different times have different cycles—not only on your own world, but on countless other worlds. These civilizations all have their own timing for their convergences, and their own bringing together of harmonics, of resonances, of frequencies. One large-scale cycle —although small perhaps in one perspective, but one that generally repeats itself over and over again in your particular Earth society— is the 40-year cycle. In plain terms, it seems to be that in your particular brand of consciousness you will generate a cycle of 40 orbits. This is a 40-year period in which to create changes that allow there to be the ability to see things which are 180 degrees polarized from the way you used to see them 40 of your years ago.

Forty years has been used in much of your religious literature to indicate the change time necessary for whole societies and for whole cultures on your planet, while 40 days are needed for the change of a single individual. This 40-year cycle has allowed us now to apply the harmonic wave diagram and thus show you in very clear and graphic terms how the cycles play out in your society. And to show you the determiners that portray where you are within the overall series of events that is representative of your entire transformational age—this age being generally 80 of your years long. You are now about —or I'll say *literally*— half way through.

For this to be easily translated, we have a visual aid to assist you. Many of you will begin to recognize first of all familiar patterns within this. You have seen similar symbols throughout your society for quite some time: the idea of the lotus flower. You have seen expressed in this format many different forms of vibratory energy representations which you have called mandalas, or in this sense, harmonic mantras. This is a literal mechanical tool that we utilize to gauge the momentum in particular societies with which we interact. We determine which ideas are playing out, and *when* they are most likely to be played out.

The Harmonic Convergence actually initiated the second part of a four-part harmonic. The first part, begun 40 years ago in 1947, can be called the Harmonic *Initiation.* Second: what is now going on in your society is the Harmonic *Convergence.* Third—and we will point this out in a moment— what will occur in your society will be a Harmonic *Identification.* And number four will be the idea of a Harmonic *Synchronization.*

These are the four general steps that fit this particular template. When you overlay this template on any society, once you have determined the cycle of orbits that society is using, you can utilize this template, or tool, to determine the timing within the remainder of the transformational age that will bring about certain changes to your world.

At the very center of this diagram is what can be referred to as point *a.* This is the Harmonic Initiation begun in 1947, and is very strongly connected to the fact that it was the year wherein you began to recognize as a society, even though possibly covertly at first, that other civilizations, extraterrestrial civilizations do exist. And that you are not unique or alone. Unique in the way you present yourselves, yes, but you are not alone.

That initiation, the beginning of that ripple, was like a stone being dropped into a pond of water, beginning to create vibrations that moved outward in ever-expanding spirals and circles. As each of you may recognize, if you pluck a string on one of your instruments, you see that it vibrates back and forth. You see ghost images of two strings as the two end points are fixed, while the middle part begins to vibrate in harmonic resonance with itself, in polarity resonance.

Those vibrations from the plucking are represented by the yellow petals, as designated on the diagram, the idea of the stone first dropped, and then the resonances going out and coming back together at the end, at the tip of the yellow petal. Now, the tip of these petals define a small circle within the larger circle. That is where you are now. That is the Harmonic Convergence area: the coming together of all the vibratory interstices, all the vibratory axions, that determine the particular type of opening and momentum you are going through now.

Notice in the center of each yellow petal a straight line with arrows at either side defining the widest point of polarity resonance. Simply stated, it is the farthest point, the farthest polarity experience that any cord will strike. We will get back to that in a moment. At the very tip of the yellow petal you can recognize the Harmonic Convergence of this year.

So from the center of the circle to the tip of the yellow petal represents 40 of your years. From the tip of this petal all the way to the outer large circle is another 40 orbits. Thus you have an 80-year radius (a to d). At the tips of the petals you can see that every two of those petals in turn define a larger orange petal, and at the tips of the yellow petals there is again a representation in the large orange petal of another polarity resonance. Thus the widest point in that petal is defined by the tips of the yellow petals. That is polarity resonance manifestation number two.

There are no more petals now, but only the spheres that fit within the larger sphere, those moving into the green. From the point of the tips of the orange petals outward, where the lines cross again, the next point is where each circle meets tangentially at the edge of the larger circle. So you have point a at the center, point b at the tips of the yellow petals, point c at the tips of the orange petals, and where the small circle meets the outside of the larger sphere, you have point d. . . . Thus, $a - b - c - d$.

From the 1940s to the 1980s your transformation cycle was involved with the process of forming a global link for that 40-year period, while during the 40 years previous to that you were initiating contact with all the major cultures on Earth and beginning to examine new modes of thought with regard to the religious manifestations in your world.

As we have said, at the tips of the orange petals is the Harmonic Convergence. So the outward movement, as you are passing through that apex, now brings you on an outer curve going to the tips of those orange petals. That is approximately 30 years hence, or about your year 2017.

At the tips of the orange petals you begin to see that there are no more petals. The realities you are converging, that were initiated 40 of your years ago at point c, will be represented by the Harmonic Identification. This is the point we have discussed with you which represents when the vibrational frequency of the particular reality you prefer will literally begin to separate from all other realities, literally placing you in whatever parallel Earth to which you are now most aligned.

As you then begin to separate from all other realities, all other parallel probable Earths, you continue the outer curve toward Harmonic Synchronization—at the point when that will be the only experience you have on your Earth. It will be representative of what you have identified yourselves with, and have accelerated from point c within you. In forming synchronization at the outer edge that is 40 years hence, it will then be only a world that contains the things you identified most strongly with at point c, when you separated from all other probable realities.

You may look at it simply as criss-crossing of energy, as a building of acceleration and momentum that leads you from one point, through that point to another point, and through that point to yet another point. There are 13 points including the center— and no accident that this is your thirteenth day. You may note also that 13 is the transformational gate number. It is that which allows you to face all the different portions you have perhaps hidden from yourselves, segregated yourselves into. It is the passing through a doorway; it is why it is a transformational, magic number, and why there is so much superstition associated with it in your society. It gets you to face yourselves, because you are in the limbo door facing all that you are.

These 13 points represent gateways, vortices of energy within this harmonic wave template. This is what basically has determined the Harmonic Convergence, and also what has been picked up by many individuals in your society as the reason for the Convergence going on now . . . for the gathering together of all probable realities.

Star Trek

Two more interesting points. We have generally observed that within any particular society there will be two manifestations in your culture which will indicate if and when and in what way you have begun to accept the idea that you will blend with societies other than your own. These two points occur at the two polarity resonance manifestation points, the widest parts of the yellow and the widest parts of the orange petals—indicated by the straight line across the yellow petals and the curved line across the orange petals. Number one; number two. As you can see, number one occurs by definition approximately half-way along the line from beginning to now, in your yellow petal. Number two occurs right in line with the Harmonic Convergence, because that is where all probable realities coincide.

Now we would like to play a little game for a moment. These two points, the polarity resonance manifestations, usually manifest in a culture through some art form, through some way that culture expresses itself most strongly. It is usually the strongest and most graphic representation of how that culture thinks of itself in terms of relating to other extraterrestrial cultures. So you can see that the second one, which is usually an amplification of the first, occurs now, in 1987, while the first one, being half way between 1947 and now, occurred in 1967. The guessing game is to decide which cultural phenomena in 1967, artistically speaking, represented in the most graphic way your ongoing relationship with extraterrestrial cultures.

(Star Trek.)

Yes. Now, we know some of you may find this quite amusing; however, your *Star Trek* program was initiated at exactly that half-way point in 1967, and now in 1987 is being re-initiated in a new format. It is the same expression upgraded and updated, to encompass your new understandings, and all the things you have learned to incorporate within yourselves within the last 20 years—for the second half of the yellow petal. This will usually occur in every society in a way unique to that society.

Thus you have fit the pattern perfectly; you have fit the template perfectly. Some of you may think of that program as a frivolous representation, but it is your most overriding understanding. And it has endured for so long because it represents the blending of your society with other societies in the most graphic way you allowed yourselves to represent it at that time. That is why it is a world-wide phenomenon. There are no accidents in that energy, and there is no accident in the sense that your interest in that particular phenomenon, and in expressing it in that way, has only grown and not diminished.

Your Own Space Craft

Thus you can perhaps readily understand that point *c*, your year 2017, initiates and represents the time when there will be within your society the capability of joining us with your own space craft, although it may be earlier—perhaps five years earlier. That is when your technology will allow you to develop the idea similar to our space craft technology. You will have this by 2017 if you maintain your adherence to the template, which it seems in all likelihood you will. *By 2027 you will be absolutely interwoven into the Galactic Association of Worlds.*

Forty of your years hence: not so very long. It took you 40 years to get to this point; it will take you only 30 years to get to the next point. Only ten years after that you will be part of The Association as absolute equals. You are accelerating rapidly, and you fit the pattern most strongly, as we have indicated.

As an aside—: some of you may recognize within this the natural mathematical relationships that you call the Fibonacci

Series. And if you look very closely, you may also recognize —if you remove a few lines— the old yin-yang symbol. For the yin-yang symbol comes directly from the harmonic wave template. And that is the ancient understanding that has been rendered into your polarity manifestation.

Allow yourselves to recognize that this energy wave is one that represents the frequency, the momentum, the acceleration. This Harmonic Convergence is your ability to understand that in coming together and focusing your consciousness for any such endeavor of harmony, love and light, you will create an impact on your planet, and you will allow change to occur very rapidly.

One of the ideas behind this Convergence, as the fulcrum point between an old reality and a new reality, is to recognize that as you each individually become the pattern for the reality you wish to experience, bit by bit each of you adds to the overall energy of your world's ability to become that world as you have envisioned it. It will accelerate in that direction; you will begin to see the blending and harmonics occur between what is now distinct and segregated levels of your society—sociologically, economically, politically. Through the combination of all that consciousness, individuals who are so aligned can utilize that energy to take steps to escalate and accelerate themselves to new levels of awareness—stepping stones, as you call them.

Many of you have recognized that there are many convergences and gateways occurring throughout any particular year. However, in your framework of time this octave month represents a very strong convergence cycle. The basic idea behind this particular gateway is that it is primarily for the specific blending of all places upon your planet, all energies within every one of you— especially those energies representing the masculine and feminine aspects within each individual.

The Dream

Now let us relate a dream communication in which we participated through the physical channel, and you can see the symbology referred to as this Convergence. In the dream the channel remembered symbolically being in a location that represented many different locations around your planet: Hawaii, Japan, India —many areas. There were symbologies which made it seem as if it was everywhere and yet in no one particular place.

Many beings were waiting for a particular entity to step forth from out of a gateway—a gateway on a plateau at the edge of a precipice overlooking a vast ocean and the horizon beyond. There was light and it was dark at the same time. In the dream the gate was called the Gate of the Moon, and was also known as the Gate of the Sun. It was all gates; it was the going in, the coming out, and the blending of many different avenues and motive forces on your planet.

When the being stepped out from the gate to greet all of the individuals who were waiting, it was both literally and physiologically masculine and feminine—wearing a simple white sarong from the waist down. It was to some degree a Pleiadian representation, and was marked by some of the interactions taking place on your Fuji and Shasta areas, and in your Hawaiian area. For from the Shasta area, and the Fuji and Hawaiian areas there is a triangle that encompasses the entire energy of the Pacific basin on your planet, representing the strong re-emergence of Lemurian energy. And this dream was within Lemuria as well. The being stepping forth represented the blending of the feminine and masculine aspects within each and every one of you that has been taking place at this time on your world, the equalization of all of this energy, all levels of your consciousness.

It was recognized within the dream that this represented the idealized energy of the Convergence itself, which is the willingness within each one of you to blend and pull together to integrate all the different formerly segregated aspects of your consciousness into one unified whole. Thus you will function as a representational whole being, a strong and full individual, assisting and giving to your world the necessary energy to allow your entire planet to become the single individual it must be in the transformational age. This unified oneness then can interact with other whole worlds. Therefore, any way your imagination and dreams reflect to you the understanding and awareness of convergence within yourselves, it will be reflected in the exterior format.

Now, many individuals are viewing this Convergence as a negative idea—time to shake things up, perhaps even to have geophysical changes. We can hardly stress enough the idea that if you are willing to consciously allow yourselves to understand your own symbols and what they represent in terms of your own blending, your own awakening, and your own taking of responsibility for your lives and the creations therein, then you will be awake through the time of the Convergence and thereafter. It will not be necessary to create an unconscious manifestation of geophysical changes to shake you awake.

Wake up now, and you will allow the transformations upon your planet to be ones of blending and smooth harmony, so that it will be the gate of the dawn, the rising sun, the gate of the moon and all things that have formerly represented your unconscious being. These things will all blend together into one smoothly flowing energy, that will allow you to recognize that *your physical reality is, in fact, simply a waking dream.*

CHAPTER FOUR

Living on the Edge

What about all these earth changes being predicted these days, Bashar?

Our understanding —and this goes for all such so-called predictions— is as follows: changes there will be; and there may be isolated events in which individuals may choose to believe they need to experience the transformation in catastrophic or disastrous ways. However, no one needs to experience the transformation in a negative way. If individuals are willing to wake up within themselves now, and recognize they deserve happiness without having to go through trials by fire in order to believe they deserve happiness, then they won't have to place themselves in a scenario where they are shaken awake.

Allow yourselves to recognize that any such information is only an opportunity, not an absolute dictum, to be aware of the energy within you and what reality you choose to believe is more true for you. When you recognize you do not need to experience that type of a tool, then you will find that even if you were to remain in a locale that did experience it, *you* would not. And if enough individuals in your locale understand they do not need to experience it that way, the entire locale will not.

Many of you enjoy earthquakes; you love "living on the edge." You are finding that the energy excites you and spurs you on to greater creativity, and you choose to congregate in areas of high seismic activity. That's why you are where you are (California). You are learning to direct this energy, learning to use it rather than fearing it. You are attracting yourselves to particular places that represent different degrees of energy, and in doing so, giving your-selves the creative opportunity to know you can flow that energy *through* you, and you can begin to identify with the power that is actually within you. *For no magnitude of any quake that has ever occurred on your planet matches even infinitesimally the amount of power you have to create your reality.*

You are learning to direct your energy by feeling it externally in ways that show you how much power you have, how much power you *are*. So you can get more and more used to the idea, at whatever rate is comfortable for you, of living with that much power, and of understanding what that much power is capable of doing. You are choosing to flow that power in a positive way, rather than a negative way, choosing to allow that power to de-structurize but not destroy. . . . Thank you all for being so bold.

The Fluid Future

The idea is to simply be in touch with the fact that the so-called future is always fluid. There are many probable realities; and when someone says —or you perceive— "Well, this is going to happen then, and it's going to be very catastrophic," it is sim-ply one perception of one band-width frequency, one probable reality. Now that you are aware that there is energy behind that probable future, if you don't prefer it, you don't have to stay on that frequency.

It doesn't necessarily mean you have to move. If you find you are in any locale wherein the majority of consciousness insists on experiencing the transformation in negative, or in catastrophic destructive ways, and you know you don't need to, then whether you even try to or not, you will automatically attract into your life an opportunity which will remove you from that locale with-out your even trying. Without your even planning to.

So if you are following what is most exciting for you, and you find yourself not attracting a situation in your life to remove you from the locale you are in; that is, if you do find the locale you are in is the most exciting locale you would like to be in, in gen-eral, then take it as a sign that you will be able to remain in that locale, and nothing will interrupt the path you chose to be.

What if I find that place not feeling right?

Then go where you find it to be more exciting. But recognize that it doesn't necessarily mean you are taking yourself out of the place that will experience destruction. You are simply following the flow of your own path and going to where you are most excited to be, surrounding yourself with the environment that is conducive to the idea you are being. That's it. No part of your planet *has* to experience the change in catastrophic ways; *none* of it has to. It depends on your willingness to wake up.

Atlantis

November 1, 1988: *Bashar, you said something about Halloween being connected to the destruction of Atlantis?*

Yes, from your ancient times All Hallows Eve, or Halloween, represents the day before the destruction of Atlantis. November 1 is the day of destruction, and November 2 is the day after. In some of your religious vernacular these days translate into All Hallows Eve, All Souls Day and All Saints Day, and are the idea of the destruction of your Atlantean land mass approximately 11 to 12 thousand years ago.

The issue you are dealing with on your Earth at this time is connected strongly to both the planet Maldek destroying itself long ago and a repetition of the cycle of Atlantis, although on a smaller scale than Maldek. In your current time frame the United States represents the idea of the replay of Atlantis, for you have much of the same technology and the same position in relation to politics around the world. Also you have many of the same individuals from Atlantis who have now restructured themselves to the point of deciding whether or not they will destroy the world again. **You all chose to be here in this transformational age to see that you do NOT replay Atlantis and destroy yourselves and your Earth this time around.**

It was stated in the Ra Materials, Bashar, that no one had ever left this density since Jesus' time.

Actually you have all decided to remain and return because the transformation is so attractive and exciting. It is not so much that no one has been *able* to leave; it is that no one has *wanted* to. And as you say, *"You* are where it's at." Your planet is going through such a strong transformation that not only do the individuals on it not necessarily want to leave, because they want to be a part of it on some level, physically or non-physically, but you have attracted the attention of thousands of other civilizations and dimensions of consciousness. These wish to watch what's going on. Thus, you have all wished to add to the momentum of the group karma of the transformation.

Economic Resources

Bashar, you say we are transforming. How do we transform our economy? Or will we have economic depression?

You will to some degree. But the idea is that there does not have to be a depression. You are simply recognizing that your economic structure is shifting, is changing. And yes, in your terms the old one may need to break down. But that breakdown does not in any way mean it *must* be in a depletive manner. It can be replaced; it can be regrown in a different way; it can be transformed.

But do you feel that there will be a major *shifting in the economy?*

Oh, yes.

Do the values in America reflect that in a certain unconscious or conscious way?

The values of your entire earth reflect it, because you are now becoming global. And so you need a global economy, in a sense. Although it will not be economics as you have known it.

Do you have anything to say to us about ways that we may accelerate ourselves through that shift?

Yes. **Begin by basing your economics on each other, not on a symbol!** You yourselves are what back your services. That is all there is to it. Direct interaction between individuals, with the removal of the limitations you call borders, will facilitate an interactive global economy. It is simply the idea of the reapportionment of the resources you have, and the reshifting of your priorities. There is really no lack on your world at all. And there is not actually overpopulation. Rather there is simply a particular disbursement of individuals and resources in such a way as to make it seem as if there is a lack.

Balance your economy by the sharing of responsibilities —in any task, corporation, or whatever— and the reliance upon the resources of all, rather than the hoarding of, or the fearing of, others—in terms of being able to deplete your own resources. Create a republic of ideas, in a sense.

I also read that there's an impending axis shift on this planet.

All right. There are changes of electromagnetic energy. But again, the overall fundamental idea is that any transformation can be experienced in a positive or a negative way; it's up to you. Whatever vibration you buy into most strongly will be the way you experience the shifts going on in your electromagnetic field. Individuals who have a great deal of fear about the shift will lure themselves into places of destruction. Individuals who understand they can use the energy to enlighten themselves, and elevate and accelerate themselves in a positive way, will simply know beyond the shadow of a doubt that they do not have to give themselves the idea of a trial by fire, and they will lure themselves to places on your planet where they will experience the energy as a *destructurization,* rather than as destruction. The more individuals on your planet there are who recognize they can use this energy in a positive way, rather than simply fearing or believing it *has* to happen in a negative way, the more readily the energy of the entire planet can change.

Thus the idea is that, yes, there are shifts in your energy taking place, both in you and in your planet, since in a sense you are one and the same thing. Here and there, as you have experienced this day of your time, you may see pockets of adjustment in your land mass. But it does not have to be as devastatingly overwhelming as many of you used to fear it had to be. You have already done much to change that energy; you have already changed it in a positive way to a great degree—just by being willing to understand you do not really have to truly shake yourselves completely awake. That is, if you are willing to wake up now, you do not have to suffer and struggle and go through all sorts of negative trials in order to wind up with the understanding you could have now: *that you deserve happiness; that you can create your reality to be whatever you prefer it to be.*

Choosing the Positive

A lot of the idea of someone experiencing a transformation in a negative way is that he is holding on tight to an old belief, and will not allow himself to let it go and trust his natural flow; it seems to take that degree of violence to make him break his grip. Sometimes an individual will even take himself out of physical reality in order to allow himself to start afresh. But he does not really die; nothing ever really does. It is all eternal and infinite.

However, you don't have to struggle, and you don't have to suffer. Any time you are made aware of an idea, and it is presented in a potentially negative format, take it not as an absolute prediction chiseled in steel—or neutronium, or whatever you may think is most difficult to change. The idea is presented as an opportunity: "Look," it says, "you can vibrate in synchronous accord with the negative energy of this idea, this fear, and attract yourselves to it and attract it to you. Or you can vibrate in accord with the positive energy. Experience the opportunity, the exploration, the excitement, rather than the anxiety and the fear, the limitation and the segregation."

Whatever vibration you choose will be the reality you get. Remember: no circumstance has built-in meaning; all situations are fundamentally neutral—blank, empty, zero— zip, as you say. *You* give them the meaning. Because of what you have been taught to believe these things mean, the meaning you give it is the effect you get. Positive meaning in, positive effect out. Negative meaning in, negative effect out. Simple physics; simple mechanics. *You experience the reality you are the vibration of; you cannot experience the reality you are not the vibration of.*

But Bashar, what about Nostradamus, Edgar Cayce, and the others who are predicting catastrophe?

There is no such thing as a prediction of the future. There is only a sensing of the energy that is most prominent and probable to manifest *at the time the prediction is made.* There is no absolute future; it is only a probability. When a prediction is sensed, the individual making that prediction is sensing the energy as it lies at that moment—behind whichever idea has the most momentum and has the most likelihood of manifesting, IF —important *if*— the energy doesn't change.

You always have the opportunity to change that energy. And in very many ways *the reason that predictions exist is to let you know where the energy IS. Then if you don't prefer it being there, you change it.* So predictions, when they are understood for what they are —rather than the rigidized, unmovable structures many of you have been taught to believe they are— when they are understood for what they are, then you will realize that a prediction, when it is made, and therefore when it is known in your consciousness, renders itself obsolete many times just by being known.

Let me stress that *your awareness of where it lies changes that energy!* Now if you don't prefer it to be there, you can do something about it, because your consciousness is focused upon it. If you hear a prediction, and you do not think you have the ability to change the energy —if you generate more fear— then you reinforce the energy that the prediction first picked up on, and make it more likely the prediction will come to pass. But if you are willing to realize that a prediction in no way determines that this is the absolute thing which *must* happen, then you can understand you have a great deal of flexibility with regard to the predictions.

Old Perspectives

Also, any time a prediction is made, it is made within the context of the time frame that it occurs in. Many ancient predictions, many ancient sensings of the way the energy of the entire culture in which you exist was to be experienced followed from a certain belief that existed in your culture at that time. That belief, generally summed up, is as follows: the great transformations that were sensed that were going to occur could not be understood as being able to occur without everything that already existed coming apart first. So when those predictions were made, they were made with the understanding and the belief that in order to experience the transformation, things were to be absolutely destroyed to make way for that transformation.

Now things do have to change; things do have to, in a sense, break down for another reality to take its place. But that breaking down in no way must be destructive; it can be creative. A breaking down can simply be the willingness to allow something to change, rather than holding on to the way you believe it must stay. Then the situation —then the culture, the structure— will break down. It will change; it will transform into the type of structure that is capable of representing the transformation in a less catastrophic way.

Therefore, any time you hear of these so-called predictions put in that manner, it is your opportunity to realize that what you are being told is, "Look, this is where your society is stacking all of its beliefs. It is still running off of the idea that you cannot deserve ecstasy without first going through a trial by fire."

But this is an old perspective. Your awakening to the understanding that you deserve happiness in and of itself has already changed much of the original energy that was sensed back then by those individuals. So now that you know you are made of love and light and ecstasy, and that ecstasy and happiness is your birthright, you now know you don't have to shake yourselves awake. You are waking up without that violent action. As was stated earlier, if enough individuals in that area all realize collectively that they do not have to experience catastrophe, then the energy of the entire area can change, and that manifestation does not have to occur in that area at all. 'Tis up to you.

In fact, you are all now the funnels, the channels, the valves through which that energy can be released and transformed in a positive way. You can put that energy that was going to go toward that idea of breaking you down in such a catastrophic way, shaking you up in a violent way— you can now put that energy toward constructive ideas. Any individual who knows beyond the shadow of a doubt that he is waking up, that he does not have to shake himself awake, will know that that experience is not something he needs in his reality. Therefore, even though there may be isolated pockets around your world where individuals believe they must experience it in that way, those who do not have that belief will no longer be in those areas, as we have said.

Therefore, any time you hear one of those predictions, do not take it as an absolute law of the universe: "This is chiseled in steel!" No; take it as an offering, as an opportunity to examine where you are being told the energy lies. And if you don't prefer it to be there, take it as an opportunity to change it by doing the things that excite you in life: being of service, and acting as if you know you deserve ecstasy.

Channeled Predictions

Some of the channeled entities today are telling us about catastrophes coming, Bashar, and many people are in fear and panic.

Many of you have shared with us certain information being told to you by various entities being channeled in your world, information delineated in negative scenarios, negative aspects. And you are afraid these must manifest through the idea of earthquakes, floods, famine, and much of the like. As we have said, this energy potential *does* exist, but only as a potential. It may have a great deal of momentum behind it; a high degree of backing behind it from your civilization. But recognize that —not that you are being lied to by these entities, for you are not— but recognize you are being allowed to see in these sharings that you have an opportunity to decide whether what they say is true for you in terms of what you know you need to experience in the transformation taking place on your planet right now.

Therefore, in each and every interaction that has ever taken place between any of you and any entity coming through a channel, when you hear something that does not strike a vibratory chord within you, do recognize that there is no need for the idea of accusation from you to them. For all that is being shared with you is a perception of an area in your civilization —or a potential reality— that does have a great degree of momentum and energy behind it . . . due to the fears many of you generate. But if you are willing to hear these words from entities who speak of the transformation in catastrophic terms; if you are willing to hear them as an opportunity to understand and reflect what you know to be true for you, then you can utilize the situation. You can be an equal to them, and not continue to feel that what you are being given as information is any more powerful than the information you have within yourselves—with regard to the reality and a world which is, after all, yours.

If we may suggest, therefore, the following: if you find yourselves in a certain scenario where such information is being imparted to you, and you are willing to have conviction on it, this may be shared with that entity—in the form of a letter perhaps:

"Dear Entity:

"I recognize that what you are sharing comes from your love for us and your desire to serve us and allow us to expand in our awareness of the transformation—which is a reflection of all we have ever been and can become.

"At the same time, I would now wish to share with you, dearest Entity, that your sharing affords me the opportunity to recognize that the transformation, in the terms of catastrophe you have delineated, is not the reality I, as a co-creator of this world, prefer. I choose to give energy to the idea that if I am willing to face all portions of myself, and accept and allow all situations in my life to be of positive service, to be in my life for positive reasons, that I can allow my experience of the transformation to be one that is positive, and not in need of the expression of catastrophe in order for me to understand myself and grow.

"I recognize that expressions of catastrophe may be the only way some individuals can believe a transformation will have a lasting effect. However, do allow me at this time, dearest Entity, to ask for your further love and your further assistance in suggesting to us ideas, ideas which could allow us to assist our world, so that as many of us as possible can now let ourselves also realize there is no longer any need to believe that transformations and changes of lasting positive effect *must* be created through trials by fire.

"I am willing to share that I believe ecstasy is our birthright. Will you share with us your perspective on how we may accelerate within ourselves to sufficient degrees to allow there to be upon this world that we hold dear the smoothest, easiest and most loving version of the transformation that can occur? . . . Thank you."

What You Are

Each and every one of you willing to utilize that situation — once again, not in an accusatory way, but in a sharing way, in a convicted way— to stand up and make a difference, and be the individuals you know yourselves to be and express what you know to be true for you— each and every one of you willing to utilize the situation as a reflection for that opportunity will make a geometric, a logarithmic difference in the ability of your entire world to allow its next step to be that much easier.

Even as a single individual you add that much energy to the momentum of your ability to experience your transformation in a positive and loving way. For you *are* energy, and experience it each of you will. You yourselves *are* the experience you are having. All of the physical reality, all of the emotional atmosphere, in which any particular manifestation or experience does occur in your lives —in a seemingly objectified manner— all of that materiality, every subtle nuance, is all *you* in different manifesting reflections back to yourselves.

You have created the idea of yourselves to be physical reality, and there are many manifestations of physical reality. But in this particular manifestation of the idea you are being, you have been playing out, as your particular unique physical reality, a great deal of separation and negativity so that you could explore all of the ideas of what it means to be limited, as we have mentioned to you before. Therefore, you have created yourselves to be the idea of a reality whose only cognition, basically, fundamentally, immediately, is a material reflection seemingly outside of yourselves, so that you can feel as if you are *in* a material universe, rather than knowing that the material universe is what you *are*.

That is what you are now beginning to explore within the idea of integration. You are beginning to experience the integration, the blending of more and more awareness of more and more of yourselves. You are beginning to blend the dream imagination and physical realities into one, to experience all the ideas of this transformation —the disorientation, the confusion, the limbo state, the seemingly surrealistic attitudes and atmospheres you encounter from time to time— which allow you to feel disassociated from the material physicality you have been used to experiencing for so many hundreds of thousands of years.

Now you find yourselves integrating and beginning to see through the illusion you have created of physical materiality. It has served you, and served you well. But an illusion, a tool, and a creation it is, nonetheless.

Personality Construct

We have said many times of late in your time frame that what you consider to be your personality is an artificial construct, and is not who or what you are. Recognize, therefore, that although you have created for many thousands of years the idea that you are a humaniform existence, understand that the idea of your humanity, the essence of what you are, is not restricted to your humaniform existence. Begin to allow yourselves to recognize that in a non-physical state you are not human; you are quite something else. You are an essence, a primal idea of energy consciousness —a being or a soul, if you will— which can project itself as basically any form, any symbol, any idea it wishes to.

We know that your civilization to some degree does recognize, at least intellectually, the idea that you are not human when non-physical, and that humanity is only the idea of the physical reflection of the soul. But also realize that many of you, because of the habit of being human, many times may not realize that when you think of the idea of the disembodied soul, you still find yourselves making the analogy that it is a *human* soul.

Understand that the soul, the energy essence, is not intrinsically human. Many different civilizations, within the third/fourth-density reality which you are experiencing, do have similar humaniform, or humanoid appearance. From our perspective, in considering ourselves to be our own form of human, to us *you* are humanoid. Recognize, however, that our soulness, your soulness, is not actually human; it is an essence which is above and beyond, and which transcends that limited definition.

Therefore, begin to understand that one of the reasons —as you make the shift from third to fourth density, and recognize more of your consciousness to be what it is— one of the reasons you are beginning to experience many ideas which disorient you and confuse you, and do not seem to fit into the structure you are used to, is because you are beginning to view, from time to time, from a point of view that is not strictly human. It is the essential viewpoint of the beingness, the consciousness you are, which can be human and many other things.

Recognize that you can begin to understand yourselves in this homogenous sense as everything and nothing at the same time—as a principle, as an idea, as an essence. By simply allowing yourselves to view from the viewpoint of this essentialness of your existence, many of the things which are now beginning to occur to you in your transformation from third to fourth density may carry a new clarity—if you allow yourselves the opportunity to discontinue the limitation of expecting everything to make sense in humaniform terms.

For the idea, or the projection, of your humanity has been a definition which has served you, and in a sense will continue to serve you through the idea of your fourth-density experience— although the type of humanity you will be in fourth density is not the same type that you were in third. You are rapidly evolving, once again, and you will find, to speak linearly, that further on in the middle, and very much so toward the end of your fourth-density cycle, you will not be humaniform in the way you have considered yourselves to be at all.

As you progress from quasi-planar physical reality to non-physical existence, going from fourth to fifth density, you will allow yourselves the opportunity to experientially become the energy matrix of focused consciousness within the homogenous energy field of All That Is that you actually are. And the idea of expressing yourselves as humanity will be a tool no longer necessary for your experience.

The idea of humanity, though well it has served you in this way, again is but another tool within which you have clothed yourselves. It has suited the purposes that you chose to explore and experience. But do recognize that as you all exist on many different planes of reality simultaneously, there are many other guises that you also exist within that are human, humanoid, and not human at all.

By simply shifting the perspective of your consciousness, as you make your transformations from third to fourth density, you may even begin to understand that from time to time, as it suits you, there may be opportunities to look even through the eyes of the aspects of your selves that have nothing at all to do with humanity. For it will broaden your perspective in many different ways. Though you will remain focused for the most part in the idea of your humaniform fourth density existence, as long as that suits the purpose of this fragment of your consciousness that is channeling through the prism of this artificial personality construct that you call your human body.

CHAPTER FIVE

The Second Coming

Bashar, are you and your people familiar with Christianity?

To some degree.

Well, I believe in Jesus Christ as our savior—

When you say you believe in Jesus Christ, what does that mean?

That means that I believe in a God who created the universe, including all of us, and that because we are all sinners, Jesus—

One moment! You believe you are a sinner?

Yes.

What is a sinner? Will you define this for me? I understand the concept of sin, but have not heard the concept from *you*. Would you therefore define the concept of "sinner" for me in your own way—as it relates to how you see yourself?

A sin for me is anything I would do or think that goes against something God would want.

What does God want?

God wants —I guess very simply, in order to answer it within the time limit allowed here— God wants me to show unconditional love in all situations. And any time I don't do that—

One moment! Did you say unconditional love? Do you understand what that means?

I understand it to mean that as far as people —whom I'm supposed to unconditionally love, for example the people in here— no matter who they are or what they have done, as far as I'm concerned I love them because God loves them. If God loves everybody in here, I have no right to overrule that.

All right. Now, you know you can create the reality of over-ruling it, but we do understand what you mean when you say you have no right. You *can* do it, but that does not mean it is something you'd want to do. Nor are we suggesting this is something that would create harmony on your world. No. But simply take yourself literally. People have very blatantly judged others, have they not? And it is not a matter of whether or not they have the right to do it.

Is it wrong?

There is no right and wrong. It is a matter of whether you choose to create a positively manifesting reality or a negatively manifesting reality.

Which would you suggest?

I would suggest the positive one. Because choosing the positively manifesting reality will be integrating yourself with All That Is, whereas knowing yourself as separate from All That Is creates an idea of isolation that does not allow you to feel your connection to All That Is. This leads to the need to dominate. For when you separate yourself from All That Is, controlling and dominating others is perhaps the only way you will feel you can collect what you see around you, *to* you. Thus you create many ideas out of separation and negative manifestation that are, in your terms, unpleasant: war, disease and many other ideas you say you do not like. This is why we would always suggest the positively manifesting reality.

However, recognize that we perceive the idea of judgment, in and of itself, to be of the negative manifestation. Thus we do not say anything is right or wrong, because that to us is to judge All That Is. To us even the idea of judgment is the choosing of the negative. To know what you prefer does not mean that you have to judge or invalidate anyone else—in terms of the way that individual chooses to explore his own Godhood, to relate to himself as his portion of All That Is. If he has chosen separation, negative reality, limitation, judgment— then it will be less likely he will perceive his connection to All That Is.

On the other hand, one who is integrated has already chosen

the idea of unconditional love, and will recognize that there is no need to judge those who have not chosen It. For unconditional love is the granting of validity to everything within Creation— for its own sake. Because that portion of creation has seen fit to learn about itself in the way it has chosen, then you, in choosing unconditional love, generate the faith and the trust to know that in an ultimate sense he is always going to be all right. Ultimately every idea is still contained within the overall idea of All That Is, and cannot become lost. There is nowhere to lose anything *to*— until you create that type of separation. There is nowhere to lose anything *to* until you, in choosing negativity and limitation and separation from yourself *as* All That Is, choose to create a dimension in which you can remove yourself from the rest of everything. Any idea you call a lost soul is a contradiction in terms. A soul always knows where it is.

What do you mean by a lost soul?

The idea we are ascribing to many individuals expressing the specific ritualized expressions through which they channel the idea of their love. Many times, even though they express it to be unconditional, it still comes with conditions. We are not saying this is your case. We are saying that we are relating to the terminology you are using, by being so specific about what you have described as the way you believe and what you have called being a sinner— which by your ultimate definition means someone who is outside of —has placed himself outside of— his recognition of himself as God.

*My recognition of myself **as** God?*

Yes.

I'm God?!?

Of course. Understand this is what we are talking about: many of your beliefs or religions on your planet speak of the idea of God —or what we call All That Is— as being omnipotent. Everywhere, all-knowing; omniscient and all-seeing . . . everything, everywhere. If God by your definition is everything, how can you be outside of it? You must also be God; God must also be you. God knows you are God. Why do you not know you are God?

Well, say I create a model . . . of an airplane. I created it and put it together, but it's not me.

Yes, it is. Understand that what you experience as your physical reality is all a symbol. If you wish to use the term illusion, all right. That may clarify it for you.

Well, doesn't that illusion, or symbol— it needs a representation, does it not?

It is a representation of an idea.

*(Other): If you are the idea of making the plane, then you are the plane, too. Whatever idea you have, you **are** that idea.*

Yes. You understand that everything in your universe is a matter, physically, of vibration. You cannot perceive anything that you are *not.* The vibration you *are* creates what you perceive the physical reality to be. Thus, if you have created this idea of a model airplane in front of you, then you are extending a portion of the idea of yourself and reflecting it back to yourself as the ability to do that outside yourself, seemingly. But everything you perceive, every individual in the room, is your creation. You have to create your version of them in order to perceive them. You follow me?

Kind of. If I am dedicating my life to following Jesus Christ—

Why would you want to do that? He did not want you to do that.

He did not want me to do that?

No. He does not want you to follow him; he wants you to be *like* him.

Well, that's kind of what I mean.

Then say what you mean. Understand that your terminology is what we were discussing; that upon your planet many times the terminology you choose reflects how you go about relating to the ideas you *think* you believe in. And in this case you are saying that by *following* someone, you are separating yourself from, and making yourself less than, rather than being equal to—which is what he wanted you to know. That all of you are Christ consciousness like he is. The idea of following "the way" was not a matter of being subservient, but of being equal and reflective, being that energy that was being demonstrated. That is "the way."

(Other): Do you think that's why maybe we are so limited? Because we —or Christianity— put trust in Jesus Christ and not in ourselves?

The idea is that any time you take the power that you *are*, and remove it from yourselves, you place a limitation that actually denies your very existence—what you have been created to be! So yes, in that sense the definitions are what is responsible for creating the limitations. To some degree, the idea of what has been described as many of the attributes and experiences are all valid; any tool is a valid tool if it gets you where you want to go.

The Second Coming

But the idea is that your society, as we perceive it —and again this is not meant derogatorily— has placed many labels, many definitions, which in and of themselves are really the only thing responsible for limiting your ability to see that you are all the Christ. And that is what it is all about. If you want to find the idea of the embodiment of Christ consciousness, go home and look in a mirror. And then start acting as if you are that embodiment, and you will be fulfilling the idea that the Christ consciousness sought to impart to all of you. *What you have referred to in your society as the "second coming" is not the coming of an individual. It is the recognition within each individual on your planet of the Christ that each and every one of you is . . . and living like it. That is your second coming!*

Know that the manifestation in physical terms of what you call the Christ actually happened far more often than once. And the idea is that in every endeavor, in every projection of the Christ as a physical expression, what was being shared with your population was that you are all part of the Christ. The idea was not that only Christ can create the reality you desire, but that your power to create that reality is a part of what God *is*.

The idea is this: at the time the information was delivered in your society, the concepts that were understood by your civilization then could only translate the idea in terms of being a ruler and being ruled. And so you created the idea that the Christ was a savior who would do everything *for* you—rather than understanding that Christ is only a reflection, a reflection to each and every one of you that you are aspects of the Christ and have an *absolute right* to create the elevation and ascension of your own energy as a representation of that energy.

Well, when Jesus said, "I am the way, the truth and the life; no one comes to the Father but through me," what did he mean by that?

He was saying, to paraphrase, as you understand your language now, "What you perceive in me is the vibration of integration, wherein I know myself to be on the same level, equal to God, All That Is. The only way you will know yourself to be that idea is to be like me, to be of the equal vibration of recognizing yourself as All That Is." That is why he said, "I am the way." He did not mean, "I know the only thing that will get you there." He simply meant that you, in allowing yourself to know that everything you do is valid in the overall sense, are granting support and service and validity to the ultimate idea of the Creation itself, and recognizing your own equality to Godhood. That is *being* the way.

You said something— and people kind of laughed when you said, "He didn't say I know the only way." But he did say, "I am the way, the truth and the life. No one comes to the Father but through me."

Understand this as well: what you are calling your biblical literature contains less than 10% of what that individual ever said in his life; and what was even written down is very much misinterpreted, according to the understanding of when it was written. Recognize that your Bible was not written to record history; it was written to *convert*.

Is the Bible not true?

It is true for those individuals who wrote it, in the way they understood it. But recognize that there is still much misinterpretation of what was actually said.

How do you know that?

We are sensing into the mass consciousness, your higher levels of consciousness. Now, we cannot expect you to take us at our word. It is up to you to believe what you want, as we have said. But we will discuss with you what we perceive to exist within your own higher consciousness, which knows itself to be equal to the idea of the Christ consciousness. We can talk to it, and so can you. We are simply here to let you know that you can talk to your own higher consciousness; and once you allow yourself to do so, you will find that it will tell you exactly what I am telling you now.

Well, that's what I believe, okay?

Absolutely! It gets you where you want to go, and that is what matters. We support you unconditionally on your chosen path. And as we often have said, every path is valid; no one belief is any more valid than any other belief. They are all equal.

(Other): All ideas are valid, including the idea that no other idea is valid.

Yes, very good.

The Only Son

Was Jesus Christ the only son of God?

The individual you call Jesus of Nazareth is but one facet of the overall Christ consciousness, or world spirit. Each and every world, each and every civilization, has its own version of that Christ consciousness. In our ancient remnant language —which we no longer use, as we are telepathic in our society— the combined consciousness of our entire world was called Shakana. Our Shakana, your Christ consciousness, and the combined consciousnesses of all other worlds together form the Infinite Creation.

Our relationship with your Christ consciousness is very direct and interactive, since we are interacting with the combination of all the consciousness upon your planet in order to be of assistance to you. Therefore we experience a direct interactive and unconditionally loving relationship with the vibration you call the Christ consciousness, *because it is all of you.* Since we come from outside of your sphere in a sense, in order to be of service to you, we

must interact *through* that sphere. Thus we will take upon ourselves the patterns of the unconditional love it expresses in order
to translate into your dimension of experience the symbols to
which you can relate. So our experience, our relationship, with
the Christ consciousness in many ways is very direct—sometimes
very much more so than many of you allow yourselves to be.

You may also note that one of the physical manifestations of
the direct Christ consciousness that many of you have not recognized is the being you call Mary, the mother of Jesus, who is the
female polarity of the Christ. There is always male and female in
the collective Christ consciousness. From our perspective, what
this basically means —in relating it to what you now call your
New Age, or your transformational age— is that, as we have said,
the so-called "second coming" is no longer the manifestation of
the Christ consciousness in a single embodiment. It is the awakening of the Christ consciousness within all of you, so that you
may literally create heaven on Earth—all of you doing so as children of God.

Recognize that the idea, as it has been translated into your
language, is usually interpreted as Christ being the Son of God,
whereas Jesus Christ actually referred to himself as the son of
man.

He called himself the son of man?

Look in your own Bible. He calls himself the son of man. Do
understand that the writings of what was verbalized by Jesus of
Nazareth were not even begun to be committed to paper until
approximately 57 years after the death of the physical Jesus.

*Well, you talked about the Bible being misinterpreted through
the years.*

Yes, every single written idea contains some misinterpretation
where it regards placing ritual around the idea of what happened.

God couldn't have watched over it?

Why should he?

Because it was His work. He wanted it—

No, no, no. Understand: it was a reflection, an offering, a gift.
Unconditional love. God is unconditional love, and will not force

you to interpret something in any way, shape or form. It is up to you; that is why you are here.

So the word of God, the Bible, according to you is not the word of God?

Yes, all of it is. As all the people who wrote it were also God. Understand this: it is all relative. The word of God is all relative . . . to itself. God contains every paradox, every paradigm, every dichotomy, every blending. God is *all* that is; there is nothing outside. You are All That Is; your space in which you live; your time —which you spend so much of wondering who and what you are— all of those things are creations from your idea of who you think you are. You are one idea of God. Every being, all beings in creation, are all the different ways God has of looking at Itself. That is what it means to be All That Is. Every dimension, every being, every thing, every thought: it is all God. And many of those things come into creation simply for no other reason than the fact that they *can*.

Many times when you ascribe more importance to this passage or piece of literature than some other passage or literature, seeking for some ultimate idea of truth, you are at that moment diversifying, focusing and fixating a portion of All That Is, and not looking at the whole—which always sees *Itself* as whole. The idea of knowing yourself to be God is simply allowing yourself the broadest possible definition of that concept, and knowing that for God that is real. God knows itself to be its own being, but also knows itself to be the compilation of every being within it. And knows every being within it to contain the totality of the whole. For as you say, nothing is impossible to All That Is; if you can conceive of it, it is real to All That Is. On some level, some dimension, some aspect of consciousness, it exists.

Now, when you do this separating out and searching through and analyzing all of the different passages in literature, many times you go about doing this because you are looking for this ultimate purpose. Recognize this: existence *is*; All That Is *is!* It always was, is now, and always will be. Existence does not have its existence *within* time; time exists within All That Is. Therefore it is eternal. Therefore understand that the concept —and any concept that is created within All That Is— is in a sense subordinate to it. Ultimate truth as a concept and purpose as a concept are things that exist within existence. And existence existed before there was the concept of purpose. That which existed before the concept of purpose does not need a purpose to keep on existing. Thus All That Is will express and manifest in all the ways It can— for no other reason, for no other purpose other than It *can* because It *is* the Creator. And the Creator creates . . . again simply because It can.

Changing Symbols

Your symbols are valid for you. You have changed your mind before, and you will change your mind again about what symbols are relevant in the understanding of who and what you are. It does not matter in the overall sense what you choose to believe. If you know that you are believing what you are believing out of unconditional love for All That Is, and also equally important, unconditional love for yourself, then there is no need to worry about what you believe. There is no need to worry about what anyone believes, since you know that whatever you believe is going to create the type of reality you will be experiencing. And experience *that*, you will.

The only thing I'd like to say is if that's what you believe, what you're missing is a relationship with the God who made you.

Why? Understand again, you yourself are missing the idea that I perceive both ideas. I contain the totality of the dichotomy of the polarity of the seeming opposites. I know myself to be All That Is; and I also know All That Is relates to me as a higher consciousness. I can create the idea of knowing I have a relationship with All That Is; at the same time I can also see myself as the one creating that relationship, and therefore *being* All That Is. To me this is not something which is mutually exclusive.

I can create whatever sense of relationship I wish; and I know that whatever sense of relationship I create is still going to be as real as any other sense of relationship I choose to create. And for me all of it is valid, and all of it is being created out of joy and ecstasy and unconditional love, the expression of the same unconditional love that the Creator created us to be. That is how I perceive the relationship. I am always in the relationship of All That Is, within joy, love and ecstasy. For us in our civilization the feeling of this ecstasy *is* the expression and the experience of what you are defining as the sense of that relationship.

Why is that not happening here?

Because for the past 25,000 years, approximately, you have chosen as a group consciousness to explore the idea of separating yourselves from your memory of being All That Is. And now you are turning over a new idea. You are through with the separation, and that is why you are are creating this idea you call a new age of understanding, a new age of awareness—in light and love.

Well, who's doing that?

You all are.

These few people here?

No, the entire planet. Or you would not be on it. Because that is the idea of this planet that you are on: to create the transformation; to begin to recognize yourselves as All That Is and create a positive world. Now that you know that you are the Creator, peace, harmony, light and love can result. Now you are through with the tool of separation. Within the time span of approximately the next 30 to 50 of your years, all of your civilization will also recognize this. *For when you created separation, you created the experience of more time.* That is why experiencing all the limitation and separation has taken you 25,000 years.

When you now choose to create the idea of integration, of knowing yourselves to be All That Is, then this experience can be played out upon your planet in a mere two to 3,000 years. And after that point you will not need to reincarnate upon this planet, for it will have served its purpose for you. You will move on to something else.

What I want to know is: if all of the people here know that whatever they choose to do is okay, then why do they need to keep coming back to get questions answered?

It is not necessarily that they need questions answered; it can also be an opportunity for sharing, for blending, for appreciating all the different ways All That Is has of expressing Itself through all the different individuals you are. Each one of you is a different path, a different way. So recognize that *if there were only one way to do something, there would be only one person.* . . . Take a look around you.

Also understand that it is not the original person who comes back. Each being who returns "again and again" is a completely new being, a completely new idea of him or herself, and a completely new universe. So as it is not the same person, in that sense no one comes back, even if "he" has been here 40,000 times.

How does the Holy Spirit work in this world?

The idea is that our perception of your Holy Spirit is the collective electromagnetic mentality, the actual energy out of which all of your individual minds are created. Spirit meant in this sense is literally a physiological phenomenon, an electrical phenomenon, an electromagnetic phenomenon. It is the literal light of your world, of your consciousness.

And again the way it works is as follows: it is an energy sea in which all of you as individual components are immersed. And being immersed in that sea, when you align with it electromagnetically by accelerating your vibration in ways we have discussed —excitement, service, positivity, and so forth— you then become of the spirit. What that basically means is you flow in harmony with all other beings; you telepathically link with all other beings, and know all thought. Because the idea is that telepathy is actually more precisely defined as tele*m*pathy—emotionally activated by love. And that is what the holy spirit, or world spirit, is.

Catholic Church

Bashar, what is the origin of the Catholic Church?

Many of the rituals now embodied in Catholic ritual came from ancient Druidic practices, remnants of the priesthood hierarchy in the Atlantean civilization. These rituals were redefined to fit notions of the different councils and leaders, and so these misunderstood notions of hierarchy were handed down to the congregation. Mostly it is one of the offshoots, as are many other religions on your planet, of ancient Atlantean priesthoods. It went through a phase redefinition through Druidic practices, emerging in areas on your planet that would support the definitions of intermingling—of not only the ancient Druidic practices, but also some of the interminglings that took place a few thousand years ago with many Orion incarnations—on certain levels.

Especially where rules and regulations are concerned; especially where structure is concerned; especially where very deep and heavy energy is concerned—there was to some degree a reaction to some of the negativity spawned in the sinking and the destruction of Atlantis. The idea of placing a very strong hold on certain aspects of the will, so that through that belief it would be believed you would regain reconnection to the Infinite through suppression, through order, through domination.

Well, it's a pretty popular belief that Jesus Christ actually instituted that—

Oh, no, no, no. The individuals around that individual instituted it to some degree, but not that individual. That was never the intention of that individual. But you see, the point is that those disciples, or apostles, were also full of the knowledge of some of the ancient Druidic practices at that time. Their interpretation of the Christ consciousness was dispensed according to those ancient understandings, and interpreted through that flow line into the basic structure you now have. That was their understanding at the time of the arrival of the Christ consciousness through that particular manifestation.

It was not the intention of the Christ consciousness to establish that particular type of structure. It was the intention of the individuals surrounding that individual, because that was their understanding at the time, based on what they already had learned of some of these ancient practices. They were, to some degree in their own understanding, continuing the lineage. But there was much misinterpretation.

After Death

What happens when we die, then?

Different things. You will, first of all, obviously no longer consider yourselves to be physical, as you now understand physicality. And when you remove yourselves from that physical state of limitation, then you will know you chose everything you experienced in that life, and thus you can create any other type of reality on this planet, or any other planet—or not reincarnate at all. You can choose to know on that level, and see very obviously that you are, in fact, the Creator.

Now, what you will first encounter at physical death is the idea that you are a thought form in a world of thought forms, and thus will usually experience whatever represents the strongest beliefs you had in life. You will experience the realization, the seeming physicalization of those beliefs, whether they be heaven or hell, or anything in-between.

For instance, if someone had the idea that there is a hell and that it would be extremely painful— if he immediately finds himself in that self-created scenario, he is very unlikely to be able to sustain that degree of pain. For as soon as he knows the pain he is enduring is not something he can tolerate, it will lessen—because the mind in the non-physical reality instantly translates into the seeming experience he is having. The instant he becomes aware that as soon as he changes his thought the scenario around him changes, then he will get the idea pretty quickly that he does not have to hang around in that scenario. It becomes clear to him that whatever he believes at any given moment, even on that level — and especially in a sense on that level— is what most quickly manifests and realizes into the experiential reality he is having. Not meaning to sound flippant, but "hell," the concept you usually hold it to mean, could only be populated for very long by masochists, by true masochists.

Further Reincarnation

So I could go on to another plane and not be reincarnated?

You do not have to be. It is always a choice. Now, since you are here, I will assume you did choose to reincarnate at least one more time—into this lifetime you are in now.

It's not my first life?

No. There is, on the average, 2 to 3,000 lives for every individual in the room, with regard to the particular Earth cycle you all have been involved in during the last 50,000 or so of your years.

So why?

Why not? Because you chose to. Because you chose to explore the idea of limitation as it is being expressed on this planet. And to do so, you chose to manifest yourselves in many different lives; to explore all the different ideas of beingness you can explore in this society. Thus you have been everything there is to be in your world at one time or another—sometimes more than one time. *Everything!* As this is now the transformational life, this life can be the last physical life you may choose in this cycle, since it is now over and turning into another cycle.

*   *   *

Bashar, I want to ask more about Jesus. I've been reading a lot on his last years, and I want to know about the period of time when the information was erased from the Bible. Did he go to India? And at what age?

There was the idea of travel to the area of India. We perceive that there was a connection at age 17 and also age 30, approximately. And also a connection in the area you call Egypt. In addition there was the idea of many out-of-body experiences in order to travel to many different places other than those mentioned. Do recognize that what the being was allowing himself to know was his own Godhood, his own Christ consciousness. And he was simply reflecting to you that you can do it too.

When you repeat exactly what he said, that reveals the whole thing: "I am the way, the truth, and the life."

If you repeat it and mean it for yourself, yes.

There is no big mystery there, no debate.

Yes, it is self-evident. You see, that is why we are suggesting you do what he did, and not simply follow him. For if you follow, then you wind up saying, "He said this; he said that," rather than repeating what he said and feeling the vibration within yourselves for what it gives you.

We are the ways, the truths and the lives.
Yes!

PART II
Transforming Self

CHAPTER SIX

Life Works!

Being in Love

Let us begin with the understanding that the transformation of consciousness you are undergoing on your planet at this time involves the very simple concept of learning to be in love with the entire world in which you exist; in learning to be in love with the entirety of the multiverse, the entirety of creation. Love is the primary vibration out of which everything has been created by the Infinite Creator. It is the very substance, the very fabric you all experience as your manifestable reality. For each and every one of you is *made* of love, and thus in a fundamental sense everything you do is an act of love.

You have talked about love for quite some time in your civilization, but many of you have not realized that what you are actually talking about is the very essence of creation itself. All of physical reality, all of non-physical reality —any experience, any conception, any imagination— pulls from the fiber of love the energy required for the idea to blossom into a type of reality that can be experienced by your form of consciousness—whatever form you have created your consciousness to be.

In the idea of learning how to create the realities you wish to create in the way you wish those realities to be, it is all the process of learning how to be in love, how to identify with that vibratory fundamental basic out of which you create everything anyway. You are all natural creators; you are all automatic creators. We are not suggesting you must learn something new that you do not already know how to do; we are here to assist you in realizing that you create your reality anyway. And thus if you are willing to shift the focus of how you create that reality, you will be able to perceive and experience the type of reality you say you prefer.

Do allow yourselves to recognize that the whole process of understanding is not the idea of learning something new, but the process of remembering more and more of what you already are. When you allow yourselves to truly work *with*, and not against, the fabric of love out of which all reality is created, and blend with that flow, you will be able to sculpt your reality out of that love into any form that represents your true heart's desire.

Could you clarify what it means to create our own reality?

As most of you have been learning these past few years, you *are* the creators of your own physiological reality, but not many of you understand what the mechanism is by which you create that reality. This mechanism is directly interlinked with your definitions, your belief systems, of the physiological reality you think you ought to be experiencing, the physical reality you have been *taught* to think you ought to be experiencing.

The idea always falls down on the notion of definitions. Your own physicists now —many of them— are beginning to realize that your physiological reality really does not have an empirical existence apart from you, that there is no such thing as physical reality without your definition of it, without your imagination to give it life, to give it existence.

Systems of Belief

Definition: Systems, structures; that which forms a pattern. A series or a cycle of ideas or observations which allow you to create a perception of continuity and cohesion. Systems of belief.

We often discuss the idea that it is your beliefs that create the physical reality you experience. Every one of these beliefs is the representation of a particular vibrational resonance, a particular frequency of the fundamental energy patterns that give rise to physical reality, a particular vibration. And so as that vibration is manifested into your physical reality —*as* your physiological experiential reality— because it operates on a certain wave length, it will have a tendency in physiological reality to gather to itself patterns of vibratory frequency similar in nature to the original vibration. It will key into other beliefs, other vibratory patterns that will aggregate around this primary belief so as to set up what appears to be a frame of reference in which to perceive and understand the original belief by surrounding itself with slightly out-of-phase vibrations. It is similar but not exact, so that you have a reference point, some surroundings, some illusion of background against which you can see the primary belief.

This aggregation, this drawing together of similar belief systems so as to allow the primary belief to stand out, occurs quite automatically and naturally within you— as you say, quite second nature. It occurs so rapidly you may not even realize, or *have* not realized, that this is what you are doing . . . creating the seeming background of reality that in your society you often think of as, "That's the way reality is." Your life happens in this reality; in the specific beliefs of your reality they manifest themselves against this backdrop of the overall reality.

But this overall reality is not simply, "That's the way it is." It is the background *you* create by surrounding the primary belief structure you have with similar belief structures so that you can create a gradation, a variation of beliefs to expand outward from you in order to create a backdrop against which to see the primary belief of your life, the primary focus of your life. These structures after a time have become ingrained within you to the extent that you take this background for granted. And as we have said, you think of it much as if it is something that exists without you. Thus it has been one of the primary mechanisms that has allowed you to experience the illusion of the universal reality as seemingly outside of yourselves.

Changing the Primary Focus

You may recognize that in your society, because of the repetition of this idea, and because this is now the way you automatically "set the stage," you have often created the idea that there is only one way for this stage to be set. And it is against that background that you measure everything in your lives.

As soon as you change the fundamental primary focus beliefs that represent the beings you are, the entire background changes with it. Everything changes. Everything is connected; everything is the same one thing. A change in the primary focus creates what you call the domino effect, and changes occur all the way down the line in the entire pattern, the entire backdrop. They may seem at times to be subtle, but are far-ranging and quite widespread—if you allow yourselves to recognize they exist.

Therefore, when you seek to create changes in your own primary belief system focus, often you will only continuously weigh that primary focus or change against a background that you will not allow yourselves to see has changed. But if you are willing to recognize that *everything changes when you change anything,* then you will not still see the primary background in the same light. You will begin to realize that something is different—somewhere, somehow.

This is why many of you create the seeming contradictions in your lives. You say you wish to change the primary focus, but when you look around, you are continually seeing the same background—in a sense, seeing the idea of your primary focus against the same background, rather than allowing the entire background to be a part of the primary focus, and changing along with it. When you look at the background in the same way you used to, you immediately cancel the change you made in your primary focus, because it is all one and the same thing. The echo, the background, carries its origin point from the original sound.

You will look to this echo to see changes occur in it before you will allow yourselves to validate the changes you know you have made, or you desire to make, in the primary focus of your being. But if you seek validation in the echo, then you will only continue in the reality in which you have already focused yourselves. The validation must come in the primary sound, the primary signal, *first*—before you see it in the echo of the background reality you consider to be your exterior universe.

Therefore recognize that in physical reality one primary belief will always extend itself to create a seeming system of beliefs with which it becomes surrounded and supported so that the primary belief can have an existence in physical reality. No belief will exist unto itself in a void; every belief brings with it a complete and total entourage, a set of props, backdrop and stage, and a complete and total audience receptive to that particular play.

Thus if you truly desire to change the primary focuses in your lives, the primary beliefs with which you are allowing yourselves to be in touch, do not play them out on the same stage. Let yourselves know you are in a completely different locale. Everything has changed—*everything!* Then you can recognize that the total system of reality you perceive your lives to be will change from system to system. Not just particle to particle, but everything will transform.

You have but to realize that many of the things you desire to see validations of in a particular specific sense will also occur if you will change the entire system first. Then all the particles that go along with the representation of the new system will be there as well. You can do it either way. As we have said: cause and effect are the same event. You can have a cause which creates an effect; you can have an effect which creates a cause. You can change the whole system; you can change a specific within the system. In every case both the specifics and the system change. You can work it from either end—or inside out, backwards/forwards, upside down. It doesn't matter.

When you do make the change, allow yourselves to function as if a change has occurred across the entire spectrum. Otherwise all you are doing is focusing yourselves into a localized specific effect, and not allowing yourselves to see how the change you have made within has made a change in the reality you desire to see around you.

Know that you are capable of getting in touch with the definitions by which you have created the physical reality you have been experiencing for many thousands of your years. If you can change those definitions to form whatever pattern you desire them to form, then you can very easily create the realities you desire to create—when you want to create them, in exactly the way you want to create them. As long as you understand that you are doing what you are doing, that you are expressing the desires you are expressing through joy, through love, through light, through service, through integrity, there is absolutely nothing —nothing, nothing, *nothing!*— that the universe will withhold from you.

Different Frequencies

Everything is energy; everything vibrates at different frequencies. The only reason one thing is different from another thing is because there are energies and frequencies which are different rates, different pitches than other frequencies. That difference in frequencies is exactly what determines what you perceive to be this object from that object, this person from that person. Everyone is made out of the same one homogenous substance. The only reason you appear to be different is because of the pitch, or vibrational rate, at which you operate, the level at which you define yourselves to be. Every being within creation is a self-aware, self-reflective, free-will entity, a holographic representation of the Infinite Creation. You all have the ability to operate on any number of frequency levels that you so desire. Those frequency levels are automatically determined by the beliefs you buy into most strongly, what you believe is most true for you.

As we have said, due to the type of society you have created, for a long time you have been heavily into self-invalidation. Being self-invalidational has allowed you to buy into belief systems that are not necessarily representative of the belief systems that would precisely reflect who it is you have created yourselves to be, who it is you desire to be. If individuals put invalidations and judgments upon you, you may —sometimes without even being consciously aware of it— buy into those invalidations and say, "Yes, I'm this; I'm that. It's not what I really want to be, but you must be right, because so many people tell me this."

All right. But do stop looking outside yourselves for the things that will allow you to be who you want to be. *Be* them—because you are the idea you imagine you can be. Act like you are what you imagine you want to be and you will be it. That will create the experiences, seemingly outside yourselves, that will represent who you now are willing to believe you can be. You are being rebounded from thing to thing, situation to situation, and bumped around because you are looking for the answers externally. They are always going to kick you back into the center of your being . . . *because that's where the answers are!*

Allow your life circumstances to change by knowing you will now accept another way for the answers to be delivered instead of the way they have been delivered up to now. You are now willing to be open to letting messages manifest themselves in the daily events of your life. But you will not see them if you do not believe you are the persons creating them. By looking for those effects outside of yourselves, you are denying that you are the ones who can create them in your lives.

Believing is Seeing

In a sense —to put it in very pragmatic simplified terms— you are saying that what society has taught you is that "seeing is believing," whereas it is actually ***believing is seeing!*** That is how it works. Now, your belief could be unconscious, so that by the time you see the manifestation of it, you think, "Oh, it is the *seeing* of this idea that has created the belief within me." And so you are looking to see things that will generate in you the beliefs you think you want. But the *only way you see those things to begin with is to already have the belief that you will see them.* Then your physical external reality forms the symbols that are reflective of that belief. Seeing it in your reality is what lets you know you *have* the belief, so the belief no longer has to remain unconscious. But seeing it is an indication of a belief already in existence. . . . Is any of this sinking in?

I hope so.

Oh, you do not have to hope so. Hope implies despair, uncertainty. Do you know personally, beyond the shadow of a doubt, that the being you desire to be, you are capable of being?

Yes, I know that.

All right. Then start using that certainty to your advantage. If you know you have the capability of imagining what you would like to be, understand, as we have said, that your ability to imagine what you would like to be *is* your ability to be that person, that version of you.

Whatever vibratory plane you are on is what you experience. If you have the ability to *conceive* how you want to be, at the moment you conceive it, you *are* that person. But when you deny your imagination its reality and say, "Okay, I've imagined what I would like to be; now what do I have to see, what do I have to do, to become this idea?" you are placing all of the steps in your way that it's taking for you to get there. Your ability to imagine that person is *being* that person—because if you weren't of that vibration, *you wouldn't be able to picture it!*

All you need to do in realizing your imagination is real, and at that moment is who and what you actually are, is to *act as if* you are, *believe* you are that person. Then your life will contain the things that are representative of the life of that type of person. The events in your life can only be 100% reflective of the person you have decided you are. So if you are experiencing events in your life you no longer prefer, then allow yourself to recognize that your ability to even imagine there is another way to be, is *being* the other way. All you have to do is to put into physical action the certainty that your ability to imagine there is another way, *is* the reality of being that other person.

You, as a *persona*, are an artificial construct of your consciousness; when your consciousness changes the idea of itself, the person you are is a different person—literally. Only the things that are conducive to that type of person's life will be what you will experience in that life. It is only mechanics, only physics. Whatever vibration you believe yourself to be will be the life you have. Plain and simple. Anything that is not of the vibration you are cannot be experienced in your reality. So if you are now willing to know you no longer need to batter and invalidate yourself, then allow yourself to be whatever you imagine a person would be like who didn't contain a need to batter herself. *Be* that person you imagine you would be like, and your reality will be reflective of a person who no longer contains the vibration of the need to knock herself down in order to show herself something.

What about the idea that you choose your parents to learn certain lessons? I think that's what trips me up.

All right. But do remember that even though you have made that choice, the idea does not mean you are incapable of expressing what it is you are learning in a positive way. You always have the opportunity to also recognize that fundamentally many of the reasons for why you choose those scenarios is to realize what you are realizing now: that at any given moment you are absolutely self-contained and quite capable of determining what your reality is going to be like—regardless of what agreements you have made. Many of those agreements are for the purpose of getting you to the point of realizing you can create your reality the way you wish it to be. Relax and lighten up on yourself. You are an empowered being; you are right now your own unique chosen reflection of the Infinite Creation. Act like it.

Guaranteed to Work

But Bashar, I want to know that my life is going to run as smoothly as I want. . . .

All right! Allow us to say this: recognize that we cannot in any way prove any of what we say to you. However . . . I can, in your terminology, absolutely 100% guarantee! —that is the word you like: guarantee— that you can prove it to yourself.

All we are saying is that if you are willing to act as the person you can envision yourself desiring to be, your reality —100% guaranteed— will reflect that idea, and *only* that idea to you. It can do nothing else; I guarantee it 100%. **LIFE WORKS WHEN YOU LET IT—100%!**

Yes, yes, yes, I know: "It sounds too easy." But life *is* easy— if you let it be. Life always creates more life without any difficulty whatsoever. Existence always continues to exist without any effort at all. No struggle. It just is. It is ecstasy itself. Therefore, allow yourself the opportunity to realize that whatever you can image IS real! You cannot imagine non-existence. Go ahead; try.

It hurts.

All right. Recognize, therefore, that anything you imagine is, on some level of your existence, a real reality. And much of it is manifestable in various ways within physical reality—according to the agreements you have made with everyone else to share the idea of this transformational time frame.

Now, let me reiterate a crucial idea mentioned earlier: All of you are as powerful as you need to be to create anything you desire in life without having to hurt anyone else or yourselves in order to create it. Believe in the power you are as the reflective representation of Infinite Creatorhood. As you think, as you picture, as you imagine, that is *real*. *Be* it, if you prefer what you imagine—and that will be the reality you experience.

Understand something: all you need is a basic trust that at any given moment you have what you need; you know everything you need to know to be who you are being in that moment. As soon as you redefine who you are, you will know the things that person needs to know—regardless of what you are seeing around you. Paradoxically, the way to see things change in your world most quickly is to change the idea of who *you* are. You see, the idea of total knowledge of all things is not necessary in order for you to function in the physical reality you are in; in fact, total knowledge would actually *hamper* your existence.

So maybe it's not so much knowledge I want as the love.

Then feel it! For it is all around you. But feel it within you first, or you will never see it out there. Know that you cannot change anything out there; you can only *allow* other people and situations to change. **If you wish to see anything in your world change, change yourself!** Then the other changes. Then you will be being a representative example to everyone else of what kind of unconditionally loving being they can also be—by allowing them to see the example you are setting, regardless of what they are choosing. If you are buying into their reality, and becoming frustrated and hateful and so on, because *they* are choosing to be frustrated and hateful and so on, you are only reinforcing the reality they are already living. You are not giving them an example; you are not giving them a chance to see any other way.

Trust. *Be* the life you wish to be. Act as if you are that way. We are not suggesting you ignore the fact that other people are choosing to suffer. But the way to assist them best is to first and foremost be the being that at least shows them there is another way to be. Otherwise they cannot see an example of how they could also choose to be . . . loving to themselves.

You must take the first step if that is truly what concerns you in life: be the example of what being an unconditionally loving being, to them and to yourself, is all about. And trust that your love will make a difference and will create the changes you desire to see. Because you will then be taking yourself to the world, the Earth, that already exists in the way you desire it to exist. You will take yourself to that program, to that level of frequency that already is represented by the idea that your Earth is peaceful and harmonious and expresses abundance everywhere.

That Earth exists now. However, **you will never see it if you don't make the vibration of that world your own.** All the programs, all the ways all the Earths have to be, already exist. We are not talking about a vibrational difference from a different frequency, not something that is physically "out there." It is all right here right now.

Tuning In

Let's use the analogy you call the radio in your society. Now, you know that all the programs are coming to the radio all at the same time; but the only one you hear is where your dial is tuned. As all those Earths exist right here right now, the one you get is the one to which you are tuned.

So create the image of the one you prefer. *Live* in the fashion you would live in that world. You will be the receiving beacon for that energy, so that *that* program can be broadcast in this reality, and others can pick up on it and decide to tune their dial to that frequency as well. If they don't know that such a program exists; if there are no examples, then others will never know the program exists, and will never tune their dials to that frequency.

If you have an image in your mind of how you would like the world to exist, exist in *your* life as if that *is* the reality for you. All the ideas of the suffering and the warfare and the hatred and the frustration: they are illusions, old programs. And you know beyond the shadow of a doubt that sooner or later everyone will tire of them and go looking for other programs. And if you are not already tuned into that new program, then when they ask you, "Say, have you heard any good programs lately?" you will not know what station to tell them to tune in to.

Right. But I have trouble staying tuned to that because of all my fears—

Oh! Oh-oh-oh-oh-oh! When you say you have trouble, that's what creates the trouble. Maybe that's how it was in the old program, *but this is day ZERO!* This is the idea of your conscious commandment. Are you going to decide to continue that idea, or are you going to decide to be the new idea right now? And if you are the new idea right now, you are not the person who can say, "I have trouble with this; I have difficulty with that." You are no longer that person; it's not within your make-up. To say that it is, is to still believe you are the old program. For remember that the present is the only place you actually ever exist, the only place you ever *will* exist, and the only place you *have ever* existed. It is always now, and always shall be now, no matter when it is.

Well, I get excited about something, can start out with it, and then it just doesn't manifest— it just doesn't continue on.

All right. Allow yourself to recognize one of the things we have discussed with many of you: that you have on your world an assumption. This basic assumption that you have been taught is that if it does not manifest in the way you think it should, you think the process has stopped. Rather than assuming that the next thing that excites you is a part of the on-going process, you assume that if it changes, that means it has stopped.

It hasn't. It is simply that everything will always transform into what is most representative of the path of least resistance. And you may not always have conscious analytical awareness of what that might be. So if you know you have initiated a certain vibratory energy, a certain excitement, and you see it progressing in a certain way, and then all of a sudden it changes, why give it the meaning that it has stopped? Why not give it the meaning that it is still going, but in another mode, in the mode perhaps necessary to attract to you the individuals you originally wanted to attract in the first place, but who were not likely to be attracted to you by the original way you were doing it.

No Interruptions

Begin to look at life as a continuing series of the energy you have initiated, but changing its form chameleon-like, over and over again, to make all the connections to the different vibrations you say you want to connect to. It has to transform into a different frequency in order to be attractive to individuals who think differently than you. It is a completely different viewpoint, a different outlook, and one that can have a profound difference as you allow yourself to know your life *is* manifesting what you want. It is only the assumption that it stops and is interrupted that creates the interruption you experience.

If you truly trust that what you are doing is representative of who you chose to be in this life, then no matter how it changes, no matter in what way the excitement continues, the fact that the excitement does continue is the sign the whole idea is still continuing. Not necessarily in the way you have been taught to think it must, but in the way it needs to in order to represent the path of least resistance to get you where you are going. You cannot have a conscious analytical awareness of all the probable paths it could take to get you where you want to go, so don't even try.

Let yourself trust that how it does take its course, even if it appears to have nothing at all to do with the course it started out on— if the excitement is still there, it is the excitement that lets you know water is still in the river, no matter how many tributaries it may take to get to the ocean. Excitement is the representation of the flow; so you still know the river is flowing. Follow it! Go down the channel it leads you on, for that represents the quickest path to the sea. If you think, "Oh no, no. I can't go this way; that is not how I was going before," but you still sense the excitement is there and the water is flowing, you are the one imposing the dam in the river. Allow yourself to go with it no matter how it meanders. The way it meanders is representative of the path you chose to be, and the meandering is necessary in order to arrive at your destination in the quickest possible way.

We are simply saying the same thing in many different ways. If you allow yourself to know that you *are* following the path at any given moment that you have created for yourself, you will then be more strongly in touch with all the different levels of your consciousness. And that will let you know you do not need as much *unconscious* time in which to connect to those levels during sleep, because you are doing it consciously. That means you will probably sleep less, and therefore you will probably experience the idea of having more time. But also recognize at the same time that you have all the time you need.

Everything is in perfect timing; you do not have to rush things along. You are an eternal being; you are right in step with the transformation. What's your hurry?

There always seems to be the question of how to be more open, but these blocks within us— what are these blocks?

It is only your assumption that there is some mysterious "how" that needs to be known before you will act in the manner you desire. In other words, laugh; be happy . . . because you want to. As soon as you do, you'll match that frequency. There is no mysterious "how"—none that has to be there. And if you really want a bottom-line definition, then: "Live now; that's how."

Any time you live right in the now, utterly in the moment, any energy that comes along, any difference you feel, you will match instantly—due to living fully in the now, accepting it all, open to it all—through absolute vulnerability. This is not weakness, but openness, strength, self-empowerment. That's how. Live in the now with it. Assume that what is happening *belongs* in your lives. Accept it; acknowledge it; integrate it. Live through it; get into it. Explore it; examine it. Get excited.

You know those blocks are there for your reasons—whether you are conscious of the reasons or not. The more you act like you know they're there for your reasons, with or without the consciousness, the sooner you *will* become conscious of them. Very often the only reason you discover is that they're there for you to accept the energy and accelerate. By the time you accelerate, you've used them for the reason they were there, and there's no other reason to discover. That's it. You go on to the next thing and the next—forever. Always in joy and ecstasy. It's that easy.

Be happy. Remember cause and effect are the same event. You don't have to wait for a reason to be happy in order to know you prefer to be happy. **Create the effect of being happy, and you will attract into your lives all of the causes to support the happiness you have created** . . . just because you want to. And just because you say so. Because you are the creators of your reality, there doesn't need to be any other why or how. What you say goes!

Victimhood

Let me interject a note here. In interacting with some of you, we have come to understand that you at times take what we are saying in a very negative way. One example recently was an inter-action in which we were discussing the idea referred to as victim-hood. We do know this is a big issue with many of you, and it has been for a very long time on your planet.

Understand that we always come from the premise that you are the creators of all of your experiential reality. The whole idea of sharing with you is that we will always hand you back your power and let you know you have the ability to create the lives you want, regardless of what we say—or any other being says, on this or any other level. We will share with you the perspective of life that has worked for us, what we know can result in absolute control over your own lives, in the creation of what you desire in a positive way. For that is our particular preference.

Now, we understand the perspective many of you have been brought up with regarding the beliefs and fears most of you have. In the interaction we had with that individual, we understood him to believe that it was a dangerous philosophy to tell someone who is creating himself to be a victim that he is the one actually creating the whole scenario. He believed that we were in a sense rationalizing and condoning the idea of victimhood. But no, this is not our intention at all.

We are able to *explain* the mechanism by which victims can be created, but an explanation is by no means a rationalization or a condonement. But it was feared, because of the way that individual had been brought up, that to be able to explain the mechanism was, in a sense, to rationalize it away, and to support the idea that there are victims in your society. But always our intention is to put you squarely in touch with the fact that your hand is securely on the lever of control in your lives; even in the idea of the creation of victimhood you are still in control at all times.

We know that you do have to create the idea of victimhood in order to experience it yourselves. You have the option and the opportunity at any moment in your lives whatsoever to cease creating victimhood, and instead create a reality of unbridled joy and ecstasy. And there need be no end to this. In our understanding, and this has always worked for us, there must first of all be within your belief system an absolute acknowledgement and ownership of everything in your life you experience, both positive and negative. For you cannot change what you do not own. Therefore, in all the interactions we have with you, we would request and suggest that whether or not what we have to say is workable for you —and we do not care if it is or not, because what we have to say comes from love— if you find it workable, use it; and if you don't, don't.

If you can understand from a neutral point of view what we are sharing, then you can assign whatever meaning you decide is the one that relates most strongly to your life. But we do suggest that first and foremost you take neutrally anything we or anyone else says. All philosophies can be applied either positively or negatively; there is nothing inherently dangerous about any neutral philosophy. If there is any danger, it comes from the belief that any particular philosophy might be dangerous. Thus the individual who is fearful of a philosophy and believes it to be dangerous is the one creating the danger in that philosophy. And of course, since every belief is an absolute self-fulfilling system of reality, he will then experience only the idea of negativity and danger from that philosophy, should he then apply it to his life.

Neutral Situations

We would like to continue discussing the idea that all situations and circumstances within your physical experience, your day-to-day reality, are basically neutral props in relation to each other, and have no inherent meaning within them other than the meaning you give to them yourselves. Everything being blank, empty, neutral allows you to extract from the circumstance the effects you desire by assigning to it the appropriate meaning. It is simple mechanics: positive meaning in, positive effect out; negative meaning in, negative effect out.

Now let us take this understanding a little bit further. We have discussed the idea that what you experience to be your physical reality in a sense is a combination of vibratory frequencies. This combination represents all the probable or potential realities there can possibly be. They all exist right now, right here all at once. They form what can be called the background reality, so to speak. Not that there is any one "real reality" any more "real" than any other. Not that there is any one truth against which to measure all truths, or other realities for their validity or truth. No, the background reality is the composite of all realities, all truths, in a holographic fashion: overlaid, intertwined, interwoven. In a sense, lying in wait for a specific stimulus to bring to the surface of that general background any particular reality that you may choose to call a dimension of experience, or a universal realm.

How you call those particular vibratory frequencies to the surface and allow yourselves to experience that particular reality, is through your beliefs and attitudes, through the vibration you create yourselves to be. Thus, in a sense, it is not so much that experience gives rise to meaning; it is that meaning gives rise to experience.

When you project yourselves into physiological reality, and determine as non-physical consciousness that you will create certain types of experiences, that is the meaning you are giving to the particular life you are creating for yourselves as non-physical entities, to experience as limited physically-focused entities. That is the meaning, that is the overall desire which vibrates at a certain frequency, and which then calls out of the background vibration, through a sympathetic synchronization, all the circumstances necessary to represent the meaning you have injected into the general life theme or structure you are about to live as physical beings.

Or, to put it in a more simple fashion: the idea is that **all circumstances are neutral.** The meaning you choose to believe; the meaning you choose to create in life, about your life, is what generates the particular types of circumstances you experience. These reinforce, reflect and represent the meanings you are creating. *Giving meaning is the actual act of creation itself!* To give meaning to something is to create it into existence in your particular experiential realm.

Now, to illustrate this idea, let's say you are on your way to the train station to catch a train. You arrive at the station; the train has just left. That is the neutral situation. There is no meaning in it: you are standing on the platform; the train is moving; you are not on it. Period.

Now the old you might have had a negative reaction. "Oh gosh, oh darn," you might say. "I have done something wrong. This is very bad; I am now very angry. Those train people! They were too early. I was not late; no, no, no. They were too early. I will now go and complain to someone." All right. Your choice.

Or again: the new person, the person you now know you have changed into, is going for the train. You arrive at the platform; the train has left. Once again, the neutral situation: you are on the platform; the train is moving; you are not on it. But now you know you are different. You *know* that everything in your life is there for a positive reason; it does not matter that the symbol is the same. Because you now trust that, and do not go stomping off to complain, your anger no longer blinds you to the fact that having just stepped off that train is a friend you haven't seen in ten years. If you had reacted in the old way, walking off in anger, you would not have met her. But you will now discover, in the course of subsequent events, that you did need to meet her at that time, and for positive reasons.

Therefore, allow yourselves to know you are the definers, ultimately, of the life you experience. And as you define it; as you give it meaning, your life takes on only —and *can* only take on— the coloration, the characteristics, the flavors and the atmospheres of the meaning you decide your life will have. And that is what you will see reflected in the holographic background, the matrix of all universal probable reality.

Dual Nature

Bashar, If I have two sides to my personality, one of them I like and one of them I don't like . . .

One is positive, one is negative.

Okay, but let's say the negative side wants to eat too many twinkies, for instance, and has all kinds of urges. Now, if I don't satisfy those urges, I feel discomfort. But if I do satisfy them, I feel remorse. How do you resolve this dualness of human personality?

By recognizing first and foremost that all polarity exists as one thing, outside of the physical reality in your whole nature. And that you do not have to continue seeing yourself as a dichotomy. You do not have to continue seeing yourself as a struggle against, or between, this and that; you have at any given moment free will of preference. If you recognize that the idea of the ingestion of those substances does not vibrate with the being you prefer to be, then if you act like that preferred being, you will find you do not have the urge—because you are not of the vibration containing the idea, "I have the urge to eat this."

Could that be called will power?

Not will power; recognition. Ceasing the judgment of yourself; ceasing that belief; the changing of the belief that changing is difficult. The changing of the belief that having the concept of what you would prefer to be is not the same thing as *being* it— when it really is. The changing of the belief that having the concept still implies you have to *do* something to become the concept you have imagined, when imagining it is *becoming* the concept. Believing that is what will make the change.

So what is my so-called bad side showing me?

That you have the opportunity to prefer something else; and to recognize that as soon as you conceive of what that something else is, you're it.

So the concept I have of my so-called good side which I prefer to be is not really what I want to be; otherwise I would be it?

You are assuming that the concept itself, when you have it, is not being it. But it is. You are assuming that merely having that concept of the good side is not being it. But having the concept *is* being at the vibratory level of that good side. Otherwise you wouldn't be able to conceive of it. Again, you have to be tuned to that program to hear it coming through the radio. If you find you have the ability to even conceive of what the so-called good side is all about, you are at that moment tuned to that frequency or that notion could never have occurred to you.

But why does this tremendous interference keep coming in?

Because you assume that when you conceive of it, it is not real, as I have said. You assume you have to do something special in order to make it real.

To stay on the station you mean?

Yes. You are the one flipping the dial. When you have flipped the dial to the point where you can perceive what this so-called positive side is like, leave the dial there.

What if I'm sitting there, and suddenly a twinkie switches on?

You are missing the point. The station you will be tuned to does not advertise twinkies. So it will never occur to you; the urge won't be there. Understand that you are contradicting yourself.

You are thinking that one being contains both of these urges. . . .
No. When you are the vibration of the positive side, you only
contain what is relevant to *that* you. If you find yourself experiencing the urges of the twinkie, you are no longer the other *you*.
You are the *you* who can experience the urge of the twinkie.

Well, how do you hold that? I find it difficult to hold that.

That is your belief. The concept is this: understand that your
statement, "I find it difficult to hold that," is a belief. It is its own
reality, and thus it is what you get: a reality in which you are a
being who finds it difficult to hold a concept.

So you merely assume the viewpoint and—?

Yes. Act like it. Assume that if you can conceive of it, at the
moment of conception that is how you are born. You give birth
to that being. And that is the only being that exists.

We will use the idea we have shared with some of you already,
one called the library analogy. As an integrated being, you have
the ability to be cognizantly aware, while still consciously being
the concept you are now, of all the other probable realities that
exist. You can have the definition, "My reality is what I am, and
it contains the ability to be what I know myself to be—while at
the same time being aware of all of the other probable realities I
know I am not."

The analogy is one in which you are in a library. You can read
every book on the shelf: the one about twinkies, the positive one,
the negative one. Only the one you make the conscious choice to
check out of the library becomes your reality. So it is not a matter of having to fight against the urge. You have the type of reality
which says you can think about the idea that such a probable reality exists, but that's not the idea you *are*. You know the library
is there, but you didn't check out that book.

*So the fixidity of the human condition, as I see it— most peo-
ple are—*

What you consider to be the fixedness is something you believe to be real. That belief is the only reason you experience the
human condition as fixed.

But at what point do you go off the rails, though?

Never. *But*— Never, never, never! You are never off your path, because you are never *on* a path. A path is what you *are!* You cannot be off yourself. Everything you do —everything, *everything!*— is an opportunity to decide what you prefer. Everything. You can learn from everything.

As we have said, every situation is fundamentally neutral. Your attitude toward the neutral situation will determine the effect you create in your life. The idea that you can have an urge to eat a twinkie is a neutral situation. It does not come with any power other than what you put into it. You could look at it as a string of words. You empower it; you power it up. "Oh yes, that concept of 'twinkie': that creates urges I cannot fight!" . . . You have just written the script and decided to act it out—by imposing definitions onto a fundamentally neutral series of props.

Well, let's say my next-door neighbor doesn't have this urge, and he never has the urge; but I do have the urge.

So? Knowing your next-door neighbor never has the urge is an indication for you of a reality you can also choose for yourself. That may be why that neighbor is there reflecting that reality to you. Perhaps you are reflecting the same thing back: that he can choose to have an urge if he wants to.

I'm sure that would make good neighbors here. But I guess my question really is: has it anything to do with a particular lifetime?

Only in the most general of senses, certainly not with the degree of specificity of whether you eat a twinkie or not.

No, well that's a ridiculous example.

It's not a ridiculous example. But the overall idea of any predestination is only expressed in physical life in the most general of terms. In other words, let us say that what you are discussing falls under the general category you are predestined to explore—of self-empowerment, and the creation of what you prefer. So you are using twinkies as your prop. Somebody else will use alcohol; somebody else will use drugs . . . or ice cream.

I see. Do you have dual personalities in your civilization?

Because we have a degree of physical manifestation, by definition we do express that portion of ourselves in some polarity.

But it is a type of polarity which recognizes the validity of each other's side, and so functions as a balanced unit.

So as you go up the scale, you lose polarity?

In a sense, yes. Polarity is only a third-density, fourth-density perspective of a wholeness that exists.

So you're saying that individuals in the third or fourth density who have that experience of polarity: they're experiencing the positive and negative as if they were two sides of a coin?

Yes. We only experience the coin, the idea of the oneness of the coin, and do not so much see it as two sides. But recognize that you need the whole coin in order to buy your twinkie.

Both the positive and negative are in harmony?

Yes. Blended into one concept. Male, female: one thing. A soul is *not* both male and female; it is neither. It is one thing. It can express itself in that polarity in physical reality, but it does not become a blended thing separated. Male/female polarities only exist from a physiological reference point of view, and not within the combined soul. Again, the soul to itself is only one thing.

The concept of negative and positive polarity is one of the defining terms of physical reality. It only comes into existence as physical reality does—or as different levels that contain that idea come into existence. The idea of the unbroken oneness is not so much literally that it contains an actual side by side cohesive interaction with the polarities you experience; it is simply one thing that can create itself to become different things. For there are many different universes that express the unbroken wholeness of the soul when it chooses to differentiate itself in many ways other than the idea of positive and negative polarity.

And now let us remind you that every situation has the potential for you to learn something from it in whatever way you wish to apply the idea. It is completely up to you. When you are as clear as you can be about the definitions of life you have bought into, then you can use every situation to see how it matches up to the definitions you prefer to have. You can take advice where it works for you, or let it go where you believe it doesn't. And later on if you change your mind, that's all right too. You have that capability and that capacity, and you have that right.

The first step in the whole idea of creating your reality to be what you desire it to be is in *ceasing to invalidate yourselves.* Because you —you, you, *you*— are the only thing you have to work with in your universe. You are the representation, in your way, of the Infinite. And if you invalidate any part of that, then you do not allow yourselves to function as whole beings capable of using whatever information may come to you from others in a constructive way.

The idea is to remember that everyone is a mirror; that is how every being in creation has been designed. But a mirror doesn't mean that what you see in it is an absolute one-to-one reflection of exactly the things you need to work on. Sometimes an individual will attract into his life others who seem to be invalidational, because in attracting those others, and in not accepting their invalidations, he then reflects back to them an opportunity to see what it is like for someone to stand on his own two feet when he is absolutely sure of what it is he desires to do. He gives back to those invalidating individuals an opportunity to stand on *their* own two feet for what *they* believe in. For any belief that anyone has is just as true and just as valid as any other belief.

If you do not allow yourselves to love yourselves unconditionally, then you do not know who you are, and you do not have something to stand up for, something to reflect back to everyone else so that they can see in you the shining example of what they can also be in their own way. The idea, therefore, the bottom line, in all of the interactions we have with you, will be to remind each and every one of you of your own personal power. To remind you that you already are aspects of the Infinite. And to put you squarely in touch—or roundly in touch or triangularly in touch— with your definitions. Thus you will know why your reality is the way it is, and you can create it to be the way you prefer it to be . . . as soon as you believe you are capable of doing so. It is completely up to you, completely in your hands. . . . Completely.

CHAPTER SEVEN

The Orchestration

Coincidence?

June, 1986: We will begin this discussion with the laying out of what you call in your society coincidence, or synchronicity. You will find that what we will specify within this context will be a simplification according to the idea and the understanding of the mechanisms that allow your life to work.

Things in your consciousness are now accelerating again; thus it will be important to us that you have a clear understanding as to the control of your own lives. We will discuss some of the exemplifications of the idea of synchronicity, and outline and delineate and define, in a very straightforward, simplified manner, exactly how you might utilize your understanding of this concept to recognize that you are, and always have been, in control of your lives.

As we have often said, there is no such thing as an accident. Nothing happens by accident. When there appears to be such, what you are recognizing are overlapping incidents —co-incidents— that describe and define the patterns and paths you have chosen yourselves to be. Now we will define the idea of synchronicity as this and delineate a little further in clarification.

Synchronicity, coincidence, is your conscious perception in a physiological time track —spatial reality— of the simultaneous manifestation of the multi-dimensional existence of all. We will now, through your examples of day-to-day existence, indicate the following idea: that synchronicity is your conscious recognition that all of the events, all of the objects, all of the relationships, all points of view, all perceptions, all interactions— these are all one thing. Every single thing you experience and every differentiation you create in your reality— all are the same one thing from a different point of view. The same one thing, manifesting itself simultaneously as the illusion of many things. Everything is one thing—one.

Therefore, to put it in your practical terminology, observe the following. Give yourselves the opportunity to recognize that what we will now begin to delineate is that in order to understand consciously that you are in control of your lives, you need to do but two things, and that is it.

We will render everything we have discussed with you to date —concepts of ideology, beliefs, emotions, thoughts, perceptions, perspectives, interactions— into two ideas you can utilize as the mechanism itself of recognizing that you are in control of creating your reality. Two things. Very simple: one, two.

Number one: everything is synchronicity. Everything is synchronicity. Now what this means is this: as you are driving, as you are walking, as you are doing anything in your day-to-day lives, remember that every single object, every single person, every single sound, every single interaction, every crack in the street, every leaf on the tree, the number of the leaves, the color of the leaves— all are there for a reason. No accidents.

No accidents! Now recognize, therefore, that while certain interactions, while certain objects or certain people may not have a strong direct relationship to you in a particular given moment, it still does not mean that they are not there for a reason. They may have more conscious meaning to the person just ahead of you, or the person just behind you, but because you are also there, you are playing the part of being willing to act and interact with all the other individuals. And their degree of importance as to their relationship to what is going on is also enhanced by your presence, just like your degree of importance is enhanced by theirs.

The idea, therefore, is to recognize, to use an analogy that you have shared with us quite often: if you are driving in your car, and someone cuts you off; or if you are in a traffic jam— if you are in a situation that you would usually label as something negative, recognize, again, that *nothing* ever happens by accident. NOTHING! Every single thing— say you are in one of your traffic jams: the car next to you; how much farther ahead or behind it is; what color it is; what way the light from the sun strikes it— none of it is by accident! None of it!

The Orchestration

Therefore, begin to be fascinated by how well orchestrated everything is that you are participating in—on an unconscious level. You are drawing into your lives every single particle of dust, every single atom that is there, everything! No exceptions. None. The way somebody may look at you; the way you look at that person; what he is wearing . . . no accidents. It all plays a part in the idea that everything is one single event, experienced from different points of view simultaneously. One event. The idea of degree of importance is simply to recognize how you relate to the event.

In other words, you may find that . . . let us say someone is walking down the street, and he is wearing a certain color of shirt. You could simply recognize it as synchronicity, knowing it has a reason. You could explore the idea of the relationship for you, and find it does not bear any reason that would stand out as anything important to you at the moment. The person behind you may get more importance out of it than you do, but that merely means you recognize that the reason for why you are there is not an accident. For you are part of the enhancement of the entire experience for the other person. That is what we mean by degree of importance.

Look at it this way, another analogy: you have the idea of a rotating propeller. It rotates at a certain frequency, a certain rate. You have also a strobe light. If you are in a dark room; if the propeller is rotating; if your strobe light —along with everyone else's strobe light— is synchronized to the rotation of the propeller, such that when you decide to turn your strobe light on, it begins to flash, on-off, on-off. . . . Whenever you decide to turn it on, that will be the first position you will see the propeller in. Because your light is synchronized to the rotation of the propeller, that will be the only position you see the propeller in.

Now, if you were independently able to see your particular synchronization, and someone else was independently able to see his —and thus your strobe and his strobe did not clash, so to speak— then he would be observing the same propeller in a different position. Same propeller! Different aspect entirely. The same single event that appears to be completely and totally different, simply because of the rate and the timing of the frequency of each individual strobe. Everything is the same thing!

The only reason you might see the same one thing as different is because of the rate and timing of your strobe of consciousness in physical reality. Everything is one thing; that is the first point. Everything is synchronicity; everything is there for a reason.

Point number two: act upon the opportunity that your conscious recognition of everything as synchronicity brings you— with integrity. Act upon all opportunities synchronicity brings you; that is all you have to do. One: recognize that everything is synchronicity. Two: act upon it with integrity. Those two ideas are all you need to do to create the life you desire. That is it. Period. That is all there is to physical reality: everything is synchronicity; act like it. That is all that is needed to be in complete harmonic resonance with your conscious understanding of All That Is as it expresses itself *as* physical reality.

One–two. Acting like it will always generate more conscious awareness of number one, which will always then give you more opportunities to act like it—point number two. They are self-perpetuating. One breeds two, breeds one, breeds two, accelerating into infinity.

Acting with Integrity

Bashar, what do you mean by "with integrity"?
The recognition that if you are aware that everything is one thing, and you are a part of it, then you recognize that you have

everything you need to be anything you want without having to force yourselves upon anyone else to do it. Integrity: integrated. Integral: integrated. Blended. One. Wholeness.

You do not have to force your opinions on anyone else; you do not have to dominate anyone else to get what you think you deserve. Act upon the opportunities that synchronicity gives you, with integrity, knowing that you are as complete as you need to be to act upon it, in exactly the way you need to, to get exactly what you need. You do not have to rely upon anyone else to do it for you, or force him to do it. Act with integrity upon the opportunities you create, and it will always perpetuate more of number one. Always. Because you, in acting integrally with All That Is, with synchronicity, will always maintain your connection to it consciously. Acting outside of integrity separates you, and stops the process between one and two. It does not allow the acting to generate conscious awareness of synchronicity.

Understand that everything is synchronicity, including negative synchronicity. You always attract the ideas you believe you are willing to act upon, in the manner you are willing to act upon them. Negative occurrences are still synchronicity, because they are fulfillments of your own negative beliefs. You are acting in that manner. What we are saying is that acting with integrity, in positive attitudes, always will consciously maintain the connection. That is what will allow you to perceive the connection as an acceleration and not a stagnation.

So you could have negative acceleration also?

In a sense. But the idea is simply that if it is negative acceleration, you will find, first of all, that you consider it destruction and will perceive it in that form. And also it may not allow you to recognize the reasons for the destruction, for the negativity, just because you are disassociating from the fact that everything is synchronicity. And then it leads to the question, "Why is this happening to me?" So it creates victimhood. **Negative synchronicity creates victimhood.** Thus, in recognizing you are forming a conscious, positive connection, and because once you recognize what it is you know you are in control of it, then you can choose what you prefer by acting accordingly—through integrity. That is all there is to it.

Do you mean by everything is synchronicity that every aspect, as you enumerated them, is a reflection of the same idea?

Yes, they are all the same thing, All of them are the same fundamental one thing —what you call Creation, or God— and it is holographic. Each contains everything; it is all *all*. Everything is all. Every separate concept is its own thing *and* its own version of the same one thing. If you are familiar with the idea you call cloning, then recognize that each and every cell in your body contains information for a whole body. That is the idea. Each and every single separate concept is a different manifestation of the same one thing. Cause and effect: the same event.

Analyzing Everything

When I try to apply that idea to tiny little events going on in my life, I have difficulty understanding it.

Again, do not forget: we are not saying that conscious recognition of everything as synchronicity means you will be able to consciously analyze every single aspect to your conscious understanding. That is not the point. The point is to recognize that some aspects will have, as we have said, varying degrees of relative importance to you. You will not form a conscious analytical recognition of the ones that do not have a great degree of importance. It is, once again, a matter of trust.

I can trust. But are you saying that it will be obvious and that we will know which ones have the highest degree of importance?

Yes. In other words, "What a coincidence! Just what I needed. Right place, right time." Everything else doesn't matter. It will appear that another variation of those same circumstances will matter to someone else, although it may not matter so much to you. But it is all the same one thing. The point is not to have the conscious recognition; the point is to act as if you know that what is occurring is synchronicity, and what stands out is what you need to know. The way you need to know it is the way you need to know it.

If you simply move upon whatever you can move upon, the things that excite you and feel correct, all the circumstances that have occurred in your life will fall into place and make sense. And in retrospect you will understand what they meant. Many times you don't *want* to know what they mean until after you spontaneously live through the circumstance, discovering in a spontaneous way what you wanted to discover, and understanding why those things happened in the way they happened. But if you trust that they are happening for a reason —your reason— and you use them in that positive way, you will always discover sooner or later how they served you in a positive way.

Trust your instincts. Examine what they bring up within you. "Why do I have this hesitation? What do I really believe about my situation, about my part in this co-creation? What are the beliefs I have? What is this hesitation allowing me to look at within myself, within these other individuals?" Learn all you can about it; apply it, and the obvious choice will simply fall into place. Then act on it.

Didn't you say that it might be detrimental to always analyze everything?

In a sense, you can recognize that many times you will allow the synchronicity into your lives; and you will have made a decision to not become analytical about it—because becoming analytical about it may not allow you to *live* the experience. You will turn it back into pieces instead of allowing it to be one thing.

Trust. It is a knowingness. You simply take it for granted that everything you are perceiving is synchronicity. No accidents. And the way you relate to it is the way you need to. Plain and simple. That is all there is to it.

What about the times when there's a lot of synchronicity and you're acting on it, and nothing happens?

That is a contradiction. Recognize that you are postulating two completely different viewpoints of synchronicity—a positive and a negative one. Know that it will always manifest in whatever way it needs to. And again, it may not be consciously obvious, so that you can take advantage of the way it has manifested. For perhaps if you were to become consciously aware of certain ideas, you would not be able to move on them; you would be fixated on the mechanism. It would be as if all of a sudden you became fascinated with the concept itself, analytically, of being able to drive a car and forgot how to just get in and drive—because you were too fixated on, "Well, this piece: how does it relate to that piece? How does it relate to this— how, how, how . . .?" And in the meantime you are late for your appointment.

That is putting it into an analogy, but it will have the same effect. Many times you will notice that synchronicity will occur in the appropriate timing. The idea of saying "it shouldn't happen" is a judgment call. You are putting expectations on how you think it should have happened. That is not allowing it to be synchronicity. Synchronicity *is* what it is, the *way* it is. Not, "Well, it should have been this. It didn't happen. I didn't see what I expected. . . . Should have been."

Well then, if we have no understanding of the outcome . . .

You do have an understanding in the way you need to. Conscious analysis is not the only definition of understanding. Again recognize: the second you act like everything is synchronicity, the more obvious it will become.

Planning and Free Will

If everything happens as it is meant to, does that mean there is a sort of plan? But within the plan there is free will?

Yes. It is both: simultaneous, because time and space are illusions, and also synchronicity. Time/space is also another manifestation of one thing; it all occurs now. It all occurs here, for lack of a better term.

Bashar, do you understand what you're talking about?

Yes, because that is how our civilization lives. That is why we do not need the idea of the tools of government or economic systems. We allow synchronicity to always let us know that we are interacting with exactly the beings we need to be interacting with, and sharing services with those beings. And they are sharing with us the only services at that moment that we need.

What about those times when we can't follow what we wish to create? There are often those times.

Again, you may be creating the idea of beliefs of negative synchronicity. And it may not let you know you are following it in a negative way. The idea is this: if you do not act according to your own instincts, what you know to be true for you, then all you are saying is that you have a belief that in not doing so you will create a reality which will force you to recognize that is what you are doing — which very often in your society can manifest in a negative reality. In other words, "I didn't follow my feelings. I find, therefore, that I still hate my job, hate this, hate that." You always reinforce the choice you make.

It's a setback.

Not a setback, no. For you are giving yourselves the opportunity to learn that the choice you made is what the reality *is* you are experiencing. And it gives you that much more opportunity to recognize that if you redefine your choice, that will be the reality you will experience, since you are experiencing flawlessly the reality you believe you will experience now.

Symbolic Reflections

The idea is to recognize that synchronicity will bring with it the idea of symbology. Many times you find that everything in physical reality is symbolic of the actual interaction, the exact fundamental energy exchange, that you are creating within your being. As long as you are in physical reality you always create an identifiable symbol to reflect to you the idea going on. Since you have created physical reality to be something outside yourselves, then understand that everything you perceive in physical reality is a physiological symbolic extension of processes, interactions, which are actually going on, more or less, inside yourselves. Not truly *outside* yourselves, but *inside* yourselves.

You *are* the actual interaction, the actual process. **You are the experience you are having!** *You are the experience you are having.* It's not that you are *not* interacting with other consciousnesses, but anyone you imagine yourselves to be interacting with, in any symbolic experience, is generally the only thing you perceive in physical reality. *It is your own self-created version of that individual with whom you are interacting,* and you are creating that interaction in a particular manner—in a necessary manner. That manner contains any specifics needed by you to allow you to see in that other individual the things you need to see reflected back to you about yourselves. Thus always in that interaction you can understand that you are dealing with different aspects of your *own* consciousness.

Once again, in recapping: realize that the idea of coincidence and synchronicity is when you allow yourselves to recognize that life always works when you let it. That everything you attract into your lives is the product of what you believe your lives to be; that you can only attract the vibration you are equal to; and thus synchronicity, whether it is manifested positively or negatively in your lives, can only be a reflection of what you believe your reality to be.

You create the idea of the attitudes, the meanings you wish to impart to any given situation, and it is your attitudes that determine the effects that will manifest in your physiological reality. Trust that whatever comes to you in your physical lives is symbolic of the paths you chose to be. Take it as something that can synchronistically serve you, without assuming it is fundamentally, automatically negative. You will allow yourselves then to take advantage of any fundamentally neutral situation in a positive way by understanding that every situation you create and attract into your lives can serve the paths you chose to be. And therefore, as soon as you adopt the idea, the perspective and the attitude that every situation can be viewed as a positive situation and can create positive effects in your lives, you will understand how you relate to the entirety of what we call the multiverse.

No Future

This brings me to a question I've been wondering about for a long time. If everything is happening right now, then why can't the future be predicted?

It is, but not in the terms you call prediction. Recall the idea of the propeller and the strobe lights. The idea, as we have said, is not so much that you are predicting a future; it is more that you are sensing the energy at the present that is most likely to occur because it has the greatest degree of energy behind it. The strobe light is on that particular setting at the time the sensing, or prediction, is made. The prediction itself might change the setting of the strobe light.

Understand what your physicists now understand: you cannot make a conscious decision that doesn't affect the reality you are deciding about. Every thought changes the reality you are thinking of. Therefore, so-called predictions are only sensings of the energy most likely to manifest at the time the prediction is made. The prediction itself can change the energy. However, if what has been sensed has a great deal of energy momentum behind it, it will be unlikely to change.

But it is not the future you have predicted; it is the present, and it doesn't change to the point where it manifests. . . . Keep it simple. The past, the present and the future are all *now*. Understand it this way: remember the radio, where you have the idea of being able to turn to different programs. Just because only one program at a time is coming through your speaker, that doesn't mean all the other programs aren't there. And you can make a prediction that if you tune the dial, you will get another program. That is making a prediction. But it is only because you are aware of the fact that the program already exists that you can do so. It is the same thing.

Is it that everything is happening now, and there's only the present, the past and the future created out of the present? And all of the infinite number of possible futures exist right now?

Yes.

So the question is not whether they are there, because they are. The question is which one you will wind up choosing.

Perfect. Thank you.

So why talk about the future at all, since there is no future?

Yes. It is all present.

The Limbo State

Well, Bashar, I think I have the opposite situation. Instead of things humming along synchronistically, I seem to be at a sort of standstill. I don't know which way to go; I'm feeling at a loss.

We have mentioned this idea of a limbo state with many of you. Usually individuals assume that when we say "limbo state," we are referring to those times when it seems you are floating, stalemated, where no particular direction makes itself any more apparent than any other direction. You do not necessarily have a particular momentum or impetus to move in one direction more than another. You seem to be at a standstill for some reason, and cannot fathom why. Sometimes you don't even want to know. But the idea of the limbo state has a more precise, and in a sense a much more profound definition, which we will share with you at this point.

The idea generally, as we perceive your consciousness, has been perceived as meaning thus: a state in which you must now wait for something to happen. Having done all you can possibly do, there is no more you can do now. You are floating in a limbo state to see what falls out of all the things you have set up. You are now, in a sense, coasting. All of these are real definitions, but they do not touch the essence, the mechanics, the structure of what that waiting is all about.

Film Strip Analogy

The idea can perhaps be best explained by going back to another analogy we have discussed before: the film strip analogy. We have talked about the idea that different moments in time are, as your scientists say, discrete *quanti:* that is, every single moment is its own *now universe*, and in the next moment is a completely different reality altogether. Whatever it is at any given moment you decide you *are* will utterly determine what the next moment will be shaped like, in a sense—how you will experience that next moment. One moment does not have to be connected to the next until you impose upon that frame, and upon that entire film strip, the idea that there must be continuity, one leading to the other. We have talked about the idea that your life, and your many lives, are like the frames upon a strip of your film: one frame at a time, one life at a time. In linear time it seems they come one after another; but that's the nature of your physical reality.

Hypothetically, from the point of view of the projectionist all the frames exist right now. Your entire life is there all at once; all your lives, all the frames, are there all at once. From the point of view of the hypothetical projectionist, which is the same as your higher self, or your oversoul, any frame can be viewed at any moment in any order, regardless of the way you think you have to view it in linear time. It doesn't have to be from A to B to C. . . .

This idea of the limbo state can be looked at from the negative or the positive way, just as anything else can be looked at. As we perceive it, the way your society generally has interpreted what we mean by limbo state is from the negative side—and this is not meant as a derogatory statement. But the negative way to look at this is to view the following analogy: Let us say you are looking at your life as a strip of film running through the projector and playing out on the screen at a certain speed. When most of you talk about the "standstill limbo state, when things do not seem to be happening," you usually look at this as the product of the film somehow slowing down, going into a static state where all of a sudden you are focused on one frame. And you don't know when the film is going to start up again.

Looking at the limbo state as if your life has slowed down is the negative way to look at it; so let's look at it from the positive point of view. You will get the same effect —the focus on the now moment— if you realize that while the film is still going at high speed, *you* have accelerated. Your ability to see the frames has accelerated and sped up to match the speed of the film. You are now going as fast as the film. It is like our earlier analogy of the stroboscopic effect. Many of you have seen the idea that when something is moving, such as falling water, and you place a strobe light upon it, you can freeze the action and allow one drop of that falling water seem to remain suspended in the air before you.

In a sense this is what many of you are now doing: you are accelerating your perceptive abilities up to the speed of your creations. And so it seems as if things are standing still; it seems as if they have slowed down and nothing is happening. But understand there is a very profound difference in how you look at this. If you look at it as if your lives have slowed down, as if the film has slowed down, then you usually wait around for something to happen and do not take action, do not move in life. However, if you understand that the only reason things seem to be standing still is because you have caught up to the speed of your creation, then you can understand that that point of view is now a point of power. *You are in perfect equilibrium with the rate at which you are creating your reality.*

Balanced Inertia

What this means is as follows: when you are in perfect equilibrium with the rate at which you are creating your reality, moment by moment by moment, then that means that everything around you is moving at the same rate. Inertia is balanced, and therefore everything has the equal ability to be moved by you in the direction you prefer. They all have the same rate of speed; you are all moving parallel, synchronized to each other. There is no great inertia to overcome, therefore. Your motion relative to each other —you and the events in your life— are now moving at the same pace, and you can gently push them in any direction you want to.

That sounds like what happens when we practice the martial arts, Bashar.

Yes. This, in a sense, is the "secret" of your martial arts. Your master of those martial arts will tell you that the reason a small, seemingly weak person can move a stronger, larger person in any direction he wants to is because at one particular moment in the action of the movement of the larger person toward the smaller one, the smaller one matches the speed of the larger person. At that moment they are exactly equal in inertia. Neither is moving relative to the other, and therefore it's a very simple thing to cause the larger person to move in any direction the smaller person wishes him to. There is no mass or momentum to overcome, as everything is moving at the same pace, and they can interact with each other any way they want to.

So this limbo state, this time of seeming standstill where it seems as if you have done all you can do, is actually the time when things can happen most magically, most quickly. The only reason it may not seem to be doing so is because you are standing there waiting for something to happen. Allow yourselves to look at the limbo state from this point of view: truly see your point of power. Understand that you are now pacing, synchronizing the rate—the literal rate— at which your consciousness is creating the moments of your reality.

Each and every moment is a discrete moment, a discrete definition, a discrete reality. They all flicker, one after another at an astonishing rate—so fast that your physical reality seems to be an unbroken continuum of time. But it isn't; it is discrete moments, discrete definitions. When you find you are floating in that limbo state, you are at the point of power to allow any factor, any event in your reality, to move in the direction and in the style you prefer to. All you have to do when you arrive at that point is act in your direction of preference, act as the representation of the reality you prefer to have. Things will fall into place in your lives immediately, happening synchronistically.

Now, I do not say this to set you up, but the only thing that would cause you to hesitate is perhaps when you see that when you are in that state where it is so easy to create the reality you want, some of you may be afraid of the power you finally realize you have and back off a bit from it—because you will realize in that moment how powerful you actually are. *The creation of your day-to-day reality is second nature to you. You are so powerful in doing it that you have been able to forget you are the creators of that experiential reality. That's how easy it comes to you. . . .* It is so easy that you've been able to overlook your responsibility for all that creation. Every single second, every single moment, you are exercising choice of what you believe is the most likely reality to manifest in that moment—every single moment. That's how powerful you are.

Infinite Speed

When you allow yourselves to match the rate at which you are creating that reality, you will feel like you are standing still. You are traveling at infinite speeds, and when you do that, you are everywhere at once. And when you are everywhere at once, it's like you are standing perfectly still. The only way you get a sense of the motion is when you have a relative measurement between your reality and what you are calling another reality. If you know that all realities, all events, all creations, are equal to you because they come from you— when you allow them to all achieve that equilibrium, then you are all falling at the same rate. Nothing is moving faster; nothing is moving slower. You can move the pieces around effortlessly, because they are all gliding. You are all together as one event, one idea, and you begin to see all the events in your lives truly as extensions of your selves.

I am not speaking figuratively; I am not speaking philosophically. I am speaking physically, mechanically, literally. You are the creators of your reality. *What you have called the limbo state is your point of power; it is living in the present, in the now.* You are, shall I say allegorically, about *that* far away (holds two fingers very close together) from having everything you want. All you have to do is go that extra little step. Of course for many of you —and again, not to set you up— that last little step is the most difficult. You have been taught over and over and over again: "It can't be that easy; I can't be that powerful."

But you are! As we have said, because you are aspects and reflections of Creation, you are made in the image of God. To be made in the image is to be an echo of God. And in that sense you are that powerful. You are Creation itself. You are the dreams of God, the hands of God, the instruments, the tools that all beings in creation are. As I tell you over and over, you —and we— are all the different ways the Creation has of expressing Itself within the creation It is.

It is your nature; it is the very fabric of your existence to be the power itself. You don't have to develop swollen egos to recognize that. You can allow yourselves to be at balance with all things, and still at the same time know that because you are at balance with all things, everything is an extension of you and will move in the direction in which you allow it to move . . . because you say so! Because that's your job. In a sense, as aspects of the Infinite you are given the responsibility to create your immediate reality in any way you desire. That's why you have free will.

Just as a side note, and just referring to some conversations we have had with a few of you from time to time, it seems quite contradictory to us that there are members of your society who insist that Creation instilled free will within you, and then at the same time sought to control your lives with *Its* will. You have free will, and you can create any reality you desire; that *is* being made in the image of God. Act as such and you will have heaven on your Earth—guaranteed.

A Long Limbo?

So it seems we are going to be in a limbo state for a while.

That is up to you. Remember: limbo states are not only collective; they are personal. If you find yourself in a personal limbo state, while you may recognize that you can exist in an overall bubble, a collective bubble, you can still as an individual do many things within that overall bubble, things which will allow it to not necessarily remain as long as it might have had you as an individual not acted.

Once again: the present *is* your point of power. In the limbo state you are not waiting; you are not at a standstill. You are at infinite speeds. Move in the direction you prefer, and all will automatically, synchronistically fall into place. In your own personal world things will change. Just because there is a collective limbo state doesn't mean you cannot have everything you desire in your own personal reality now. The more you create the reality you desire to live in now, the faster you will represent a living example to everyone else as to the type of reality they can create collectively also. And that will speed up the whole process. So it's really still up to you; it is in your individual hands. Remember: *one individual can have an impact over the entire planet; you've seen it done many times.*

Once again we remind you: because we love you, no matter what you choose to think of yourselves, we will always believe in you totally. You can create any reality you desire, and we will be with you no matter what that reality is you choose to create. But the type of reality you choose will determine exactly how we are able to interact with you. As you recognize that you can serve each other and create a reality of joy, then you open to us the invitation that is necessary for us to have from you to enable us to interact with you, and together blend our race and your race into a larger civilization that can continue to explore creation in ecstatic ways. There is no end to it—at least no end that we have ever found in the thousands of years, in the thousands of civilizations, that have explored creation. There has never been found even the minutest inkling of an end. As far as we are concerned, there never will be.

We rejoice in any opportunity you give us to share creation with you, but only if you are willing to be fully who and what you truly are. For if you are not, then it is not with you we will be interacting, but only with your idea of what you think you ought to be, only with your own illusions and delusions of self. We prefer the genuine articles; we know the genuine articles of you are creative beings, spontaneous beings, loving beings, beings who can create anything you desire.

CHAPTER EIGHT

Welcome to Fourth Density

February, 1986: *Just what is this fourth density you talk about, Bashar?*

Time: what a wonderful creation! But a creation it is: your own illusion, your own understanding of the idea of the way in which you have chosen to express the separation of yourselves from All That Is.

First we will discuss a particular aspect of this idea of fourth density, and we will do it a bit differently than usual. This new idea, this singular notion, will be representative of the timing and certain allowances on your part, within yourselves. All the ideas we have shared with you these past two years have, in a sense, had a particular structure, a particular focus.

Those ideas now can function as the soil, as the foundation, into which the singular crystalline seed, this new idea, can be planted. Recognize this is not against your will; only according to your allowance will this idea take effect. But in the sharing of this idea with you, it will then exist within your consciousness consciously; and in your own timing, according to your own degree of willingness, you can then allow this seed to burst forth and take root in the soil, now that we have laid down the foundation. It can bring forth a blossom that will be what you could call a revelation, one allowing you to finally physically perceive the idea of your own transition into fourth density. By physically perceive, I mean that your physical reality —once you allow full recognition of the idea we will share with you to exist within you emotionally, knowingly— your physical reality will change as you have not seen it change for thousands of years. And it can be in "the twinkling of an eye." It will be up to you.

There will be no reason to judge the fact that in certain ways the understanding will come at different times for different individuals; that is still all part of the timing. But this idea, this speed idea, will be what this revelation change will hinge upon. And now we can discuss this with you consciously, rather than subconsciously or unconsciously, as we have been doing.

But first, to review the ideas we have already discussed with you: we have discussed how you create your reality; that you create the past and the future from the present; that one moment is not connected to the next; that you create the idea of time; that memory is also still a present creation; and that the present is the only time in which you ever exist—because it is the only time you can ever experience.

We have shared many of these ideas with you, and they have all gone into forming their own portion of the structure of the foundation that we have been laying down, co-creating together with you by your own allowance. Now the structure is intact in whatever way it needs to be within each and every one of you. We have discussed that your imagination is real, that your dream reality is real, and that it is only your degree of willingness which allows you to perceive these things as real or not.

This one idea we are going to share with you will be delivered in much the same manner as all the other ideas. It will seem to be a phrase like many other phrases, but there is a difference. For this is what will function as the key; and when you decide to turn it, the reality you unlock will not be the reality you have known. And you will begin to experience —not just think about it, not just philosophize about it— but truly physically experience it.

We have discussed with you many ideas about what you call sanity and insanity: the sensing of other realities that are no less real than your own, but are not the mass agreed-upon reality. That what you call sanity is only the mass agreed-upon *insanity*— the idea that everything is an illusion, and yet everything is real. Because you *are* the creator; you are the gods. The universe is your creation. What you imagine is real is a portion of that universe, and can be really experienced on every level, including the physical one.

We have discussed with you many times the idea of prophecies, patterns, rituals, tools, things that you may choose for yourselves to create in order to understand yourselves in the way you chose to understand yourselves, in the path you chose to be, and the manner in which you chose to unfold yourselves. All these things will still be valid once we have shared the single idea with you. But you will have now incorporated this new idea, which will allow all that we have discussed to create this congruency, this concurrency, this simultaneity, this synchronicity, this explosion of reality within you.

Before we share this one idea, we will share something more. We have discussed a few ideas about your brain. We have told you, and your own scientists have since discovered, that every thought you have, every idea you create, physiologically changes the pathways in your brain; it rewires you. *Every* thought you have creates new pathways and eliminates the old ones. I do not mean it opens and closes pathways that do not change. I mean there are pathways where there were none before. And where there were pathways previously, there are none after the thought.

So in revelation you have the aligning of many different ideas, many different levels of your consciousness at once. The conscious recognition of your alignment in one moment: that is revelation. You allow there to be a majority or a totality of rewiring in every portion of your brain, for you emerge from that revelation a completely new person. You are, in all reality, a completely new person in every moment of time that you create, for, as we have said, one moment is not connected to the next. You recreate yourselves over and over again in the various moments of time that you also choose to create, to create the idea you call a continuity—which is an illusion.

Now, recognize this: for what we have to say, it will not matter if you have shared with us once, never, or a million times. If you are present at this time in this co-creation, you will understand what you need to understand. You do not ever have to have been near these ideas before. The fact that you are in the vicinity of them now will allow you to know that you cannot be anywhere but where you are supposed to be. Therefore, trust that you will understand the idea on whatever level you need to, and trust that you already have the foundation prepared to understand the idea.

Know that when the phrase is delivered again, it will not be hypnosis; it will not be implanted against your will. It will simply be allowed into your conscious recognition, and you will do with it what you will when you will. But again, recognize this is the fulcrum, the seed crystal idea, for if you can understand this, your reality will change.

One more thing about the brain: when you scientifically delve into the brain to understand your mentality, to understand your consciousness, recognize that your brains are wired according to your beliefs. And when you study the brain, you study it *with your brain.* So do be aware, therefore, that a brain cannot study a brain objectively, for it will only see what it is wired to see. Your reality exists in total. What you see of All That Is is only what you are wired to see. Thus, only by changing the idea of yourselves will you allow yourselves to rewire your brains in ways that will allow you to perceive the reality existing all around you, but to which you are blind, to all intents and purposes. You will reconnect, connecting in ways which will give you different sight, different sense.

Once this phrase is delivered, many of you, once again, may feel you understand it intellectually, but not emotionally. "All right, I understand the words," you might say, "but I do not feel any different." That is all right. That is the way your imagination chooses to accept the idea and the understanding now. But understand it will be there. That seed is what will explode in your mind, in your brain. Not physical explosion, but energy explosion that will, from the inside out, completely rewire your brain. And then the reality you perceive will be a reflection of that rewiring. It will be the fourth density, complete.

At this time, therefore, all of you close your eyes and relax, while taking a deep breath. If you are feeling feelings, feel them. If you are feeling fear, feel it. Live it; love it; enjoy yourselves. For you are now all you need to be in this moment to understand anything you wish to be at any other moment. Take two more deep breaths.

Now, simply relax into your imagination, and pay attention: . . . Your present is *not* the result of your past. . . . *Your present is **not** the result of your past.* . . . **Your present is not the result of your past.** . . . *YOUR PRESENT IS NOT THE RESULT OF YOUR PAST!*

Take a deep breath, followed by two more. . . . And you may open your eyes. . . . You may emerge into your natural state of existence.

Recognize that once you allow the explosion of understanding to truly —*emotionally, experientially*— understand that your present is not the result of your past, you will, once and for all . . . *BREAK THE CONNECTION TO THE THIRD DENSITY!!*

* * *

You will experience things in your physical reality which will be a reflection that you no longer have the need for what you call memory. For you will know everything you need to know in the present; in any situation that you create in the present, you will know what you need to know. You will begin to lose the ideas of the methodologies you have created that you call learning—in the way you have created it. You will understand that you do not need to learn by process that which you can know by experience in the moment.

Right now you are creating yourselves to be the idea of persons who have habitual patterns from the past. And now you are creating yourselves to be the idea of persons who have habitual patterns from the past. And *now* the same thing, over and over again. But you do not have to have that definition of yourselves. When you are willing to know that you *can* change that definition, and changing that definition will change the physical reality in the way you experience it, then you will understand that your past has nothing at all to do, in a controlling way, with what you are experiencing now.

The present is *not* the result of the past. The present is the result of what you *think* it is the result of *now*. If you think your present is the result of your past, that's the effect you are creating. But you are creating that effect *now* in the present. So you create all the apparent linear continuity manifestations that seem to fall into place to make sense out of the theory you have of who you think you are at this moment. Change that theory and you will no longer experience anything that has to do with supporting the old theory. You will now only experience the manifestations in your life, the feelings in your life and the belief systems in your life, that go toward supporting the new theory you are being at this moment.

Now, this is sinking in on many different levels. We realize that some of these concepts may be new to you. But allow us to remind you of one very important thing: never is it possible for you to hear something you are not ready to hear. So if you are now in this conversation with us, that is an indication that on whatever level you need to, it's sinking in and making sense. And bit by bit, at whatever rate you are comfortable in changing those frames, your outer reality will also change.

Only Now

But do fully grasp the major idea here: you create the past from the present, and not the other way around; the present is the only experiential time in which you ever exist. Any time you look at yourselves, it is always now; and it always will be now. It may be a different manifestation of *now*, but it will always be now. Therefore, you are creating from now any idea of the so-called past; you are creating from now any idea of the so-called future. It can be anything you desire it to be.

When you change the *you* you are now, you will then focus on the particular ideas of the past that will represent the *you* you are being now. Because the so-called idea of the past has many probable ways of manifesting, just as many as there are of the future. So whatever idea you are being now will determine the way you relate, and what it is you perceive to be real about your past—and about your future.

Bashar, you say our present is not the result of our past. Couldn't that be true for one person, but not for somebody else? If someone thinks he is the result of his past— well, he is, isn't he?

Yes, and he will then reflect that idea by remaining in the third density.

Since everything is true, does it mean we have to really believe that, or have that concept fully, to be able to go on to the fourth density?

If you are creative enough to create a type of reality for yourselves which says you can have a reality that is the idea of believing whatever you want to believe, and still be wherever you want to be with it, then *that* will allow you to be in that reality. You may find, however, that you will simplify and eliminate definitions bit by bit, so that your reality will be the simplest definition it can be. You can have a reality containing what seems to be both of those ideas, and still be where you want to be, for since you know you are always where you want to be, then that is what the definition of your reality can be. You will not really need created symbols that reflect where you are; you will be where you are no matter what definition that carries with it.

Acclimating

Now, this fourth density experience is a little bit more rarified, a higher degree of energy expression. And thus many of you now are finding that as you are beginning to acclimate to the idea of the new accelerated energy —but are still thinking you exist in the old third density— many of you will be, or already have been, feeling this energy in different ways, as long as you are attaching comparisons to your body and what you think your body can and cannot tolerate.

Many of you are feeling the acceleration of this energy in various ways. For instance, perhaps you are experiencing fevers, flushings, adrenalin rushes, anxiety rushes. Many times there will be pain in the spine, the shoulder blades, the base of the neck; even migraines; sinus pressure; palpitations of the heart or rushes of anxiety in the solar plexus.

I've been feeling disoriented and tired and off balance, as has my son. We were told it's from the energy being beamed to Earth. Can you tell me any more—?

In a sense, but keep it simple. Recognize that you are now allowing there to be the idea that there is more energy than there used to be, even though there isn't. But you are becoming more aware of the energy that is available; and therefore, to you it is the same thing as having more energy.

Again, the disorientation is simply the time you are creating for yourselves to get used to the new level of energy. You are *dis*-orienting yourselves from the old reality, and *re*-orienting yourselves into a new one. New definitions. Thus the importance of having clear intention, clear definition, clear desire, clear deservability and clear action. They will reorient you very quickly.

Use the energy, use the limbo state, to define what you prefer. Then act accordingly, and you will be aligned; you will be reoriented. Remember that some of this disorientation, as we have said before, is also part of the process, if you wish, of literal, *literal* disillusionment. You are redefining your physical reality as an extension of you. It is the same energy you are; it is the idea you are; it is made of your consciousness. So in a sense, now that everything is dissolving in its old definitional sense, you are becoming disoriented because there isn't as much solid structure to hold on to. You are floating in the center of your being, making up your mind as to what the new structure will be like.

All of these ideas are fourth-density symptomatic of new awareness of new levels of energy that you are, but still couched in old terminology. You will assimilate; you will acclimate. Do not fear. It is simply one of the ways you can begin to consciously be aware that you are changing, you are transforming.

All of these different manifestations let you know something is going on. Because you have created yourselves to be a reality which feels the need to rely upon processes in order to become something else, then many of you still have a little bit of the remnants of some of these processes. And that is the only reason why you are feeling these ideas to be taking seemingly so much time to work themselves through.

But work themselves through they will. For you *are* the idea of the transformation itself. Transformation is now what you are all about.

I still don't understand what a density is, Bashar. Could you make it more clear?

Now, this is to some degree a colloquial terminology for what you have called dimensions of experience. All it really refers to is different frequencies of existence—a different density, a higher density, being a more accelerated frequency, a less material frequency. It is a label, one way to say that there is a separation, a separation of vibrational resonance. You can make an analogy with your visible light. You have visible light and you have light that you cannot see. You may therefore understand that the reason you can see some light and cannot see other light is because of the rate of their vibration. All reality you call physical is of this nature, and it all vibrates at different rates. Some of it you will perceive and some of it you will not. Usually those that are realities you do not physically perceive the way you do this one are ascribed to what you call other realities or other dimensions of All That Is—or within All That Is.

But we will also say this about the idea of densities and your transformation through them, your acceleration and graduation through different densities. You, as a planet, are now going from third density to fourth density. And what this basically means is that fourth density is the last level on which you can experience yourselves in an accelerated state and still remain physical.

Our civilization is going from fourth density to fifth density, which is a non-physical state. Above the fifth are non-physical states, up to and including seventh density, and then you go into an entirely different octave of dimensional experience, for which right now there aren't very many words to describe it accurately in your language. And even *we* are only beginning to explore that idea. However, the idea itself of going from level to level, density to density, is —now pay attention!— is the process of realizing that you actually *are* the dimension itself that you previously thought you existed *in!*

Being the Dimension

One more time: you now exist, you think, in a physical universe. Your fourth-density transformation is where you begin to realize you are the creator of your reality. What that means is that physical reality is your expression, is your projection, is your creation; that it's actually made of you. It means you are actually *it;* that physical reality is *you.* When you really grasp this, you then see yourselves literally *as* the dimension of experience of which you previously thought you were only a component.

That's how it is for every level. You begin to realize you *are* the dimension itself that you previously thought you were only a part of. And here's the wonderful paradox of the whole circumstance. Each and every single one of you, as an individual, will experience yourselves becoming the whole dimension. Each of you will think that all the other consciousnesses you have seen as individuals are being in a sense absorbed into you. You will all have the same experience because the universe is holographically structured. That means that any point of view can exist equally everywhere within creation. And that all points of view are relevant and all true.

Every being, in a sense, can be called a God-thought—one of the ways that God has of thinking of Itself, of expressing Itself, of experiencing Itself. So here you are, being God manifested as physical individuals, with individual personality and individual identity. That's one of the ways the Infinite can experience Itself. There are an infinite number of ways, for there is no end to the growth; there is no end to the transformation. The idea of going from level to level and density to density, as least as far as we can tell, will never, never end.

About the wiring in our brains: our neurophysiologists, first of all, have not been able to understand or describe the processes that make up consciousness.

That is because consciousness is not a product of physicality. Physicality is a product of consciousness.

Right. But as far as the memory mechanisms are concerned, I don't think they are considered to be pathways, as such. They are more electrical activity—

Yes, that is the point. Pathway is the root of electrical activity, the interaction of electrical activity. As we have said, the brain —which is what they are using to explore the brain— cannot see itself objectively. They will not discover in a mental way what they are after. When they include consciousness in their equations, they will understand what they need to understand. They will not find it analytically, because **you never do find anything analytically. If you think you have, it is only because your consciousness has created an understanding, and then you take yourselves through the process of analyzing to find what you already know.**

You have talked about parallel dimensions, and slipping from one dimension to the next. In applying that information and coming up to a situation that I didn't prefer, my methodology has been to close my eyes and decide that I was in a different dimension. Then when I opened my eyes, I would be in a different dimension, and my preference would be manifested in that different dimension. It was quite outstanding, even to changing a traffic jam on the freeway.

Yes! There are all possibilities, for the ebb and flow of physical reality is but an illusion.

Well, you stated that our mass consciousness hasn't permitted a lot of this. But I presume it's beginning to allow it now, and that is why it's been working.

Yes, this is the timing. All ideas we have discussed with you in the past have been related to the processes allowed by your mass consciousness. Now instantaneousness is allowed.

Yes. Within that context you have said that we could be losing our memories of the past. So I presume any moment in the past is a moment currently in another dimension.

Yes, you will recognize that you are creating it in the present. *And it acts as a connection to that other dimension.*

In the present. It is not that you are now reaching into a past for the information. You are *becoming* the idea in the present, in order to have the information you need. So you won't exactly really forget anything. However, you may find that you will not relate to the idea of a past situation in the way you related to it previously: feeling that your present situation was a result of it. You will make a disconnection emotionally. This so-called past event you have had will just be one more way you choose to experience the present. Nothing more.

In fourth density, for the most part, you will still be able to relate to linear time. Once you find yourselves at the end of fourth density, emerging into fifth, you may not relate to it any more.

Being in the Moment

In your fourth-density life, everything you do will be as if you are doing it for the first time. You will be living in the moment and truly understanding that every single moment of time is literally a new moment, and it isn't really connected to any other moment—except in the sense that it occupies the same place the last moment occupied. However, it isn't the same moment, nor is it really a direct continuation. Continuity is your illusion.

Well, wait a minute. You're still here at 8:00 every Thursday night—

It isn't 8:00 to me; that's your time frame. Every time we have an interaction with you, it is totally new—for the first time. It is that we live that much in the moment; everything is really that new to us. It is the same way —before your society unteaches you— that you as children live in the moment and are fascinated with everything. You see everything as if you are seeing it for the first time—which you are. A child knows this.

So it would be the same thing as if a child would see an opportunity every Thursday night at 8:00 to do this thing?

If you wish to put it that way. But the child does not see it as an opportunity every Thursday night at 8:00. He notices an opportunity; he acts on it. It does not matter where or when it is. It is simply the expression of who and what he is. He has not yet keyed into the notion of linear time as specifically as many of you have. He is simply acting in the moment with whatever is there that represents the vibration he knows he is. And so it is always new—always new.

Understand that when you see a flower —and every day you approach that flower— you are always, always approaching it from a slightly different direction, a slightly different time. Therefore, it is never really the same flower, is it?

Because we're not the same people?

Correct. So when you understand that every moment is absolutely new and truly for the first time, then it isn't a matter of saying, "Well, I think I'll do this for, oh, two to three months." Right there you are setting yourselves up to experience the idea in a linear fashion, and that makes it wind down. When you really no longer need to express yourselves in that way, you will start expressing yourselves in whatever way is most representative of who and what you are, which is what I will do.

When the energy itself shifts, we can translate this idea into your linear time, saying, "Well, it will last such and such for so long." But that idea is not really how we experience it. We just go with the flow, and we know that when the flow changes direction, it is representative of the collective energy that we and you are, together in this interaction. Then we follow it; we act on it. It is not that we actually plan it out, time it out: "All right; this channeling is going to take 3,287 Thursdays." We do not approach it that way. We simply live in the moment. And in a sense, as a civilization we are now gaining the ability to actually experience every single one of the channelings we have done with you as one interaction—in a sense approached from a different point of view, simultaneously. Is this making any sense?

Creating Less Time

A little. You're saying that you are beginning to experience all time as now?

Yes. *Because* we are moving from physical to non-physical, our reality is almost completely blended as one idea.

Okay. I think it's going to take a while for it to sink in.

If you say so. But that's how you create more time, with that definition. 'Tis up to you. For the time you will experience will all be worth experiencing and will all be beautiful. The sooner you allow the time you do create to be worth experiencing, the less of it you will perceive, paradoxically enough.

Wait a minute. Say that one more time.

All right. One more time—for the first time. When you allow whatever time you do create for yourself to experience to be experienced in full joy, then paradoxically you will actually experience less time. **When you live in the moment, you don't create as much time. Only the waiting for something else creates the time that happens in-between.**

Do understand: from one particular point of view, one I shall now choose, each and every one of you is actually always spontaneous. Even when you create hesitation, it's still a spontaneous creation. So the idea is to look at everything in your life as a spontaneous creation, if that's what you desire. And then you will start to see everything being redefined in that way, and you will see the result of that attitude in the actions you perform.

In other words: if you see hesitation as just one more way to experience spontaneity, then that attitude —seeing even the idea of planning and hesitation as a spontaneous creation in the moment— will actually allow you to manifest in physical terms the idea in a truly more physicalized spontaneous manner. The attitude of how you look at things, in other words, will determine the way your life unfolds, the way the opportunities come to you, and how you will act on them in a more spontaneous fashion. Does this make sense?

I think so. Might this help to explain how sometimes we create feelings of being stuck?

Oh, yes, yes, yes. It is only because of the definitions you give to the circumstances. You see, what you're saying is, "This means things are in stasis, not moving. When you see this, that's what it means; it means you're stuck. It means you are not moving ahead." Instead of having the attitude that what is happening is a part of the process, not an interruption in it. And you dive *right* into it to find out what part of the process it is. As soon as you dive into it, you are in the middle of experiencing it. Therefore it goes right through you very quickly; and before you know it, you're through it.

So if you think you're feeling stuck, and you just do the next thing, you're really not stuck.

Correct. Explore the idea of your definitions of stuck. Remember that anything you call a block is not actually a block, unless you choose to treat it like one. Unless you treat it as if it's something to go around, instead of something to go through. Discover what a block usually is: information you really need to know, but which comes in an unexpected package. You may not recognize it on the surface, but that doesn't mean it doesn't belong in your life. Dive into it; unwrap it. 'Tis the time for unwrapping presents on your world.

When something comes you think is a block, find out what you would have to believe in order to experience it that way; find out what information it is bringing you. Absorb the information, and the idea you have called the block will unfold—as a direction, as a path, in a very obvious and clear-sighted way. Understand?

Yes. I think this must be the real meaning of the statement, "This, too, shall pass."

In a sense, yes. Because everything, though real, is transitory, because it is all the product of your imagination. Physical reality is only what you dream it to be, what you imagine it to be, what you define it to be. That's all. But that's the reality of it.

Third Density Pain

You said earlier that a bunch of symptoms you mentioned— all of which I've had— were symptoms of moving into the fourth density.

They are symptoms of moving into fourth density, while still retaining some connections to third.

Okay, I have a little confusion about pain being created by friction.

You have a habit of thinking of yourself in a certain way as a third-density being. When you begin to have the notion, or become aware of the idea of fourth density, you will find that you usually begin to explore that understanding from a third-density point of view. One of the things you all have created in your society, to begin the exploration of fourth density from a third-density point of view, is the creation of a belief that as third-density individuals you have a slower vibration than you will have as fourth-density individuals. But this is still the remnant of a judgment: the creation of the idea or belief that the third density is somehow *less* than the fourth density.

So you create a separation while you are "forcing yourselves" to explore fourth density, and allowing yourselves to experience some acceleration of energy. You still hold on to the idea that while you are doing the exploring, you are still somehow something less than what it is you are becoming. You are moving at a slower vibration in that way.

Therefore, as you create the idea of fourth density to be represented in your mentality as a so-called higher vibration, and at the same time still retain a notion that while you are doing this you are a slower vibration, this judgment and this comparison of separation then creates the scenario wherein you have two different vibrations within the same body. This causes friction, which causes pain.

When you know that you are what you are at any given moment, and what you are is what you need to be, you will then accelerate as a smooth oneness of vibration and not create comparisons between something you think is *less*, and then become something you think is *more*. You will become one vibration; you will erase the friction, and there will be no pain.

A Strange Disease

Bashar, last April I experienced about three months of very strange events and symptoms.

You experienced three months last April?

Yes, I did—all in one moment. I was absolutely fascinated with every moment, and every moment was almost like jumping off a cliff—and it was okay.

Yes! Living in the now.

It was lovely.

Was? Why *was*?

Well, you'll see. A strange thing started happening. These very morbid, horrible thoughts started coming in . . . one by one. In other words, I could look at the news prior to that time, and it all looked good. Even the starving faces in Ethiopia were brilliant reminders to everyone to open their hearts and all that. Then it all started looking ugly, and it all started looking malevolent, as if this thing that I'd experienced was all a joke, and as if it was all an illusion. And I know it is; I know I've created all of this.

All right. How does seeing it that way serve you now?

I don't know. Then the next thing that happened was an experience one night. All of a sudden all these dichotomies, which had melted— I swear, every single dichotomy in the universe came rolling in on me, and it seemed to be not in my control. My heart started beating a mile a minute. I actually thought I was having a heart attack and dying, and I almost went unconscious. Parts of my body disappeared, and I was just terrified; I even had the paramedics come up. . . . They did nothing, but I did have company then. So then I took myself to the hospital. I was not having a heart attack, but everything looked very strange to me.

Disorientation.

I couldn't even go out of my house. I actually cringed from the sun—and the moon even. It was too much. And I thought, "I know I'm creating this, but at the same time I don't want to be creating it." It was almost a dichotomy of the original thing I experienced. So I tried various ways of dealing with it.

Then recently I've been experiencing again driving in my car, my heart starting to beat a mile a minute, and then starting to faint. I feel very, very disoriented from life. It's boring to me. . . . Well, not really boring, but— am I ill? I want to know if I'm ill.

Ill? Yes. You have symptoms of transformation sickness. You are experiencing the idea of fourth-density disease.

Well, what is the remedy?

To live. And cease to judge what is happening to you as something negative.

Yeah, well there's less fear now about it.

Yes. Make a friend of your fear. It is there to show you something. Accept the message it delivers, and integrate that message within you as a part of you. You will know that in your ecstasy you will at the same time also remain grounded enough to assist others.

Uh . . . I don't quite get it.

Just take it in a general sense. The idea that when you accelerate to infinite speeds, many times from your belief systems you will create within you the idea of losing sight of the ideas that you wished to exemplify in choosing this physical life on your planet. So you give yourself the opportunity to experience the polarity of the ecstasy. Now you will be able to blend the two dichotomies, as you say, and form a balanced state of being, one which will allow you to exist in the fourth-density state with equal ease.

Now I get it.

Thank you.

Fourth Density Life

So if I understand you, in fourth density we will experience time in a different way, and then each life span will continue for a much longer period?

The idea is that as you begin to live more in the now, in the present, and not so much living in the past, not so much living in or worrying about the future— the more you live in the now, the less you experience the idea of time itself. You will simply lose track of when it is. The days —even though they may be observable by the coming and going of daylight— will not necessarily have as much meaning to you in the sense of absolutely having to know what time it is, what day it is. You will move as you feel you need to move, and you will automatically be exactly where you need to be when you need to be there—whether you know what time you got there or not.

Days will blend into days, years into years. Years will pass; hundreds of years will pass. And to you it may still seem like a day, so much in the present are you living—in the now, the eternal now. That is why many of you will find that your life spans are increasing. This, in a sense, is an abstract misnomer. It is not literally that you are having more time; it is that you are creating less time. So you come into your primal now continuous existence and simply span the ages. They become reduced by comparison to you since you are no longer counting.

Now, because you will accelerate at that rate, it is our perception that your civilization does not need to remain physically embodied for any more than approximately two to three thousand years more. Then at that time you will go on to other realms, other dimensions.

As we progress through our transformation, and we experience a lightening of our bodies, will we see a difference on our bathroom scales?

In a sense, you may choose to create that type of a symbol to represent the enlightenment of yourselves, if you wish, yes. Gravity will no longer hold you quite so hard.

So it would mean we will begin to have lighter, more resonating bodies?

Yes. Things will appear to be brighter to you; you will see colors more clearly. You will see energies that are now invisible to you. You will be able to truly see auric fields, the ethereal-magnetic field, and any other interactive vibratory field that connects the idea of your total consciousness upon your planet.

You will find that you have no disease; you will sleep and eat less. You will create your dreams upon your planet, and also will interact with many other civilizations. You will rebuild many sections of your world, landscaping them into pleasing forms; you will cease to build on many sections of your world. You will build in space; you will explore space and dimensions of time, and other levels of experience.

You will begin to truly see through the illusion of physical reality as your own projection. You will be able to come and go, in and out of your body at will. You will find you no longer need to reincarnate at all, and any time you wish to have the experience of a physical form for a brief period of time, you will all share a very few bodies.

What will be the approximate population size?

Within a thousand of your years, it is likely —not absolute, but likely— that you will be down to 50 million.

What about in 60 years?

You may be beginning to reverse the trend down from approximately 6 billion. As we have said, you will find that you really are not overpopulated; you just do not apportion the land you have in equal ways. But again, once you begin to move out of the phase of reincarnation; and once you allow for more longevity of the lives you already have, then you will decrease your numbers. Many individuals will remain to function as non-physical support systems for those others who wish to continue for a time in physical reality—until such time as you no longer need to be physical at all. Some of you may still stay around as non-physical support systems even then, for other beings who might want to use your physical reality as a new experiential reality, and thus begin their cycle anew.

Now, you say our present is not the result of our past. So will we be using our imaginations differently?

You will be *living* in it. You will be experiencing your imagination in as real a way as you have been experiencing physical reality. You will —as we have said many times— be living your dreams. Did you think we were being figurative? When we said you will be living your dreams, we were being quite literal.

I'm not talking about the night dreams; I'm talking about day dreams.

What is the difference? Night dream, day dream . . . All we are saying is that now the barriers are dissolving, the definitions that allow you to create the idea that night dreams, day dreams, and awake physical states are different. It is all going to be one experience. We do not, in your terms, really ever sleep, because since we are living in the dream, we never need to wake up into physical reality. We are awake. That is what is meant by living your dreams. Through experiencing your life as if it were the type of reality that you think is only relegated to your night dreams, the impossible is made possible. You will no longer be making a distinction between the dream reality and the physical reality, and feeling that physical reality is more real.

Bashar, you said that nobody is going to go faster than anybody else.

Not in an overall sense. There is a bubble, let us say, of leeway that you will stay within, in general terms, even though some individuals may be more accelerated than others. But you will stay within the bubble of acceptability, thus allowing you all together as a bubble to move into fourth density at once. You will not get ahead of anyone else, although in a sense you may be ahead of someone else on a personal level.

All Together

What proportion of people will be going into—?

No, no, no. To ask for that type of information causes separation and is quite meaningless. Everyone who chooses to be fourth density— well, 100% of those people will be in fourth density. 100% of all those who choose to be in third density will be in third density. And so forth. There is no way to give you anything that is meaningful, in terms of what percentage will be in fourth and what percentage will be in third. It is a constantly shifting idea. Choices —at the moment they are made— completely eradicate the percentages. So you could say, right now— 70%. Right now— 63%. Right now— 82%. What difference does it make? It is always changing.

Okay, I got it. But it means that we as individuals can talk to people and plant "seeds" allowing them to change their minds.

You can always share what you are, of course. You can share this idea with anyone with whom you come in contact, because you wouldn't have that contact if you could not share with them.

Bashar, if a person reaches the stage where he no longer blames or points fingers, does that mean he has more or less achieved fourth density?

In a sense, yes. That will be the beginnings of the fourth density experience. There will be more and more changes: physiological changes, energy changes, sociological changes—all of which you will be able to witness as you go along in fourth density. But that will be the beginning of your willingness to consciously know that you are now, in fact, in fourth density.

And is that how you would sum up the fourth density, where the subjective creates the objective?

Yes, in a sense. Knowing that there really is no such thing as objectivity; knowing that you create your own reality totally. Fourth density is taking responsibility for the creation of your reality—acting like you actually do, in fact, create your reality. That is fourth density. Recognizing that everything, as we have said, is synchonicity, and acting like it.

Everything is interconnected holographically; everything is the same one thing manifesting in all the different multi-faceted, multi-dimensional ways that it can— simultaneously, with regard to any particular event. Everything you experience is the same one thing. Knowing that, and acting like you know it, is living in the fourth density, living in the now, living in the moment.

Will we be dissolving the unconscious as we move into this fourth density, so that by the time we are fully into it, the unconscious will be completely dissolved?

In a sense, yes. You will simply know what you need to know when you need to know it. You will be living in the moment and will fear nothing, and you will be consciously aware of everything in your life as your creation. Nothing mysterious; nothing hidden; nothing occult.

Then we will eventually move into integrating with our higher selves?

That is still a form of integration with your higher selves in a way, but remaining in physiological terms. Fourth density is the expression of synchronous harmonious congruency with your so-called higher self, while still remaining to some degree separated. Fifth density, then, is actually *becoming* the higher self, and is non-physical, as we mentioned..

I guess the idea seems to be that normally an individual would proceed from third to fourth to fifth to sixth to seventh, and so on.

That's how you think of it linearly from the third-density point of view, yes.

Is it possible to simply pass from third dimension to the twelfth without—?

To some degree, yes. Because you already exist on every level there is to exist upon simultaneously. On the twelfth level you know this; on the third you may not. But the idea is that on the third you can become whatever representation of that connection you need to be. But allow me to now ask you a question: in your terms of linear thinking, what would be your reason for going directly from third to twelfth without experiencing all of the ones in-between?

Enjoy the Third

My experience with the third density hasn't been particularly enjoyable.

Then you will probably remain in it until you realize that it can be. The idea is that when you invalidate an experience you obviously chose to have, then you are not getting out of it what you can get out of it. And it will usually allow you to remain in that experience until you understand the reason for why you chose to be in it to begin with. The quickest way to get to the twelfth level is to realize that you can —absolutely, in every way— enjoy the third.

Well, I haven't reached the point yet where I find limitations particularly enjoyable.

All right. But understand there are many different kinds of limitations. It is a form of limitation just to be focused in a specific way. Even in what you would call twelfth density there is still the idea of a particular awareness or focus that allows you to conceive of the fact that you are in twelfth density. That is still a type of limitation. Limitation, in and of itself, does not have to be inherently negative. You are simply buying into the belief system, or one of the belief systems in your third density reality, that *all* limitation is inherently negative—or that there can be situations that are inherently negative. But there aren't.

Let me say again that no situation has any built-in meaning. Whatever meaning you give to a situation is what you have been taught to give to that situation; it's what you have been taught to believe that situation means. The meaning you give to a neutral situation —a neutral set of circumstances or set of props— the meaning you give to it utterly determines the effect you get out of it.

So if you do not find third-density pleasant, then it is because you have been taught to believe that it is not. Only that belief —*ONLY that belief!!*— creates third-density to be effectually unpleasant. *Only* that belief. There is nothing built into physical reality that says physical reality has to be unpleasant. Just because it is a limitation in a particular way does not mean you cannot soar with exuberance in third-density reality.

Again, paradoxically, since you obviously have chosen to be in third-density reality, it is our suggestion that when you finally let yourself realize you can become absolutely ecstatic in the third density, that is when you will have cognition of the fact that you already exist on all the other levels already. And allowing yourself to know that will be the simple matter of shifting your perspective, rather than feeling you have to climb your way out of some thick dark mire into which you have fallen. It is all point of view.

Now, perhaps this will be of some assistance to you, if you are willing to absorb it directly into your heart. Pay close attention to the following definition, even though we have stated it before. Your idea —and we are speaking in general as well— of going from level to level, plane to plane: that idea, or process, is simply one of recognizing that *you actually are the dimension itself that you previously thought you existed in.*

So if you find yourself thinking that you exist *in* third density, think again. You *ARE* third density; you *ARE* the physical universe; the physical universe *IS* you. When you know that you *are* all you experience the physical universe to be —when you are in control of what it is you *do* experience the physical universe to be— then it will be heaven on Earth, twelfth density on Earth.

All levels align at a particular way of thinking, in a particular mode of thought. All levels align. All you have to do is realize that going from level to level to level is the recognition that you already exist *as* that level, and think of yourself in that point of view. When you allow yourself to operate as the collective totality that you are, then no one level will seem to be overwhelming—because you will be drawing on the totality of all that you are.

You are not cut off from yourself in twelfth density; you are always able to draw from *all* of the power, *all* of the existence, the totality of the spirit and the soul that you are. Then no one level will seem to be overwhelming, because any one level will seem to be a small fraction of the total being, the total creator that you are. And when you function in that way, enjoying where you are when you are there —living in the moment, living totally in the present— that is paradoxically exactly the way you allow the future and all the levels to accelerate most quickly into your present experience. For you do not *go* anywhere; all happens within you. You bring those experiences to you—and even that you are not literally doing. Nothing in the universe truly literally actually moves or goes anywhere; it is all perspective and point of view— all of it.

Do remember this— and this also may assist you greatly when you allow it to sink into whatever portion of you it needs to sink into: many of the ideas of what many people in your civilization believe to be entrapment —"I'm stuck here; I'm stuck there"— is because you have been taught to believe that consciousness exists *in* the body. It doesn't. **The body exists within your consciousness.** There is a vast difference in the realization of those two definitions, and the idea, therefore, is very unlimiting, very expansive. For you can recognize that what you think of as your body is but one focal point within the combined idea of the consciousness you are, out of which is created all the physical reality you experience. You have much more mobility, because you can diversify your focus, disperse your point of view, broaden and expand the way you look at yourself—the way you look *through* yourself, the way you look through the idea of yourself that is expressed in bodily terms. Thus it is important to remember that the body is immersed in the collective consciousness that you *are.*

*   *   *

And now as a final note to all of you: from this point forward, you will begin, at your own rate, your own timing, to notice the increase of synchronicity in your lives, the ecstatic explosion of coincidence. And perhaps, just perhaps, you will begin to forget your past. Do not fear that forgetting, for that forgetting is what will allow you to live in the moment, knowing everything you need to know when you need to know it, and recognizing that you are indeed unlimited beings. *Now you are unlimited beings!* I thank you for your co-creation.

Welcome to the fourth density!

CHAPTER NINE

Follow Your Excitement

Bashar, What is my purpose for being here? What is my mission in life?

Within any given life which any of you live you can create many so-called purposes, as there are many projects, services and circumstances by which you express who you are. *None* of these projects, in and of themselves, is your purpose; they are your chosen method of *expressing* the purpose of your lives.

Now, we recognize that, generally speaking, when you ask that question, you are usually referring to this idea on a much more foundational level. Because of the society you have created yourselves to *be*, many of you spend a great deal of time searching for your basic purpose, and often become frustrated, tired and discouraged about not finding it.

First of all, please remember: *every single thing is a choice— everything!* Yes, you chose to be where you are; you chose to be born. So first and foremost allow yourselves to recognize that you made a decision to be physical. You knew what you were doing when you made that decision. And whether you have conscious recognition of it or not, you still *do* know what you are doing. At least begin by relying upon the assurance and the trust that you are doing whatever it is you are doing for a reason. It is not pointless; it is not aimless; it is not so scattered as it may appear to be in the illusion of the physical reality you have bought into.

Recognize, therefore, that for every single one of you **your fundamental purpose is to be the person you have designed yourself to be.** It is no more complex than that. It is to do what excites you the most and to be of service by doing so; *to be the fullest you you can be, because you will never be this you again.*

Only One Life

The idea is as follows: you have had a saying for a long time in your society, "You only have one life to live." Well now, reincarnation notwithstanding, this is true. You, as the *you* you are now, only have one life to live. You've got one shot at being *this* you. Even though the soul you are may experience many lifetimes, each one of those lifetimes is unique, and a distinct expression of the overall soul you are. Therefore, since you have never been *this* you before; since you will never be *this* you again, the foundational reason for this life is, again, to fully be the *you* you chose to be. That's it. Period.

Everything else —any way, any method, any point of view, any methodology of experiencing and expressing the idea of being fully who you chose to be in this life— is up to you as the physiological consciousness. Now, many of you go through life looking for a specific thing that would seem like the purpose of your life, but create difficulty in finding that thing because you don't recognize that it's up to you to *decide* what that thing is. The idea is that the choice was made by the higher self, and *that* —the fact that you are present in this physical reality— is almost the entire extent of what you usually refer to as predestination: just the fact that you are here. Period.

There may be some generalized themes that are also representative of the overall predetermined reality decided upon by you when you were the higher self in a non-physical realm before you became physically born, but they are only generally represented in your life as overall themes. The specifics of how you go about living the life, and the themes you find yourself exploring within it, are completely up to your determination as a physiological being. The methodology is in your hands.

The higher self, the whole self, may say, "This hallway is the hallway you will walk down as a physical aspect of the total being. But *how* you walk down the hallway is up to you. You can run; you can walk —backwards, forwards, upside-down, right-side up, sideways. In the dark, in the light; alone, with friends. Swim, fly, crawl; look in all the doors; walk all the way to the end— that doesn't matter." It can be positive; it can be negative. That's up to you and your free will. You are the representative; you are the emissary in the foreign land of physical reality. It's up to you to decide how best to blend in with your environment. But the overall "mission" more often than not has been decided by the free will of the higher self.

Give Me a Sign

So what do you mean, then, by following your excitement?

Excitement, excitement: what is excitement? Mechanically speaking, the idea as we perceive it is as follows. Excitement— what you feel to be the physical sensation, or the knowledge, the knowingness of yourself that is translated as excitement—is your physical translation of the vibratory energy that represents the path you chose to *be* in this life. So when something excites you more than anything else, that excitement is there to tell you three things.

First: this *is* who and what you are. The circumstance and the situation that comes into your life at any given moment that excites you more than any other is letting you know, "This is who you are; act on it!" You see, excitement *is* the sign that many of you ask for. "What can I do in life? Why am I here? What is my mission? Oh Universe, *please* give me a sign!"

"Hey, look over here; here's a very exciting thing you could be doing!" "Don't bother me now; I'm looking for my purpose. I'm too busy searching for my mission in life. I'm supposed to be serious about this."

But you see, the things that come with excitement *are* the answers, *are* the signals, *are* the signposts; that's what excitement *is*. It's tapping you squarely on the shoulder, saying: "This is what you want to be doing right now." The reason it excites you is because it is aligned with the idea of who you are; that's what excitement is.

The second thing it tells you is that because it is who you are, if you act on it with trust and conviction, it will be the thing that can be the most effortless thing you will ever do—because it is who you are. You are being yourself. And so of course it will be effortless. *The only time you have struggle and pain is when you are trying to be someone you are not,* again fighting the flow, buying into the definitions of what other individuals say you ought to be.

The third thing that tells you when a situation comes along that is more exciting than the other is: this is the thing that if you do it, will support you in the most abundant way to allow you to keep doing it in a more expanded, ever spiraling way. Therefore, you will automatically be able to attract the opportunities to allow you to do the thing that excites you the most.

Excitement is the thread that leads to all other excitement, as long as you are acting on the things that excite you the most, *with integrity*—which means functioning as a whole idea, and not stopping to think of yourself as a collection of parts, or compartments, that is scattered here and there. Recognize that all the different things that have your attention are all part of the same whole idea, and will all fall into place automatically when you act on the one that represents your strongest intention. Then you can flow. That is focus and trust; that is allowance; that is willingness to understand that by definition everything that excites you must fit, and will have a perfect timing in which to do so.

Abundance

So, one: excitement tells you it is you. Two: it tells you that because it is you, it will be an effortless creation. Three: it tells you that because it is you and will be an effortless creation, you will be able to attract the abundance you need in whatever form you need it. And understand that abundance is more than just money. Money on your planet is one of the valid ways to represent abundance, but it is not the only tool, and is not always the shortest and quickest route. Abundance will always express itself along the path of least resistance, just like electricity. When you broaden your definition of what you think abundance is, then you will allow all the different ways it *could* come to you, to come to you. And now let us add one more definition.

Abundance: the ability to do what you need and want to do when you want to do it. Period! That is all abundance is. If it comes in a number of different ways, what do you care?—as long as you still have the ability to do what you want when you want to do it. Keep in mind that abundance is a general idea, whereas money is a *tool*.

Now, we know that abundance is a "big issue" on your planet. All right now, you are all abundant; you all deserve abundance— unlimited amounts of what you want, at least as far as we are concerned. So here is just one brief example—: rearrange this idea; apply it to you if necessary.

Because of the way many of you have been functioning, often you see by example that certain individuals on your planet who are physically abundant are in your eyes morally or spiritually bankrupt. This may create a type of impression on you that causes you, without your consciously realizing it, to automatically equate abundance with moral bankruptcy. You say to yourself in internal dialogue —which is perhaps not as loud as you would like it to be— "If I become abundant, that means I must also become morally bankrupt, and I don't want the moral bankruptcy. Therefore I'll keep myself from being abundant."

When you examine your beliefs about abundance, if you find you have that kind of belief, you can say, "Wait a minute. I realize that more often than not when I think of a rich person, I think of someone who is," to use your phrase, "a scum." You may realize right then and there that you have built up out of different belief components one particular belief structure. You are saying with that belief structure, "Everyone who becomes abundant becomes a scum.". . . "I don't want to have that belief any more," you can say. "That's the definition I had, but I will now disassemble those components. Being abundant does not have to be attached to the idea of being morally bankrupt. So what are the components? What are the ideas I would prefer?"

No judgment here; you do not judge or invalidate the moral bankruptcy. It may not be what you prefer; it may be a very negative thing. *But if you judge it, you change your vibration to the same level.* That's what your biblical phrase means when it says, "Judge not lest ye be judged." It doesn't mean you're going to be judged from outside; it means that *as you judge, you become that vibration; you put yourself on that level and can't be where you want to be.*

The idea is to let that go without judgment. It is one choice you could have made, but you no longer prefer it. Preference is not judgment; preference is your ability to discern what you are all about, what excites you. Examine the possibilities and say, "What components would I rather attach to the idea of abundance? I would rather attach the idea that being abundant would allow me to continue to be a loving individual. Then I will be able to allow other people to be excited by sharing certain ideas with them. I will be able to do this exciting thing and help change the world in positive ways. That's my idea of abundance."

There is a segment in your book called *Wishcraft*,* which besides aiding you in finding your excitement, finding what brings you joy, also gives you many examples of all the different ways you can go about expressing your abundance—other than the idea of having to have money. Yes, you can have that; it's a very valuable idea. But it is not the only one. You can also trade; you can make it yourself; you can win it or be given it as a gift. You can borrow it; you can rent it. . . .

So do you believe you can have what you want? Can you allow it to be that simple?

Sometimes, yes.

Sometimes. All right, fair enough. Always be honest with yourself, because if you do have difficulty believing it, then deal with that. Acknowledge that you have difficulty believing it. Don't deny it, as denial is the first step to forgetting everything about who you are. Don't deny anything about yourself, including the fact that you have denial. Allow yourself to deal with the fact that you may be denying you have a certain belief, and that you do buy into the idea of doubt and fear and self-invalidation. It's all right to acknowledge that you have those feelings. If you don't acknowledge them and don't deal with them, then you can't change them. You cannot transform what you do not *own*, first of all. So own it. Say, "All right, I do it sometimes, because sometimes I don't think I'm capable." It's all right to think that way.

You see, the whole issue is that once you own the right to think that way, you have made it clear that it was your choice to choose the negative reality. And once it's clear that it was your choice, it's back under your control. If you sometimes don't feel capable of doing what excites you the most, acknowledge that you believe that. And then get into a very honest discussion with yourself about why you would choose to believe that way. What type of beliefs would you have? What kind of definitions would you have to buy into in order to feel you couldn't do the thing that is most representative of who you are.

Struggle or Ease

Let's say there are two individuals, one with more money, one with less money: if they are both capable of doing what they need to do when they need to do it, they are equally abundant because that's all that matters to them. And that's the level they have defined themselves to be.

If someone has a more expanded idea of what it is that excites him, then perhaps he needs more symbols of abundance to flow into his life to represent what it is he is. If he already has sufficient symbols of abundance in his life, then he will be able to accomplish what excites him as smoothly, effortlessly and easily as anyone else. For let me remind you once again that the universe will always support you by supplying you automatically with whatever opportunities represent your ability to continue to be who you are—if you are willing to act that way. The universe always supports you 100% in whatever idea you believe yourself most to be.

Now, if you believe, "Well, I have to struggle in order to make a living; and I believe that nothing that does not contain struggle will work for me," then the universe will support you in *that* idea 100%. It will say, "Well, if that's the way you want it! Here are the situations that will reinforce the beliefs in your life that you already have—: that nothing will work for you easily, and that you have to struggle in order to live. Here are all the situations representing the beliefs you have." These situations are given to you by the universe automatically to show you exactly what your beliefs are. They are not to prove you are stuck in anything, nor to prove you have failed in anything, but to show you beyond the shadow of a doubt that, "Look, this is the reality you get because that's what you believe to be true. If you don't prefer it, then change the beliefs."

When you change the belief to, "I do deserve to create a reality of effortlessness and ease, and I will be supported," then that's the reality you will get; the universe will support you 100% in that direction. It will say, just as magnanimously and just as equally, "Well, if that's what you want, here it is. Because now that's what you believe." And as you believe, that's what you experience in physical reality. All you need to do is be willing to recognize that 100% trust in the direction you prefer will create the reality you desire to experience.

Do recognize that we are not suggesting that you do something you are not already doing. You are already using 100% of your trust; but you are using 100% of your trust in a direction you don't prefer. So place the 100% trust in a direction you do prefer, and then that's the reality you get.

It's very hard for me to believe that if I just go and quit my job, everything will be okay.

All right. It's hard for you to believe. But it's your choice to believe that it's hard for you to believe. You are choosing to believe it is a difficult thing to do; but know that you are never *not* supported by the universe 100%. It just depends upon what your definition of the 100% *is* that you are doing. If you have a 100% belief that you must do a job you only *like*, then the universe will be 100% behind you and give you circumstances you will *like*. And that's all it will give you.

If you are willing to know that you will not be doing anything differently in terms of the mechanical approach, but just differently in terms of what you allow the mechanics of the universe to support you in—by changing what you *like* to what you *love*—the universe sees no difference in that. If you choose to go from doing what you like to doing what you love, the universe will support you 100% by attracting into your life all the circumstances that will support you in doing what you love—just as strongly as it attracted into your life all the things that supported you in doing what you only liked, when you were doing that.

When you know there is no reason to distinguish between the two, you will allow yourself to let it be all right to do what you love to do, and the universe will say, "If that's what you want, here it is!" That's the way the universe works. So if things in your life are mediocre, it is supporting your belief in mediocrity 100%. That is all there is to it. Believe in ecstasy. It will support you with no more effort than it supports you now.

Finding A Career

But I want a career that will really excite me, and I just don't know what that is. Why is it so difficult to find that?

When we talk about the idea of doing what excites you the most, we do not necessarily mean that you must have a cognition of *the* thing that will be *the* most exciting thing you will ever do in your entire life. We are talking about living in the moment, keeping it in the moment, keeping it present-focused. If you do not have an idea of an over-riding career, then at any given moment you can still be doing the thing that excites you the most with all the integrity you have at your disposal.

Doing that step by step, a step at a time, will always lure you into the circumstances that represent the next step you need to take to bring you an automatic and effortless understanding of what it is you could be doing that represents more and more who you are. When we say do what excites you the most, we're not just saying, "Well yes, have a good time." We *are* saying that also, but it is not being left on that level.

We are talking mechanics here, not some airy philosophy. As we have said, excitement, that knowingness of what moves you, is actually your physical translation of the vibratory energy that represents who and what you *are!* Excitement tells you what you are best capable of doing. If something excites you, it excites you for a reason. There are no extraneous creations, no accidental interactions. Whatever at any given moment is the most exciting thing you could imagine doing, with all your integrity, is the path in its most synchronistically unfolding manner. Follow it; do it; trust it. It will always lead you where you need to go to give you the skills, the abilities and the abundance necessary to do the next most exciting thing, or the next most exciting step of the thing that will come along.

If two or more things excite you equally, act on any one of them; it doesn't matter which one you pick. When you make the decision, it will be obvious which one actually excited you more. All you need to do then is to act on that one, and it will lead to circumstances that will give you the time necessary to act on all the other things. They will all fall into perfect timing. If they are all representative of aspects of an overall idea that excites you, then they are aspects that will enhance each other, not exclude each other.

Let them occur in your life at whatever timing is necessary. Let it be obvious by simply looking around and seeing which ones you are capable of doing anything at all about at any given moment. The ones you are capable of doing something about, *do* something about. When you get to a point where you can no longer do anything about that, look around and see if getting to that point has given you the capability to do something about some of the other things you are excited about at that point. Then bit by bit, step by step, you will bring them all up to the same level . . . in perfect timing.

Many of you know very, very well what your excitement is, but you have been talked out of believing that what you know you really want to do is a valid way to make a living. So you shut it down and pretend you don't know what you really could be doing. Without placing judgment on it; without invalidating it in any way, at this particular moment is there any one thing, no matter what it is, no matter how silly it may seem in the eyes of your society, that actually would give you the most joy in doing as a career? Or, if you wish, just doing.

I would probably just dance for free, but I know that's—

One moment. Let me repeat myself: without invalidation; without qualification, what would give you the most joy? Are you saying dancing?

I love to dance.

Well, thank you very much. Could not have said it better myself: "I love to dance." Is it the most exciting thing you can imagine doing, above and beyond anything else? . . . yes, no—?

Well, probably in this moment; that's the only thing that comes to my mind.

Do not qualify it. Of course we are talking about this moment. Right now is it the most exciting thing you can conceive of? Yes or no?

Then that's it. That's it, yes.

All right; thank you very much. Then right at this moment —as long as you are focused on that idea— right now, *you are a dancer!* You are the *energy* of a dancer; you are the *frequency* of a dancer. And if you continue to *act* like a dancer from this moment forward, you will have the life style of a dancer and automatically attract —automatically; synchronistically— synchronistically and effortlessly, *effortlessly,* all the circumstances and all the relationships germane to the life of a dancer, to allow you to take advantage of them so you can continue to be the dancer you say right now you are.

Are you willing to act that way, though? That's the real question. Are you willing to act in the manner of what you say really excites you— knowing beyond the shadow of a doubt that by acting as if that really is true for you, the universe will support you in the doing of that thing? Are you willing to believe that, or do you doubt yourself?

There's probably a little bit of doubt there.

All right. Let me remind you of something else, if I may. . . .
May I?

Oh, of course.

100% Trust

Oh, thank you very much. When we talk about infinite trust, we are not talking about something that is difficult to do. When we say, "Trust it 100%," many times we hear a collective psyhic groan from you. "Oh, no! That's real hard. 100% trust? Everyone knows how hard that is!"

But you see, *you have all always trusted 100% in something. What your society calls doubt is not a lack of trust. It is an absolute unshakable, unswerving 100% total conviction in a negative reality.* You always use trust 100%. It's just a matter of whether you trust in something you don't prefer, or trust in something you do prefer. Now which do you prefer to trust in—what you prefer, or what you don't prefer?

As soon as you decide, however, that what you really prefer you will do 100%, there is absolutely no reason, as far as the universe is concerned, to withhold any less than 100% results from you. You will get 100% of it when you act in that direction 100%. Sometimes, because of the way you define yourself, you may find that even if you are doing something 99%, and yet there is still the 1% that you are not doing it, that 1% may be enough to prevent you from experiencing the other 99%—depending on how you have arranged the definition.

100% trust will always —I guarantee it; I promise— give you 100% absolute reflection of that reality. Absolute. You are always getting a 100% reflection of the reality that you define as the most likely reality you are capable of handling. Always. The universe will only give you what you say you are ready to handle. So as soon as you say, "Well, of course. Because I *am* excited about this more than this; because it *is* what I prefer more than that, then it must be representative of who I really am. Therefore, by definition, of course I'll be able to handle it. Otherwise I wouldn't have conceived of it."

As soon as you act as if that is true for you, the universe will say, "All right; if that's the way you want it, here it is: all the opportunities that represent the *you* you now believe yourself to be, as opposed to the *you* you used to believe yourself to be." . . . You always get an absolute reflection of whatever you define yourself to be—no more, no less. So 'tis up to you. At least, if you're going to hang on to things you don't prefer for now because you believe that's the rate at which you need to handle it, then at least —if we may suggest, because we love you— please do not spend time berating yourself for the time you are taking. For that only adds to the time it takes.

So if that's the way you are going to go about it, then at least relax, breathe easy, and say, "All right! That's the way I'm going about it, because I choose to believe that's the way I need to go about it." Paradoxically, as soon as you let the way you're doing it be all right, you will probably change. That's the whole paradoxical mechanism. *As soon as you allow where you are to be all right, you will be able to get where you want to be much faster.*

When you are always where you want to be, you are living in the now. *If you let wherever you are be where you want to be, you will live in the moment. And then everything will be able to find you.* There is no other time that exists except now. If you are living in the past, living in the future, then nothing you need to work with can find you . . . because in the present you are not at home. So again: where do you choose to put your trust—in something you prefer or don't prefer?

One Consciousness

Well, my mind says I would choose—

Ah-ah-ah-ah! When I am speaking, at least for this moment, I am speaking to the total *you*. If you now choose to segregate yourself into a mind and a conscious and a subconscious, you will spin a game that will last for years, as many of you already do. You think you have to reconcile all these different fragments of yourself you have created yourself to be—but *you* have created these levels.

I'll let you in on a little secret, which is no secret at all. You don't really have —none of you actually really have— an unconscious or a subconscious mind. You are one consciousness, one homogenous idea. What you call your soul, or your spirit, your higher consciousness, your lower consciousness, your mind, your mentality, your physical consciousness, your subconsciousness, your unconsciousness: all of these are simply different convenient ways to avoid looking at something you fear. That's all it is. You are one consciousness, unbroken.

You have created convenient compartments in which you can place things that for some reason you have been taught are dangerous to look at. . . . Why? It's only a portion of you. *There is absolutely nothing! you could ever! discover about yourself that cannot be applied in a positive way.* Oh yes, you can discover many things and apply all of them in negative ways, but is that what you prefer? Yes or no?

If it's no, then why not assume you have just as much power to decide how to apply what you discover about yourself, just as much power to decide to do that in a positive way, as you have always had in a negative way. You can apply anything you discover in a negative or a positive way. Why not choose to understand that you only prefer to apply it in a positive way; and that you will therefore only get a positive result out of that application. You cannot get —*cannot get!*— a negative result from a positive application.

Let me say again: you cannot experience any reality of which you are not the vibration. If you have a reality you don't prefer, then it's because you are buying into a belief system that supports that reality. It's as plain and simple as that. You have a saying for it: "What you put out is what you get back. What goes in is what comes out." You cannot get the opposite effect; you can only get an equal, corresponding reaction. If you put a positive idea out, positive preferential trust, you can only get a positive reality back. If you put a negative idea out, which you call doubt, you can only get hesitation, guilt, frustration, and all the other symbols your society has created to represent negative trust.

Do you believe —are you at least willing to consider the possibility of believing— that if you fully act in the direction of the being you say you want to be, that you yourself can be responsible for attracting the things in your life that will support you as that being? And that spiral will continue forever? Are you willing to believe that could be possible? And that nothing is too good to be true?

Yes, I'm willing to believe that.

All right. Then discover what stops you from believing it now; come to terms with what that definition is that prevents you from living that reality, and reinvent, redefine the reality you prefer to have. You will get that reflection; I guarantee it 100%. The universe keeps nothing from you—nothing! But the universe can only give you what you say you're ready for. If you do not believe you are ready to handle the idea of success —because you are willing to buy into, "It's got to be a struggle," or "It's got to be a striving"— the universe will only give you so much.

That is because obviously you're telling the universe, "I'm not ready for any more. Please don't give it to me. I am still creating a trust in a negative reality, and when I have that kind of a belief, I do not want these things—because they will not manifest in a positive way. Give them to me when I choose to believe that I deserve a positive reality."

And you do, you know. You deserve anything you can conceive of just because you have the ability to conceive of it. You don't have to earn the right to deserve happiness; you already have that right because you exist. Do you understand?

I hear you and I do want to believe that.

Threshold of Believability

You are on the threshold of your believability. You are exploring that threshold, what you are truly willing to believe is possible for you. Listen to the language in which you put it; it will indicate where your threshold of believability is. As soon as the threshold of believability is squarely within you in the present, then you will experience the life you desire. As long as the threshold of your believability is still out there somewhere in the future, no matter how close it is to you, if it's not *in* you, you won't experience it. Now you are exploring that threshold of believability.

How can I—?

Ah, we're getting to that, thank you. Let's do a little exercise, one which will assist you in recognizing where the threshold of your believability is. All right?

First of all begin by creating for yourself, in any way comfortable for you —it does not have to be very complicated; it can be anything at all— that represents the idealized way you would prefer to live. Have a picture of yourself doing something you would enjoy doing, and being supported fully in that life style. Not having the shadow of a doubt that you are supported; truly feeling that's the way you live. That's the way you live, and everything is just fine. Understand it as the idealized essence of the way you feel about living.

We are not asking you to have a picture that is absolutely structurally rigidized. We are talking about the life style in essence in the way you feel. Have that picture in your mind with that idealized state. And then I will ask you a series of questions. . . . Do you have that picture or feeling in mind?

Yes.

All right. Now, be very honest with yourself, and also with me for now, in these answers. Do you honestly think that within, oh, say, ten of your years— will that be enough time for you to be able to create that way of life?

Yes.

Do you believe you will be living that way in a month?

No.

Do you believe you can be living in the way you prefer to be living, no matter how that is, in one year?

(Pause) No.

Do you believe you can do it in three years?

I believe I could do it then.

All right. Are you sure? Can you really feel it? . . . A year?

If I put all my attention on just doing that, yes.

All right. Why would you do otherwise? Why would you have to put your attention on anything you do not want to do?

I guess I think I have to take care of a lot of other details.

But understand: when you are doing what truly represents the vibration of your reality, all the details take care of themselves. Not that you will not be doing anything; it is simply that when you live the essential way; when you live in synchronous harmony with the path you chose to be, everything is already on that path in the format it needs to be, and will fall into place as it needs to fall to let you continue being the person you chose to be. You will automatically and effortlessly and coincidentally attract into your life all the tools necessary to allow the details to be taken care of. It is all one package.

You see, the difficulty you are having is in thinking that your life is a series of separated ideas, rather than one homogenous event in which everything that needs to be done to allow you to be the person you need to be will be taken care of automatically. The things that don't get done, if you are truly being who you know you need to be, don't need to be done to allow you to be that person. You follow me?

The Outer Reflection

I think what I need to get is that it's more a matter of feeling a state that I want to feel than an acquiring or attaining some outward form.

Oh, yes, yes, yes! The outward form is only a reflection of the inner knowing. When you create and generate the vibration of the inner knowing, "This is the way I am!" then your outer reality shows that to you. You don't get the outer reality first before you create the inner belief. **You always get in physical reality only what you already believe to be the most likely reality you'll get.** And only when you choose to truly believe with your whole heart and soul, "This really is what I'm all about! This really is the way I prefer to be!"— when you generate that feeling and that desire and that energy within you, then your outer reality has absolutely no choice but to reflect that inner feeling, that inner knowingness.

And it *is* that simple. Letting yourself know that that vibration of truth for you is your vibratory frequency, the vibratory frequency that represents the being you chose to be, you will then tune yourself to that station. When you tune yourself to that station, and let your dial remain on that station, only the things that are pertinent to that station can be received by you. You know you can't receive anything other than what the station is that you are tuned to. But you must decide to tune to that frequency first. Otherwise you are listening to a program you don't enjoy. Change the dial, and the program will change along with it.

* * *

No Excitement

Bashar, I don't get really excited about anything.

All right. Now do realize that when we talk about the idea of doing what excites you the most, it doesn't necessarily mean you are going to be jumping up and down every single moment. The idea of a peaceful knowingness, an absolute certainty, can also be representative of that excitement, of that vibration that represents your knowing that you are in synchronous alignment with the path you chose to be. It doesn't mean you have to be running around all the time. It can be a very steady conviction, a balanced knowingness, a certainty.

Yah, that's kinda the way it's been—just relaxed. I want a little more excitement than that.

All right, the idea of wanting something to be exciting: what's wrong with right now being exciting? Do you remember the question we asked all of you as to what was the most important thing of all?

Yup.

And the answer was?

Where I am right now.

Yes, the thing you are doing right now. Therefore, if you truly allow yourself to understand that what you are doing right now is, and must be by definition, the most important thing of all at any given moment, then you will start looking at it that way.

When your attitude changes, you will start realizing that you are where you are for a reason, and start allowing yourself to get out of the moment what you really need to—rather than assuming that this moment contains nothing for you that would generate excitement.

The idea is to face your world with a child-like fascination. Then you will begin to discover that a lot more things you take for granted as being mundane are actually quite a bit more exciting than you thought, and you will be able to act on them—because you now see them for the excitement they are. Many of you have very thick skins by this time. And so things that could be exciting to you do not have much of an effect on you. You may not even be able to recognize your own excitement because of the thickness of that shell. But start walking through it. Allow yourselves to break through it by simply breaking through the conventions of your society. That will allow the skin to become much thinner, and allow the excitement to penetrate much more easily. Then it will be obvious in which direction lies your excitement and your path.

Again, the idea is to act upon your imagination. Here is a very simple mechanism: all of you—this will work for anything and everything. Very simple. Your imagination is the template, the blueprint. If you conjure up in your imagination an image—a vision of how you prefer to be—then take whatever situation is going on in your life, hand it to the *you* you have conjured up who is representative of the excited person you would prefer to be, and watch how the *you* in your imagination handles the situation you have given to it.

Then copy it. You will get the effect that it gets in its excited state of handling all things in that excited way. That's what your imagination is for: to copy. It gives you the picture, the blueprint, the path, the methodology, the ritual, whatever will work best for you. Create an image and mimic the image. Then you will be that person, and you will have that life style automatically.

That's what a child does. It sees and it becomes; it sees and it becomes. It does not question whether what it sees is valid. A child knows it is within integrity, so it doesn't have to stop to question it. It sees and it becomes; it expands and it grows. You can do that; you can play. It is up to you.

Out of Work

Bashar, I've been getting progressively more depressed from being out of work. The longer I'm out of work, the less trust I have in myself and my ability to find work in something that's going to excite me.

Then create what excites you to *be* your job; that's the whole idea. The idea is not to look around, necessarily, for the things that excite you that already exist. If you do not find something, then allow what excites you to *become* your job. Somebody had to start the jobs that exist in your society. They didn't always exist in the format they exist in now. Someone had to say, "Wait a minute! Look around; the thing that really excites me the most there isn't a job for. I guess I had better start one." And now, at this point in time, you think that's a typical job.

But if you look around and do not find something that excites you; if you look around and find that your path simply does not lead you into these things, then allow yourself to truly examine in all honesty what it is that really would be exciting. Take it for granted that you then, if that thing really excites you, and no one else at this point is doing it, or you do not attract into your life an opportunity to do it where it already exists, then take it for granted that your ability to conceive of what it is that excites you the most also represents your ability to create that to be the job that will support you—automatically.

Again, this is a matter of truly trusting that what you come up with, what you really know would excite you in life, you are capable of doing, whether any structure already exists for it or not. If no such structure exists, then it means that because you thought of it, you have the structure inherent within you, and all you have to do is let it out. Let it unfold, and then the reality will be able to build itself on that template structure. But you're not letting it out.

I feel so incompetent . . .

That means you *believe* you are. No feeling comes without a belief already being instilled within you. There is no such thing as simply feeling something for no reason—out of the blue. Feelings are not generated out of thin air, out of a vacuum. If you are feeling something, it is because you already believe that something to be true.

Feelings Are Secondary

Feelings are a reaction to a belief; they are secondary to beliefs. Feelings are not the primary experience of reality; beliefs are the primary interface. First you believe something is true; then you get the feeling; then you have the reinforcing thoughts—which may re-reinforce the belief; and then you regenerate more of the same feelings. But the feeling that you are incompetent comes from the fact that you simply choose to believe you are incompetent. It's your choice to believe that, but you don't have to.

I want to let go of it, and every time I try, I keep getting these voices that tell me, "Remember this time; remember that time when so-and-so happened . . ."

Let them come up! So what?!? You see, you are trying to shut portions of yourself off. You think that when you integrate, you will never hear those voices again. And that's not true; you will always hear those voices. As a matter of fact, the more you integrate, the more you will hear them because you are accepting everything, every way you are, into your life. And those are some of the ways you can exist. They come up not to show you you have failed, not to show you you are stuck; they keep coming up to give you the opportunity to realize how much you must have changed. You don't relate to them the same way you used to—unless, of course, you choose to do so.

When you say, "Oh well, look: the voices are still coming up. That must mean I have failed; that must mean I'm not doing the right thing the right way," you are choosing to maintain the same relationship with those voices; but you don't have to. The voices are there as an opportunity to realize you can form a different relationship with them. "All right; here comes the voice: 'Well, remember when this happened that way?' 'Well yes, but so what? That was then; I have learned since then. And because you, oh wonderful voice, have now reminded me of the way I did it then, I have a great and positive opportunity to see how differently I am going to do it now.' "

You are giving yourself a measure. It is the way to allow yourself to recognize you are going through an evolutionary process, if that's what you believe you must go through. From time to time you may find, well, the voice comes up: "Look, this is the way that happened then." And then you may say, "All right, this time it happened *almost* the same."

But there is the key word. If you are a positive individual, you will lock onto that "almost the same." It was a little bit different, and that's good enough for you, because if it can be a little bit different, it can be a lot different. Next time when the voice says, "Well yah, but remember when it happened this way?" then you can recognize that the last time it was different, and next time it will be *more* 'more different.' "So you just keep reminding me, little voice, of the way it was, because when you keep reminding me of the way it was, it gives me an opportunity to see how much more different it's becoming all the time."

Everything in your life can be used in a positive way—even the same old little voices. It's up to your willingness to allow your imagination to work for you. Trust it; have a positive attitude, and that will determine everything. If it's there, use it as a tool. Don't think that just because it's there, it means you've failed. That's your old attitude; that's your old belief.

I just get reinforcements from other people in my life telling me also—

No one can *give* you reinforcement; you have to *accept* reinforcement.

Well, they're agreeing with the voices—

So what?!? The inner reality *is* the outer reality; it is one and the same. If you have the little voices within you, of course you're going to have the voices outside of you as well. But when you start using those little voices in the way we have just described, then the outer voices will also change. You understand? The inner *is* the outer reality; the outer *is* the inner reality. They are not two different things. It is one.

Plant Something Different

As you believe *in*, so do you see *out*. As you sow, so you reap. That's what that means. The seeds you plant within yourself are what you see growing in the garden around you. If you do not like the flowers you see growing, then change your order of seed. Plant something different, and then something new will grow. The inner is the outer. If the outer is not the way you prefer it to be, change the inner and the outer will follow.

I've worked on saying those things. I guess the belief was still the old one; I didn't get rid of the old belief.

You cannot get rid of anything.

What I said was, "Okay, I can do this, and I can handle the job." But that belief was still hanging on—

Listen to the way you sometimes phrase things, as well. Many times the way you phrase things is an indication of the way you really believe. "Okay, I can handle it!" Right there it lets you know: the way you are saying it means you think it's overwhelming to begin with. And that's what the real belief is. The belief, therefore, is not really that you can "handle it" —because if you knew beyond the shadow of a doubt that you could, you wouldn't have to convince yourself. If you find yourself using phraseology that indicates you are attempting to convince yourself, then you do not believe it naturally.

Let yourself know that you do not have to think twice about something you already own. When you phrase things in that manner; when you say, "All right, I can handle it," then you are indicating that you do not really believe it is handleable. You do not have to "handle" things in that way. You already control everything. Therefore, if situations occur in your life that seem to be non-preferable manifestations, you controlled it for a reason, for a positive reason, into that format.

Even though I don't see what the positive reason is?

Let the positive reason at least be the fundamental reason that you're giving yourself an opportunity to realize you don't have to relate to the scenario the way you used to. And you may be checking yourself to see if you still are.

Something Positive

What phrases could I use that would be more beneficial to me?

"How does this serve me—exactly the way it is? *Exactly* the way it is: how does it serve me? What can I learn? How can I positively learn something from this?" When you let it be the way it is, that is when it has the greatest opportunity to change into something else. If you deny the form in which it comes, then you are not allowing yourself to see what is inherent within it. You are not allowing it to present itself in the way you have created it to present itself. You are denying your own creation, your own format. Only when you acknowledge your own format of delivering messages to yourself, exactly and completely the way it comes to you, do you then create the conscious freedom to transform that delivery system into a way you prefer it to come.

If you constantly treat your delivery system as if it is malfunctioning, then you are not listening to it. You are thinking something is going wrong within you, and therefore that's the belief you reinforce. And therefore that's the cycle you repeat: "Something is wrong; something is wrong!" So of course your reality constantly reflects back to you, "Something is wrong; something is wrong."

Everything is just fine. In what you used to consider the most dire circumstances, let yourself realize everything is just fine. "I'm in control of this; look at how much control I have, to have created such an absolutely exciting scenario. Everything seems to be wild and hither and thither and all over the place, and seemingly wild and unconnected and out of control. But since I *know* I'm controlling that, look at how much power I have." . . . Are you beginning to get the idea?

Yes.

For the only thing you are experiencing is the idea that you have old habits that are difficult to break. If that's where you are coming from, all right: "I have habits that I believe are difficult to change. So if I believe in the idea of habits, then I'll use the idea of habits in a positive way and create positive habits. I am in control of everything. Even when it seems like it's out of control, I'm controlling that." Get used to knowing and believing there is a positive manifestation that can occur from every scenario. With no exceptions! . . . None.

I felt like I was, but when I lost my job, I just went down—

But you see, you assume that not being in that job for some reason has to be an inherently negative scenario. Why make that assumption? It is only an assumption. How do you know what losing that job may be making room for —perhaps something you would just explode with delight to receive— that you wouldn't have room to receive if you still had the old job? Trust that when things like that occur in your life— if you know you are doing the best you can do at that moment, and those things still occur, then assume it's for a good reason, and let yourself see *how* it is for a good reason.

Only when you insist that those things occur not for a positive reason, do you then keep the reason from coming to you that would let you see why you lost the job for a positive reason. Because you're sitting there moping on the idea, "Oh well, the only thing I can think of that losing my job means is that it must be negative. Something's wrong." And when you are focused in that way, you can't see the positive side of the coin. You can't see it until you choose to look at it. You have to decide consciously that you will look at the positive side of the coin in every single circumstance, or you will not be able to see positive manifestation. If you are constantly insisting that circumstances are inherently negative, then, "Losing a job *must* be a bad thing. It *has* to be; everyone knows that."

If that's the way you choose to look at it, that's the way you'll experience your reality. When you insist just as strongly that to lose a job must be leading to a more expanded and broader positive experience, that's what you will get in your life. That's it; it's that simple. Honest!

I guess I got impatient, because I did state that. I said that exactly. And what happened was I did get an interview for a job that paid more—

Yes? And then what? Did you bring back the expectation, "If I don't get this, I'm failing."?

Yah. Then when I blew the interview and I didn't get the job, you know, then I started to go into my old—

Remove the expectations! It doesn't have to manifest exactly as your ego or your habits think it should. It doesn't have to! Let it manifest along the path of least resistance. Stop fighting yourself. You do not have to push yourself into a mold. You fit exactly where you are. You do not have to conform to a particular idea of what success represents. You *are* successful exactly as you are.

Anxiety

It's also very scary doing something new. Could you give me a suggestion for helping to let go of the anxiety?

Well again, it can be very easily done when you recognize, as we have suggested, that anxiety and excitement are the same energy. If you understand that, and start acting like you believe it, then you will feel the energy as excitement and not anxiety. It is not that you will get rid of the energy; it is not that you will not continue to feel the energy. It is that you will feel it in the way that is indicative of how you look at it. That is all. So know that it represents the discovery of something new; that the energy is there, the vibration is there, because you are on the threshold of more information, more awareness. And we assume that that's an exciting thing.

Since you will never go faster than you are ready for, you do not have to worry. You will always be able to handle it, because again, if something came that you were not really able to handle, there would be no point to it—and the universe does not do pointless things. So trust that you always have a built-in governor saying, "Whoa, whoa! Take your time. No rush; no hurry."

Do what excites you the most in the way it excites you the most to do it, with integrity, and you will always be being of service. Remember, the things you are exploring now; the things you are learning now, will be some of the information you may impart to other individuals who wish to do the same thing later. So pay attention to what you are going through; you can use all of it in a positive way. . . . Relax. Laugh a little more about the idea you are going through. And if you feel the anxiety, that's all right. Remember: *Anxiety is the same energy as excitement, with judgment placed upon it.* That's all it is.

Relax the judgment, and you will let go of the anxiety. It will turn into excitement and laughter, and you will giggle your way through life.

*   *   *

Follow your Excitement!

Acquire the tools and the props of what you need and use them. Do not build a prop and then sit with it, wondering what is going on. Apply it; act on it. Get out in the world, doing what you most love doing, and know that the world will shape itself to what you need. It will do so for everyone, and there is no conflict in it. *No one loses because you are winning! You all win because there is enough for everyone.* You are all learning this, and we thank you for learning it now.

A very good suggestion was given by a spiritual friend of us all: even if at some moment you may feel that you do not have what you need, you do not have what it takes, very often all that is necessary is to say, "I may believe I do not have it now, but at least I am *willing* to have it." Then act to the best of your ability on what you can do. Use your imagination, and let the rest take care of itself.

Be bold, for no one will turn you away. There is always an appropriate audience for everything you truly need to say, and you will find that audience. For everyone who wishes to be on a particular stage, there is always an audience to appreciate what you have to say—once again, because everything fits. Everything belongs; and there is never!! —*never-never-never-never!!*— an actor who is born without an audience being born at the same time for that actor.

NEVER!! It all works perfectly!! Flawlessly!! Believe it; act like you believe it, and you'll see the results—guaranteed. Can't prove it to you; wouldn't want to try. But it works for us, and you are no different. You fall under the same *one law* of Creation: what you put out is what you get back. See for yourself.

Do! . . . *Think* is wonderful. *Believe* is wonderful. *Feel* is wonderful. However, *doing* is what creates the reality you wish to experience.

Follow your excitement!

CHAPTER TEN

The Agenda

November, 1989: Whole Life Expo

It has been quite some time since we communicated with you in this fashion. I have been very busy speaking through other individuals in different areas of your planet; but in this particular area we have allowed things to "stew" a little bit. This way the information we have already shared could be applied by the many individuals who have received it already. And also we could for a moment step back and allow you to utilize the information as you see fit—to use it in the direction that excites you the most.

We speak very often about the idea of doing what excites you the most; this has been our main thrust in all the time we have communicated with you. However, now that things have accelerated and progressed a bit, we find that we no longer need to speak with as much allegory. We can be more direct than perhaps we could have been five or six years ago when we first contacted you in this way.

Therefore, let us get right down to "the agenda." Many individuals have sensed, or taken readings, of the overall energy of your society and how you are progressing in your assimilation of data, your awareness of consciousness. For you have created a momentum that is pushing you faster and faster toward certain things. Many of you are already beginning to see physical effects, not only in your own individual lives but on a planetary scale with your focus on peace. All of your walls and barriers seem to be coming down, both figuratively and literally, and we congratulate all of you. It has made us very happy to see this begin.

Many of us communicating through various individuals have talked about certain times that are specific points of acceleration. The last time I spoke with you in this area I spoke about a date, that of October 15 of this year. I said that after that date there would be much acceleration in a certain way. Allow me now to explain in a little more detail exactly what is meant.

As you begin to choose the lives, the paths, the attitudes and the habits that are now more representative of peace and creativity; as you begin to choose these things, you crystallize the events of your lives in certain specific ways—to allow only certain types of opportunities, certain types of situations to occur. It is what we call synchronicity: what you put out is what you get back, as we have said many times. As you have accelerated this, it becomes less and less likely —in fact, more and more difficult— to choose anything that is not representative of what you really desire, of what you really prefer.

Crossing the Threshold

You will find that this October 15, 1989 date was given to indicate a threshold that you have crossed, whereby you now number enough individuals in your society aiming toward what you desire that should you for any reason whatsoever —doubt, fear, hesitation, habits— begin to choose that which is not what you want, you would find it falling apart more quickly. It would point you in the proper direction by not working out, by creating more and more unhappy, stressful situations in the things you no longer want to do; to make you tire more quickly of those things that are not what you are all about as an individual.

Therefore, from that date forward you will find that the more you hesitate to do the things you know you are all about, the things that really excite you, the less well things will go for you. The more confusion there will be in your lives, in a negative sense.

The agenda now is that approximately between your time of 1990 and 1992 or 1993 more and more of this energy will crystallize. . . . I know I will be very bold in this statement I am about to make. Understand that this is simply how we are perceiving your energy at this time; but the momentum is very strong, so I will make this statement anyway:

If you have not, by 1993, allowed yourselves to do in your lives only, ONLY! what is really representative, on any level, of what you prefer, what you desire to be, from that point forward you may not be able to catch up.

The acceleration will be so great at that point that if you are not allowing yourselves to be aligned with your own truths, you may find it almost impossible —nothing is impossible, but almost impossible— to backtrack without absolute breakdown of everything you know. For the next three of your years you can do it somewhat smoothly, with some buffers, with some timing, with some pacing. If you have not allowed yourselves to crystallize in what is really important to you by your 1993, the only way it may be available to you to do so will be to completely cut yourselves off from everything and start, as you say, from scratch.

Now, some people might find this more exciting. That will be up to you. I am not telling you what to do, but only giving you a reading of your energy. Because that is how fast you are acting; that is how fast you are changing.

There is no reason to hesitate; there is no reason to delay doing what you really love to do. There is no reason to hold on to those jobs, those situations, those relationships that are not representative of you. Allow them to change gracefully —with integrity, with love— but change them.

Do not fear your typical fears . . . "I cannot quit my job; what will I do? What will I eat? How will I live? Where will I live? I will not be able to pay the rent! I will be kicked out!". . .

I will say this briefly because I have already said it enough: trust that the thing in life that excites you the most comes complete with all the tools necessary to support you in the doing of that thing. It is automatic; it is built in. All you need to do is act on the opportunities that doing that situation brings to you.

Very simple: see, feel and be. Everything we have said folds up into three steps. It's that easy. *See* what you want. *Feel* it. *Know* it. *Desire* it. Then *be* it. *Act* it. Do only that thing in the way that is representative of who you want to be. See it. Feel it. Be it. . . . one, two, three.

The E.T. Agenda

Now a continuation briefly of the agenda. Many of you have asked, "What is going on with extraterrestrial activity on Earth?" Remember, I tell you these things not to take power from you. You do not need us to make your decisions, and we are not here to save you. Thank you for your offer, but no thank you. But because we would love to interact with you freely and openly, and because of the acceleration of your energy now, I can give you a rough outline of our agenda for more open interactions. In 1993, 1995, 1997 and 1999, every two of your years in the odd numbered years —beyond that at this time we cannot say because those are critical points— depending on what you do at those critical points with regard to us, that will determine what happens beyond your 2000 mark. 1993, 1995, 1997, 1999: look for major release of data regarding your involvement with extraterrestrial societies.

You will find in your 1990s a representation of the laying away, or putting aside, of all of the peripheral issues that cloud the nucleus, the seeds, and the kernels of all of your different disciplines. You will build in your 1990s the beginnings, the roots of one interdisciplinary idea or understanding that involves the combining of all political, economic, religious, metaphysical, scientific, philosophical—and every other discipline on your planet.

All will be brought together in your 1990s. All of the clouds that surround the issues that keep them apart will be stripped bare so that all of the seeds of each issue will be seen for the similarities they possess to each other. By your year 2000 you will have begun the basic foundation for what will carry you through as an overall global philosophy for your next one thousand years.

This is your general agenda for your 1990s: to remove the clouds from your own individual selves; to strip yourselves of the things in your estimation that do not belong in the reality you prefer; to be your own nucleus —raw and exposed, as you say—

shining bright, the core of the stars that you are. As you act out what is important to you, what you prefer; as you begin to radiate to each other this energy, this vibration, this frequency, you will each become more sensitized, more sensitive to each other. You will be able to key off of each other more clearly without the negative confusion of certain habitual customs which now blind you and keep you from your heart's desire.

You will understand certain social patterns to be creations of the mind, creations of fear, creations of doubt, reservation and distance. You will understand that your core is indestructible. Indestructible! You are eternal. You are infinite; you have been around forever. You are not going anywhere. You will always exist.

Constant Change

It is said that the name of creation is *I Am.* This is absolute in its truth. It is, it always has been and it always will be. That which exists can only continue to exist. It will never become non-existent because non-existence is its own realm. It already contains all the things that will never exist. Whatever doesn't fit in that realm of non-existence has always existed, exists now and always will exist—because there is nowhere else for it to go. Non-existence is full up—of all the things that will never exist. There is no room for existence there. It is the polarity of creation. No beginning, no ending; it always is at every moment.

Therefore, since you exist —at least I will assume I am not fantasizing you— since you exist, you always have and you always will. You cannot be obliterated. You cannot be consigned to oblivion. You cannot be destroyed. You are infinite, but you are ever changing. You are never the same from one second to the next. Never.

Allow yourselves to feel that that change is the true constant in creation. The true stable foundation of existence is constant change—so that it does not stagnate, so that it is ever perpetuating. Creation is not over. It is not that everything has already been created and now God has sent everything off to run around and have fun. You are all and we are all, together, God ever creating Itself anew, ever changing and always existing.

Paradox, yes. But when you deal with paradox, that's when you know you are close to the seed at the center. Because only at the center do all apparent contradictions find themselves reconciled as one. Only *from* the center do all apparent polarities issue. They are all there. They are one thing. They only appear paradoxical, mutually exclusive—because of the vibrations in the realm that you have chosen to perceive yourselves, because of the vibrations in the realms that have the idea of polarity of opposites.

You have created the ability to take one thing and separate it into not only more than one thing, but even separate it into things that look like they have nothing to do with each other. Most creative, exceedingly creative—and I am not being facetious. It is the true measure of the power of creation that it can even, so to speak, fool itself into thinking it is not a part of that creation, into forgetting that it is what it is, that it is *I Am.* That is the power of creativity.

Now however, as we have said, you have played that game through on this world in the way you wanted to do so, and now you are remembering *I Am. We Are.* We are waking up. "Oh yes, I remember now . . . well, that was a fun game, but now we wish to remember that we are *what is,* and wish to change the rules of the game. We wish to play as integrated whole beings now."

And so you are remembering; so you are gathering; so you are discussing ideas of consciousness: What is consciousness? What is physicality? What is dreaming? What is being awake? What is real? What is non-real? All of these things in your 1990s will be understood to be simply manifestations of one thing: your own perspective. You are waking up. *Good morning!*

Time Gates

The idea of acceleration contains currents and eddies, if you will, backwashes and loops. To some degree they have the purpose of reinforcing the forward momentum. Now and then, because of the type of overlapping vibration you all create in your forward momentum, there will be doorways, gaps, more dimensional gates that so many of you could find yourselves within— and find yourselves reflecting past ideas, future ideas. These time gates allow you at that given moment for a little while to perceive the collectivity of yourselves.

So there are currents and eddies and washes throughout all of your energy, particularly for now because of the momentum you have set up. And especially around the 15th of every month. A very strong one has always been your March 15, and even more so starting in 1990 will this be so. Many things will be happening at that time. People will be finding that the time gates will be moving fast and furious. They will find confusion within their consciousness. They will find many things going on in the world that almost sound like they could not be happening in the same world at the same time.

Around your March 15 date, what you refer to as the Ides of March, very strong gates in your consciousness will also be opening up to certain probes or visitations from your own past civilizations. Very strong. You will see it reflected in your society by a certain kind of discovery and a certain resurgence of awareness of past civilizations.

Yes, all of you really are seeds of unconditional love; thus when you truly allow yourselves to burst forth with the flowers of knowingness that are within you, your planet will be such a lovely garden. Right now all the things you are doing, all the things that seem to be so churning in your society— well, you can look at it this way: you are tearing up the topsoil, preparing it for a new planting.

You are creating furrows in the ground; you are farming the richness of your past experience. Negative though that may seem to be, know that it will form a very rich compost. All that has been negative, all that you may consider to have been a waste, is what allows fertility and new growth to occur—once you place it in the proper place behind you, beneath you, and grow from it.

Let the light from your own future selves draw you upwards from that rich soil of experience, for it is a rich experience. Very rich. A suggestion: go to a natural spot where there is a richness of the soil, and sink your hands deeply into dark, dark rich earth. Breathe the smell of nature in and then look up at the sky. See where you have come from in your physical reality. See where you are and see where you are going. Make a grounded connection to heaven. Bring heaven to Earth. Experience the richness and the vitality of your souls.

Remember, for every single thing that you truly want to do, that truly is representative of you, there will always be a place and a time in which it can be done. You would not exist if that were not so. There is never one side to creation. Always it is complete. And for every desire, for every true self wish, for every soul wish, there is *always* the opportunity to manifest that wish in the reality you are in right now. Always . . . see it; feel it; be it. It's easy and it's fun.

Once again I congratulate you all. I extend our love to you all, our appreciation to you all, our joy. We are always with you; you are always with us. Let us travel together and enjoy life.

PART III
The Extraterrestrials

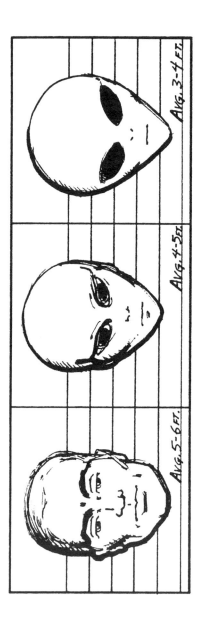

Human	Hybrid	Grey*
Earth	Essassani	Zeta

Avg. 5-6 Ft.   Avg. 4-5 Ft.   Avg. 3-4 Ft.

*One of the races of the Zeta Reticula

CHAPTER ELEVEN

Life on Essassani

November, 1987: *You said that you've been observing our culture for thousands of years?*

I was speaking collectively. Not my society specifically, but many of the societies within the Association of Worlds have, yes.

Living the life that you're living now, do you experience time in the same linear dimension that we experience it?

Somewhat, but not exactly. Our ability to communicate with you right now shows that we experience it somewhat differently. For colloquially speaking, we are actually of your future. Therefore, in a sense you could say we are speaking backwards in time. Because we still have a physicality somewhat, the idea is that we do perceive notions of time to some degree. It is very pliable and malleable for us, because our society's transformation now involves going from physicality to complete non-physicality.

So from your viewpoint you can tell what the transformational age has accomplished?

Somewhat, here and there. Not everything will be apparent to us. Each time we tap into the flow we may perceive very different things. But some general overall patterns and flows are observable to us because of our vantage point.

Physical Aspects

I wonder if you could describe for us the planet on which you live: how large it is; how far it is from your central sun, the time periods for your year and your day . . . and some of the physical aspects of your life.

On a level from which you are able to perceive us physically, we consider ourselves to be beings similar to your own species, although somewhat different. Our physiological form is generally as follows: we are approximately 5 feet of height in your counting; white/whitish-gray skin coloration; very wide upturned eyes. The pupil of our eye encompasses most of the eye, and because of our enlarged pupil it would appear as if our eyes are almost black. Actually they are not; most of them tend toward gray in coloration.

The males usually have no hair; females generally will have some, tending to be whitish in color, although there are exceptions. If you wish some type of comparative analogy between our civilization and a species of your civilization, you could use the idea of Mongolian and you would be close, but not exact. We are relatively slender, relatively frail as you would understand that idea, as we move from physicality to non-physicality.

In our ancient language, which we no longer use as we are telepathic, our planet is named Essassani. As our people are Sassani, and *Es* means place, this translates out in your language to "place of living light." Since it is our understanding that all beings are made of living light, we have called our world thus.

Our planet is not too dissimilar to your own, although a tiny bit smaller. What you would call our gravitational component is approximately 85% of your own. We do not really follow the flow of keeping track of time, but since we do have a physicalized world, and since a day is simply a single rotation upon its axis of the planet, we do have days. They are slightly longer than yours, approximately 25 of your hours. However, our year is much longer, being that we, in your terms, have an approximate 120 million mile radius from our central star. Thus our year is approximately 454 of your days of counting. Our sun is much hotter than yours; hence the diameter of our orbit is broader. Therefore, my age is approximately 139 of my years, but more like 160 of yours, allowing for the variation in our time stream.

Essassani is park-like and very green, our central star being yellowish-green. The idea is that we have no major structures on our planet at this time. In population, the majority of our civilization, which does not number very much —at least not in terms of your world— exists in what you would call city ships, or large space craft. The surface of the planet itself has been left more for recreational purposes at this time. With a very slight adjustment your species would find it most comfortable.

Our axis tilt is not very much—approximately 3 to 4 degrees at the most. Therefore we maintain a relatively constant temperature. We do not have the wide variation in seasons that your civilization experiences. In fact it never varies more than 13 degrees around the average temperature of approximately 72 of your degrees Fahrenheit. The idea is that you would find it most comfortable. It would be a bit more rich in oxygen, to some degree. You may be a little light-headed here for a while, but adjustments could be made.

Our permanent population is approximately between 200 and 250 million by your counting. There are many other species from other civilizations that come and go on our planet at various times for various reasons. Our city ships range anywhere from one to ten of your miles in length, and contain several hundred thousand individuals at a time. These ships and the large population on them is for the purpose of exploring different areas of the galaxy, for inter-dimensional penetration, and for communication with various civilizations. These make up what we call The Association of Worlds, numbering approximately 360 worlds so far. The ships are also for exploring and contacting new civilizations such as your own—new to us, that is.

Could you tell us how far your planet is from us, and in what direction we would look to see where you're going to be?

Yes; however, you will not be able to see our star because we are in a different dimensional plane. While we are in our dimensional plane we cannot see your star either until we make the dimensional shift. However, if our dimension and your dimension were overlapped, you would find our star approximately 500 of your light years of counting in the direction of the constellation you call Orion.

The Galaxy

Then can you tell me how many members are in The Association, Bashar?

Several billion, I think.

And how many in the triad?

If you mean in your world, our world and Sirius, then obviously several billion, since you have several billion of your own. There is no accurate count we can give you, for it is constantly fluctuating.

How many galaxies do you know of?

Galaxy is a collection of many solar systems. Your civilization and our civilization and the civilization of Sirius exist within one galaxy—which is a collection, as you count them, of over one hundred billion stars—and that is one galaxy.

You will find that there are other galaxies as well. Now, we have explored minutely into 5 galaxies at this time, including our own. And there are some representations from each of those that we know of in an overall Association. The majority of them with which our civilization is familiar, however, stem mostly from our own galaxy, from several different star systems within this galaxy. And as you may know, the Milky Way itself contains an infinite number of galaxies.

And how many intelligently-populated planets are there in the Milky Way?

What you would perceive in your density, or close to it, is between 60 and 70 million. It fluctuates as well, but some are within that.

How many stars?

Over 100 billion.

You said once that you had directly investigated or interacted with 359 of them or so—personally?

Not myself personally, but the Association; however, all of the 60 to 70 million inhabitations do not belong to the Association. We are simply listing the inhabited planets that we are aware of—most of which we have not contacted.

Triads

Bashar, you seem to like triads a lot, and I know your space craft is triangular in shape.

Yes. Our fascination with the triad —forming triads, working with threes, and so on— is because the triad formation, or triangular formation, first of all is the primary fundamental geometric that will always occur in the second and third densities. The tetrahedron is the most basic fundamental form of manifestation in third density that you can have in physical reality.

Now, this idea of Sirius consciousness, our consciousness and your consciousness forming a triad consciousness is so that the two are always supporting the one. Our civilization works in threes, in networks of threes, always upon the principle of forming the triad for support, the two to the one. . . . and thus our triangular scout craft.

So tell me about your craft. How does it look from the inside?

The particular craft that I use more often than not is a three-sided, equilateral triangle-shaped one. The interior is hexagonal, for the three points are isolated for machinery, the central portion being relegated to control.

That sounds great. Would it be visible to our eyes?

Oh, yes. There are many beings interacting with your civilization at this time. We will not be physically the first to interact with you, however, for we are assisting others who will be the first. In your manner of counting time, our opportunity to interact with you will occur somewhere generally within the next eight to ten of your years.

I was wondering, Bashar, if there is a possibility of a human at this time visiting your planet? And if so, what technique would we use?

Only in astral form.

What technique would you suggest to get us there astrally, then—to change our frequency so that we could be with you?

Allow yourself, when you are lying down in your meditative state, to close your eyes and think of the vibration you are feeling now that I represent to you. When you think of my identity, you will automatically be keying into the frequency of our civilization. An abstract form that can assist you is to think of a three-sided tetrahedral structure outlined in electromagnetic blue-white light. That will also align you to our frequency. Thinking of my identity will allow you to flow in the direction of our dimensional vibration when you simply let yourself flow. It is as simple as that.

Do you understand, again, that the majority of our population is composed of beings who do visit us in an energy state, an out-of-body state? In a sense they are projecting their mentality, and creating instantaneously the representational body in which they can experience existence upon our planet for any length of time they wish. And then when they are through with it, poof!

Many of *you* visit our dimension in astral form. However, when you wake up in your physiological reality, you bring back with you the remnants of a dream that may or may not have made sense to you, because there are many aspects of your own physiological consciousness that may not be able to relate, or need to relate, to some of the things that you did when you were out of your body. So it will provide convenient symbols to represent the experience you had, in terms that will make the best sense for the reality you are focused in now.

You may not necessarily carry a literal memory of your interaction with us, but you will carry back a symbolic one at least that will contain the symbols necessary for you to be able to apply in your reality whatever it is you experienced, and/or learned, and/or shared, in the other reality. But that is all you need to do: think about us and you automatically align yourselves like a dial on your radio to our frequency.

When we're on your planet, is our physiological make-up the same as it is when we're here?

No, then it will be *our* physiological make-up; you are in our type of body here, by definition.

Would that be the conscious "I" of myself here?

Are you imagining that you exist in our civilization right now?

Sort of.

Sort of. Then you are sort of there also. Understand that our civilizational energy is offered to everyone, and is that malleable. The second you form the identification, you have a representational form on our planet in our dimension. And it can interact, and does interact, with all the other members. That's why we tell you that the awareness does not serve your purpose, obviously, by definition. You can allow it to, but right now if you do not have the awareness, you are not allowing it to.

Recognize also that this is one of the reasons why we say that when we talk to you, we talk to all different portions of you. Many times while we are talking to the *you* here, we are talking to the *you* there. And you, as the *you* there, are talking to the *you* here. You have only but to allow yourselves to realize it to begin to experience it consciously.

Do you have any idea where exactly you are going to land? Which area?

No. And again —again, again— do not expect us to come. Because then we can't. The expectation is something that says, "We need you to; we place you above us." And immediately you put us out of reach.

Well, I just think it would be very exciting, and I'm looking forward to it.

All right. But do recognize that the idea is, when the excitement is in the present, that is when we can meet you.

Well, it's very exciting right now.

Oh, very exciting! Is it so exciting that you are willing to completely be the beings you know you are?

Yes.

All right. Then the sooner you begin to act like it, the sooner we will be there.

Body Death

Bashar, do you ever die?

In your terms we can physiologically leave the body approximately around the age of 300—which we do so consciously, with our eyes open. When we leave the body, it is not through age or disease or suffering, but simply the timing to go on, to go else-where, to expand in other ways. The physiological body converts instantaneously back into the energy of the world from which it was created. There is no decay—except in a very rapid form.

Know that the idea of the generation of pain in no way means it must culminate in physical death. It can always be transformed, especially now in your transformational life, where you are be-ginning to be aware of the fact that pain does not have to remain. In our civilization we no longer experience the idea of pain at all.

Are you planning an incarnation on planet Earth?

No. We are no longer in your type of cycle anymore. We are moving into fifth density, a non-physical, more ethereal type of existence.

Well, do people reincarnate in your civilization?

Yes.

With a choice?

Of course. So do you. Always.

Social Organization

Bashar, I'm curious to know about social organization on your planet. How are you all organized?

The idea is that we are a spontaneous civilization now. We have elevated trust to an art form—in a positive sense, the idea being that we no longer need a government or political system as such, or an economic system as such, because we interact directly with each other individually and in groups—more in a format now that you would call a network. It is our perception that the governments on your planet in time will also take on more of the aspects of networks, where you will facilitate individuals in con-tacting other individuals, those who have services with those who have needs.

The idea of our Association is not so much a government, nor exactly a federation, for that still implies, to some degree, a gov-ernmental structure similar to the one you know. It is a network-ing body, a serving body, that puts intelligence in line and in touch with other intelligence that matches spontaneously, need for need, service for service. And that is much the way our society interacts. We have no need for a medium of exchange, because every individual that has a service automatically attracts every individual that needs that service. And every individual that needs that service that is attracted automatically brings with him a service that the first individual needs. Everything is run by synchronicity, coincidence—because that is the way life works.

Life is a holographic matrix, wherein everything is connected to everything else automatically, as we have often stated. When you truly know that, and when you focus on that particular structure, that's the way you experience life, and you do not need a reference structure in order to organize things. Things organize themselves, and the government becomes one that serves, rather than rules, allowing the flow to take place. At any given moment, as we have said, our population is exploring in space craft, interacting with other civilizations and exploring many aspects of the universe. Very few of us remain on the surface of our planet at any given time, and thus there are no large cities such as you have, with large built-up structures. The space craft *are* the cities.

Our fluctuating population includes individuals popping in and out, taking for the moment our corporeal form to experience our particular civilization, and then flashing back into energy. There are sometimes other beings from other societies who choose to spend time on the surface of our planet, interacting with many different members of our species and other species, as we mentioned earlier. This is, in general, the idea of our life style. It is always very spontaneous, very joyful, very ecstatic. And we are always exploring, always learning and growing, always having a good time.

What about non-conformists? Are there such things?

Everyone is a non-conformist. And because each being is allowed to be the fullest individual he can be, we thus have great unity.

Does that agree with a one-mind concept?

Yes. Understand that it is a misunderstanding in your society when you believe that one mind means a blandness of individuality. Just like the person you are, when each and every one of your personality parts is as strong and as equal to every other part as it can be, then you function as a whole being. It is just like that in a society: when each individual is the strongest *individual* he can be, then you have unity—for each is equally validated for the individual he is. Therefore, paradoxically, everyone supports the totality of all the other individuals that exist, and supports the idea of each and every being *being* the strongest individual he can be. So unconditional love is the key that allows us to function as one mind, and at the same time allows us to operate as distinct and variegated individuals.

So there's no disagreement among individuals?

There are always different points of view. But the different points of view do not impede us from the general flow of our positive progress. There is never disagreement in the sense that it holds things up. There can be different points of view, different approaches; but you see, to us they're all valid. If three individuals have three different points of view and three different approaches, we do them all. Or if they finally allow themselves, by trying them all —I use your term for now: *trying*— to simply come to the understanding that what one individual or another individual did is perhaps not as efficient as what the third individual came up with. Then in recognizing that, the other two will probably align themselves with the third one.

Again, everything is done spontaneously, in a very obvious and conscious and willing manner. There is no need for argument, as you call it. All points of view are valid, and we can learn from all of them.

"Entertainment"

I'm curious about what Essassanians do for entertainment.

We have many different forms of expression. Some of them are similar to your own. There is art and music—many different ideas. Some are similar, but some are very diverse from your own. We are always exploring and learning many different endeavors, many different expressions.

In your classic vernacular, I would be considered a pilot, an engineer, a sculptor—and, as you say, a diplomat. I interact with many other societies similar to your own. These are the things that excite me. Everyone does what excites them the most, with full integrity. Beyond that, it is unlimited.

Do you have an entertainment system, such as television or films, the way we do here?

No. There was something similar in times past, but our society is mostly telempathic. Information is simply sent from mind to mind. There are within the space craft recording devices, but these are completely mnemonic, and are accessed directly by mentality into the computers. The images simply unfold in our mind; they do not have to appear on a screen.

So there's no central place that sends out these entertainment —or other images— to other individuals, and that you could tune into?

There is one representative place always on every planet of the Association that can function in this way. Also there is a chamber on every large city ship that functions in a similar fashion.

And who creates these images—every individual? I mean, if you have 200 million people on your planet alone, that would be a lot of frequencies—

Well, not every image is processed, nor does it need to be. The idea is that if an individual has a specific desire for a particular access, he will be able to get it. Remember that all individuals, including those on your own planet, have access to all the knowledge, especially that knowledge pertaining most directly to your world. It is generally referred to as the Akashic records. It is the storehouse of knowledge, of the Infinite.

To some degree we have modified mechanical representatives of that idea. It is a network, once again, of energy. But it is not confusing. It overlaps, but any individual who creates himself to be a particular frequency will only access the particular information that is aligned with that particular frequency. He will not interfere with anyone else's ability to access what information he needs. It is holographic, in that sense.

Music

I'd like to ask more about music on your planet. Do you have scales? And what kind of musical form do you have, and what kind of instruments?

We have some degree of instruments that are created, many of which are spontaneous, many of which are remnants from older times in our civilization. The majority of our instrumentation is usually percussive, bell-like. There are a few strings and a few wind instruments, but very few. They are similar to your oriental instruments—Chinese, Japanese. Very simple tonalities are created with these instruments, as the majority of the tonalities we experience are actually at this point created telepathically and shared in that way.

Would our orchestras of Indonesian bells and gongs be similar in some ways?

To some degree, although you will find that they will be simpler in structure in many different ways, and you will allow yourselves to recognize that many of them may be tuned to particular tonalities which represent the general combined total pattern of our civilization. As I say, they will be few in number, and very simple in construction.

* * *

Bashar, since you obviously still have some physicality, in what way does that serve you? And do you experience physical pleasure as we do?

To some degree it serves us by allowing us to interact with civilizations such as your own that need that type of relationship to be able to interact. Also, because we exist in pure ecstasy, in that sense, it is a very pleasurable state in which to exist—as you will soon find out on your planet as well.

There is nothing wrong with existing as a physical representation of consciousness, although we are now going from transitional fourth to fifth density, as you are going from transitional third to fourth. Soon we will not have embodiment, because we no longer need it for the idea that we are. However, as a civilization we chose to experience certain ideas of physical reality so that we would be able to exist and assist other civilizations going through a similar experience—to be able to interact with them in terms they could relate to.

Love and Courtship

Can you talk a little bit about love-making and courtship on Essassani? Since you're all telepathic, how would that be different from the way we do it here?

First of all, allow us to remind you that we always allow whatever relationship any individuals find themselves attracted into to be an obvious reflection of the things they need to understand and learn at that point. And we allow the relationship to be what it is for, rather than what we think it should be.

We find that any attraction has its reasons, and therefore we interact according to our instincts, and not so much with the idea of courtship. Any individuals who find themselves interacting know they are interacting for a reason, and thus follow their emotions and instincts accordingly, knowing that whatever comes up for them, in that they are functioning within their integrity, *is* what belongs in that relationship. Thus they will simply respond to those ideas.

Do remember: every individual within our society considers him- or herself in a sense to be married to every other individual. So since we are already married, there is no need for a courtship, and the relationships simply unfold according to what each and every individual has brought into it. No matter in what way they appear to transform themselves, as they continue to unfold and are allowed to transform naturally, then we take it for granted that is the way they are "supposed" to transform.

We do not put expectations on them for what we think they ought to be. We know they are there to serve us; we know we are there to serve them, and we rejoice in the spontaneous co-creation. We do not in any way apply any particular label as to how we think it should go, or how we think it should wind up. "Will it be this way, or will it be that? Will there be anyone else?" We continue to live our lives, allowing one relationship to blend into another circumstance, and allowing them all to intermesh together into one act of love-making, over the whole world.

So in a sense you are making love all the time?

Yes. In a sense, so are you all.

Procreation and Children

Could you also tell us a bit more about when you all decide to have children? How do you procreate?

We are always in touch telepathically, consciously, with the consciousness who chooses to be born. When we agree to recognize the timing of the event, and the purpose for which that individual wishes to experience a physiological life in our world, then we are aware of when that timing is. Conception and birth do not occur prior to that timing.

But babies are still carried in the mother's body?

Yes, there is that formation.

For how many months?

Seven.

Is conception similar to what it is on our planet?

Similar, yes. But do not forget that there is a conscious awareness of the agreement with the individual about to be born. In a sense you can say there is conscious awareness of the participation of that individual in the sexual act—when the sexual act is for the purpose of allowing the exchange to create an atmosphere in which that individual can be born.

What I'm driving at is: is there the requirement on your planet to actually have sperm fertilize an egg?

No, only the interchange of energy.

Something like what we call immaculate conception here?

Sort of. But there is still the blending of the polarities of the masculine and the feminine.

Would it be like an exchange of energy during meditation?

In a sense.

Is there no exchange of bodily fluids?

Not at this time, although there used to be. Now our bodily fluid is mostly electromagnetic in nature. As we have said, we are in contact with the entity to be born at all times—prior to birth, through birth, and into the physical life. There is a very brief orientation period for the consciousness to acclimate itself to the new matrix into which it has imposed its consciousness. No more than three of your years are necessary for the individual to begin functioning fully as a member of our society, in full consciousness. By three years of age he will be relatively independent. Then the "child" goes on his way, attracting himself to whatever other individuals he needs to interact with in order to learn what he needs to learn to live the life he is choosing to live in our society.

That does not necessarily mean that he will take up the physiological manifestation exactly in the same way an adult would be doing it, but he will go and attract himself to the teachers and the sharers and the learners to whom he needs to attract himself. He will always remember his biological parents, for we are never out of touch. You see, the child recognizes that every adult is his parent, and every adult recognizes that every child is his or her child, and acts accordingly. We are all truly one family, all telepathically connected. No one ever loses a child; no child is ever lost.

As we said, by the third year the child is off and learning, absorbing whatever he wishes to absorb to be the person he has chosen to be. It is very ecstatic, very nurturing, and very loving. You might say Essassani is one big playground. Do realize, however, that you also can be in touch with the beings who will be born unto you. For understand: *they are not children now.* You can recognize that there are services that you may want to perform, and that this non-physical individual radiates a desire to accomplish certain things in physiological manifestation.

In putting out that desire and putting out that radiation, the individual in our society automatically attracts only the individuals that have the desire to serve him. So it's automatic; there's no wondering about it. Only the individuals who can be of service are attracted to him, and he will only be attracted to the individuals who can serve him.

Is that not so for us now?

Yes, it is absolutely that way now—except that you create negative synchronicity as well as positive synchronicity. We only create positive manifestations.

Love-Making

How often do you yourself actually engage in the physical act of making love?

Whenever it comes up.

How often is that?

The idea occurs spontaneously wherein the reflection of my life so attracts an individual who wishes to interact in that way. Again remember, however, that at this time in our society, while there are remnants of a physiological act, it is more of an energy act.

This sexual exchange of energy: how is it different?

It is a direct exchange, an activation of the cellular structures within the body. That is due more to the actual flash exchange of energy, rather than what you would typify as a physiological act of procreation. It becomes less and less physical. In a sense, in many ways when you blend the physical and the non-physical together, it becomes less of a distinction. It becomes the same thing: all one act, all one idea of blending. Not meaning this to sound strange to your ears, but because of what our society is, any such exchange between any individuals is on some level actually felt by the whole society. And that adds to our overall ecstasy and sense of joy.

Our interactions are a blending, an identification *as.* It is like moving into a common daydream, sharing therein the exchanges of emotionality and desire. We recognize that this act, truly as fulfilling on every level as you are used to thinking of the idea of consummation, will cause whatever cellular and structural changes that need to change to do so within our physical forms —that which we maintain to be the belief of our physical form— and will instigate the union, if necessary, of a third identity wishing to be born. If not, then it will simply consummate according to whatever we have to learn from each other. It is not that we can give you any particular idea of regularity; it is always spontaneous. And in a sense is always unknown until it happens. We just accept it for what it is when it happens.

Is that what you feel when you're coming through the channel—sharing this daydream?

Yes, somewhat. It is a form of love-making. That is why, when each and every individual on your planet is in love with every other individual, you will also be of one mind; and then you will be telepathic. You will identify as each other, and therefore you will interpret the vibrations of Infinite Creation in a similar way. That is why individuals on your planet whom you recognize as being in love often share the same thoughts. It is not that they are literally reading each other's minds directly; it is that they are on the same wave length. Thus the vibrational pattern that they are, sharing the similar idea, interprets the Infinite Creation in a similar manner, in similar thought forms. You could therefore say that the physical channel and I are now exhibiting to you an act of being in love.

Marriage

So the concept of marriage, or the institution of marriage, is not on your planet?

Not in the ritualized form that you experience it, no. For we recognize that the act itself is the thing, and there is no need for anything else that needs to reinforce that act. It simply *is* what it is. If that desire is not there, then no ritual will make it mean anything more anyway. It is like the economic standard: something that to us would be a middle ground symbol, rather than a direct exchange.

Once again, perhaps to put it in the simplest perspective: our entire civilization is married to itself. Every individual is married to every other individual. Any relationship that occurs, in any way it occurs, with however many individuals it occurs, is a part of the marriage, is a relationship within the marriage. There are times when it takes upon it the physical appearance of what you refer to as a monogamous relationship; there are times when it doesn't—just as it occurs in your society. However, in your world there is a great deal of denial about that.

As an example, and because it is germane to your society, we do not expect one, or even know whether or not we have been in a monogamous relationship until we reach the end of the life-span. Then we say, "Well, no one else came along; I guess it was a one-on-one, wasn't it?" We know in absolute trust that if any other relationships do automatically occur, then they are a part of the overall relationship. They enhance the overall scenario, in whatever way they naturally unfold, and they cannot be an inter-ruption. It is not possible in our society.

So there is no commitment?

There is a commitment to be what we are—to each other. Any relationship that is co-created is enjoyed for the relationship it is, not what we expect it should be.

Why do you think we are so attached to the idea, in this civili-zation, of committed relationships?

Because you feel it is the only way to guarantee the idea of support. Also, you search for someone whom you believe will make you feel whole. Instead, however, what you attract to your-selves is someone who reflects your own feeling of lack of whole-ness. And you each reflect the same to the other. Thus you look for a *guarantee* that your "other half" will not leave you. How-ever, if you know you are attracting exactly what you need to attract, you will be committed to that relationship—exactly as you need to be, for the time you need to be. If and when it should change in various ways, you will change with it.

The definition of the relationship may change physiologically in many different ways, but it is still a relationship, no matter what the new definition is. You are, in fact, whether you know it or not, always committed, although you can fool yourselves into thinking you are not. You are committed to the idea you are co-creating. Now, if you choose to view the co-creation through judgment, you may not be aware of the fact that you are obvi-ously committed by being in the relationship to begin with. But understand, even if you are forming a relationship in which you are exploring the idea of commitment, or lack of commitment, you are at that moment committed to exploring that idea within that relationship.

That is how we relate to each other in our civilization. And that is why when a situation and a relationship changes, we are committed to the change as well. For we know that since change is the only constant, all change serves us and allows us to serve. In our world there may be individuals who choose to attract into their lives the situation where they experience what you call a one-to-one relationship with one individual for the period of the life span. But there are many individuals who do not, many individuals who interact with many other individuals over the course of a life span, because they have created and co-created with those other individuals *that* many reflections to learn what they need to learn about themselves and others, and different ways of being of service in that life.

We recognize that any interaction is the product of what an individual is, if he is honest and within integrity of himself, and therefore will play it out at whatever rate it needs to. Regardless of any structure that may be imposed upon him, it will not change a thing. Even in your society you truly do recognize this idea, for even though you have created the idea of a structure of marriage to ensure the interaction, when you know the interaction changes, you create the structure of divorce. We simply act and interact in all ways; and since we are always loving in that interaction, then we know that any transformation that takes place is always for the positive. In some ways we always remain in any relationship that has been created. Any relationship once created goes on forever, no matter how many different ways it may transform.

And that's what we're moving into now?

It is what we perceive your planet to be understanding, yes.

Great. Thank you very much.

Rituals

As a visiting anthropologist, Bashar, I would like to ask what the equivalencies are for your people for some rituals we have—like marriage ceremonies, for example? We have rituals to mark special occasions, like birth and marriage and puberty. And we also have myths to explain why we do the rituals the way we do. What do you all do for that?

Usually whatever we want.

Like what?

There is a type of ritual that remains in our society that you may or may not find interesting, and it takes place usually about the third year of life. This ritual is a recognition that upon that third year the individual born in our society has what he needs to begin to absorb —at his own pace— all the other information that is pertinent to whatever it is he is going to do in life. He can begin to go out into the world on his own, as we have said, and seek what he wishes to seek, gleaning information from whomever he wishes to glean it, learning at his own pace whatever he wishes to learn. This can be termed a naming ritual, or a recognition of adulthood at three years of age, even though the physical form may not be mature as you understand it.

This ritual takes place with three individuals, representing one for each year, gathering together and surrounding the child. The child will sit in the middle. Each individual will focus upon an aspect of body, mind and spirit, and will flow a sense of energy to that child. This child will, in this ritual, take from each of those three individuals a blend and a balance of those ideas that the child makes his own—his own unique formula, his own unique frequency, representing his own idea of what his combination of body, mind and spirit ought to be. In other words, he solidifies, or crystallizes, his identity within our society—because up to that point he does not really have a solidified identity. He is fluid, and he can come and go at any time, and even become non-physical instantaneously if he wishes to.

At that point if he decides to "hang around" in our society after three years, in crystallizing his identity at that point, he then harmonizes, or synchronizes, with the tempo of the mental framework of our society so that he will fit in and flow, *in* all the places and *to* all the places that best represent the path of least resistance for that individual to grow. He does so in whatever way evolution needs for him to grow to fit into our society best. We do not take names per se, since we are tele*m*pathic and are always interconnected with one another. Everyone functions in a child-like manner in our society, giving in to spontaneous unconditional love. It is very joyful, much like what your children now are teaching all of you to be like.

There are many, many spontaneous manifestations that you might call rituals. But none of them are as heavily bought into as most of the rituals on your planet. They are simply artistic expressions that are individual in the moment.

Sometimes groups will spontaneously come together and form a myth, a ritual, but only because it is one way of expressing an idea. It is not something that would be institutionalized, or rigidized. In the next minute, or perhaps several years later, it may dissolve, because the society no longer sustains the need for that particular format or matrix.

Essassani's Transformation

For how long have you been doing things this way, Bashar? And where did you get the idea to do them in the way you've described?

In your terms of counting, it was approximately between 300 and 500 of your years ago that our society made an abrupt transformation. Because of the nature of our environment and the nature of our evolution, we were always, shall we say, somewhat prone to have a little more cohesiveness than your society exhibits at this point. There has never been as much variation in our history as there has been in yours, never as much segregation, diversification. So to some degree we might have had a little bit of a head start, evolutionarily speaking, as we were pushed in that direction by the environment.

However, as was mentioned before, the idea of a tendency, a momentum, developed until it brought us to a certain point where the collective mentality of our society manifested in a particular event. This particular event is not unlike what you refer to as your Christ scenario. Now, let me backtrack a moment and refresh your memory. What you call the Christ consciousness is, from our perspective, the combined consciousness of the totality of all the individuals on your planet. It knows itself as a singular identity, but it also knows itself as being made up of all the consciousnesses upon your world.

Every single planet, every single society, every single dimension of consciousness, has its own version of the Christ consciousness—the collective soul, the world spirit. In our ancient language we called ours Shakana. Our Shakana is what manifested in our world, but did not need to manifest as a full physiological life span. It existed in physical form, as a physical birth, for approximately three days of your time. Within those three days, because we were already to some degree susceptible to inter-mental linkup, the added momentum of the combined consciousness focusing in that way upon our planet created a surge of mental linkup throughout the entire world. And in a sense, we went into a daydream, a waking dream. The entire world woke up three days later with a new understanding of our ability to expand beyond what we had understood before.

I do not mean anything derogatory by what I am about to say, and in no way is this an invalidation of the way you have done things. But to put it most simply, when we were presented with the reflection of the collective consciousness of our world spirit, we listened. That is all there is to it. It woke us up, and everything we have created from that point forward was possible because we started to function as a unit.

Contrary to what many of you have been taught to believe, functioning as a unit in no way invalidates identity. In fact, just the opposite: it strengthens it. Each of us became the strongest individual we could possibly conceive of ourselves becoming. And in becoming the strongest component, the strongest individual we could become, that strengthened the whole and allowed us to function as a unit, to be literally in love with each and every being upon our planet. We understood that the way to truly expand our reality was to be in love with *all* creation, including your civilization, which is why we are very eager to communicate with you. When certain changes take place upon your planet to make that more conducive, then nothing will hold us back from interacting with you in very blatant ways.

But let me say this, at the risk of repeating myself even more: it is not in any way critical that your society interacts with us. That is not the end-all, be-all idea of why we are communicating with you. We are not the most important thing in your world; you are! Your planet is the most important thing to you. And when you as a society begin to allow yourselves to truly live up to your full potential, you will co-create with us a vibrational frequency that will create a middle ground, a meeting space, in which your frequency and our frequency can come together in a compatible format.

You see, you must meet us half-way. The dimension in which we exist, from your point of view, is rather ethereal in nature, rather dreamlike in nature. And that is why it's actually simpler for us to contact you through the aspect of your consciousness, rather than physically materializing in your world. Yes, it can be done and it has been done; but it is actually not as easy to do. We must lower our vibration and solidify ourselves so far in order to materialize on your planet, it is actually easier to touch you on a mental level first, as that is where you are closest to the frequency in which we naturally exist. So understand that physically what to us is our solid material reality, to you is the stuff dreams are made of.

Education

Would you say something about the difference in formal education before your transformation?

As we are telepathic, a number of thoughts, or information bits, are always being fed, shall we say, into the minds of all individuals who are willing to access that stream of consciousness. There really is no formal education in that sense. An individual will attract himself to whatever endeavors he truly is most interested in—so the majority of individuals in our society learn by doing. They learn on the job by simply attracting themselves to the environment that represents what they are interested in, and allowing the individuals in that environment to teach them what they need to know.

The individuals in that environment are always more than willing to take the time to share their knowledge with an individual, because they know that there's no way that individual would have wound up on their doorstep had it not been someone who would become one of them. Thus they always want to instill within that individual whatever knowledge he needs to know. They take him under their wing, tutoring him until he feels he has received a sufficient amount of information to satisfy his curiosity. There really is no formal structure.

Now and then there are organizations that occur for specific trainings that may be necessary. One of those organizations, or associations, is responsible specifically for my ability to be able to communicate with your civilization at this time. The idea that we contact many civilizations means there are many modes of thought; and to some degree some training is necessary to allow one to become acclimatized, so to speak, to the different ways in which different alien societies do think. Without that training, and without certain other tools to assist us, I would be far too alien, and you would be far too alien for us to have a meaningful communication with you.

Going back to the issue of reincarnation: one of the other things we do, which prepares us to be able to communicate with other societies, is to have at some point a life in that society so that we can build up a framework in our own incarnational history. This allows us to draw upon that framework later on and use it as a model. Using this reference point, the society we then interact with isn't so alien—because we have had at least one life there to which we can relate.

That is the situation that is going on here before you. For I am, as I have said, the channel's future self. The physical channel before you is the one past life I have had on your planet, and thus

I created a frame of reference through which I could communicate with you more easily than coming in "raw," as you say.

Male/Female Energy

Bashar, you have spoken of Anima as being your female counterpart, and in fact, many of us have heard her speaking through Darryl. Do you know all your counterselves that are manifestations of the same oversoul?

At this point truly all beings in our society are part of the same oversoul, in an overall sense.

Do you experience that unity even though you have an individual physiological manifestation?

Yes. We experience the unity through the feelings of unconditional love that we have for every single being in our society.

What I was driving at was that I want to understand your experience on a day-to-day basis, the degree to which you experience your integration with the mass consciousness.

It can occur in many different ways, some of which are similar to the ways you experience it. It's just that we recognize it for what it is when we see it, whereas many times you don't. The idea is that anyone we interact with is there for a reason, and we take it as a reflection, as a different aspect of the counterpart oversoul self, feeding back to us what it is we need to look at to allow ourselves to grow into the beings we have chosen to be.

We still respect individuals; we do not disinherent their individuality. But we also at the same time recognize everyone as the expression of synchronicity each chose to be for everyone else.

Is there a real difference between men and women, or male and female?

There is an obvious physiological difference, yes.

Well, how about in terms of energy, or roles in your society?

Not so much.

This whole idea of blending the male and female within ourselves— as we blend them, do we then become more neuter?

In one sense of word, perhaps. But then not really, if you choose to maintain an individuality expression. Although each and every individual male and female in our society is the blended marriage of the male/female principle within him/herself, you would still experience our energy as either distinctly male or distinctly female. That is how we choose to express ourselves relative to the ideas we wish to be in the universe where we exist. This is also assistive in communicating with societies like your own that are still very much in the middle of exploring their polarities—assistive by giving them an anchor point.

But then you have a purpose for maintaining a separation.

Oh yes, of course.

But in the general progress, if you take away that purpose—

Then it would be mostly neuter.

What does neuter feel like?

Much like the idea of being non-corporeal. Although you find in your system that at first you still retain a high degree of identity to the idea of your last incarnation, it is not so with us.

So the differences between men and women are anchored in physiological differences?

Basically. They are the polarity expression that exists within the soul as a unit—expressed in physical terms, expressed in the dimension that does experience the polarities in separate ways.

But in non-physical reality that polarity wouldn't be there?

It would not be perceived as such, no.

But is there not a positive and negative concept of energy in non-physical reality?

In a sense, yes. But it is not perceived as you perceive polarities from your dimensional point of view. There is not necessarily exactly the terminology to be able to explain this to you. It is merely an experiential thing. You will understand it when you get there.

Thank you. What I'm wondering is, when you leave here, what's the first thing you do when you go home?

The Dawning

First of all, I am still at home; I am not actually physically with you. This is a telepathic link from within my scout craft, which

is at this time over my own world, at the beginning of a new day.
. . . And now allow me to describe this dawning.

Over the greenery of my world the rising of a yellowish star
with a greenish tinge, there being pale, coolish amber light that
allows the very trees to seem to be waking up, to be stretching and
expanding under the light. Opening up, spreading out farther and
farther until all the branches and all the leaves touch, creating the
canopy of a forest once again. Whereas the night before they had
been collected, singular stalks dotting the landscape, now they are
spread out to give their shade to the creatures below.

There is, now and then —when one is in the right place at the
right time, and has such a vibration— a small thin flash of red-
dish-purple that will signal the angle of the light through the atmosphere that represents the "official" new day, the new dawn upon
our world. A crispness, a lightness, a freshness, a smell, a touch,
a sound. A vitality and a smoothness, an assuredness of being,
activity and delight. The new day begins.

And so we thank you all for sharing the new dawn on our
world with us.

Diagram of Bashar's Scout Craft

Interior plan

Navigation control

Control panels

Central power

Telepathy chamber

Side view

Plan view

Light

10 ft.

5 ft. 8 ft.

SCOUT CRAFT
Type "A"

• Powered by light
• Piloted by computer mind-link with navigator
• Ship hulls are a crystalline-metallic composite "grown" on force field "templates."

214

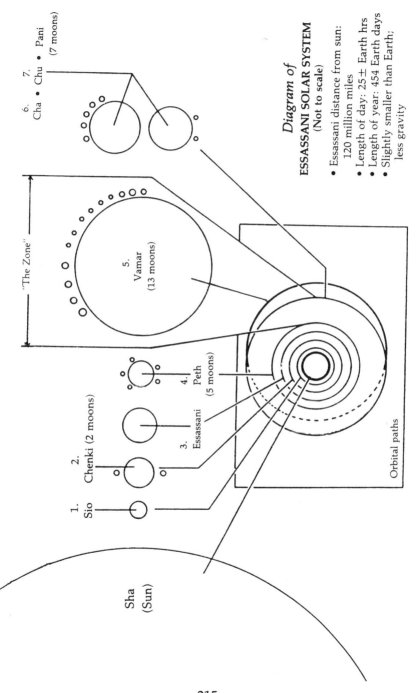

Diagram of
ESSASSANI SOLAR SYSTEM
(Not to scale)

- Essassani distance from sun:
  120 million miles
- Length of day: 25± Earth hrs
- Length of year: 454 Earth days
- Slightly smaller than Earth;
  less gravity

1. Sio

2. Chenki (2 moons)

3. Essassani

4. Peth (5 moons)

5. Vamar (13 moons)

6. 7.
Cha • Chu • Pani
(7 moons)

"The Zone"

Orbital paths

Sha (Sun)

215

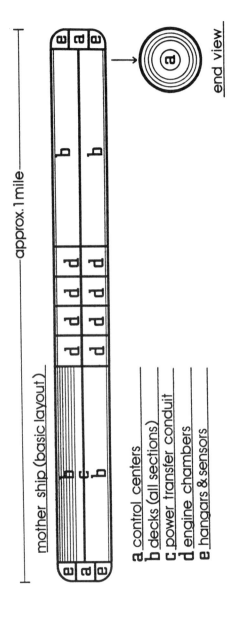

mother ship (basic layout)

approx. 1 mile

a control centers
b decks (all sections)
c power transfer conduit
d engine chambers
e hangars & sensors

end view

Diagram of Solar Wind, the Mother Ship

216

CHAPTER TWELVE

Message from Orion

June, 1986: *(With Bashar's facilitation, another entity,* **Neamon,** *speaks through Darryl.)*

I have been instructed to send you greetings. First of all, allow there to be the indication that the perception of what I have just experienced is something that is strange for me, and I am not entirely sure that what I have been told is occurring, is in fact occurring. It seems as though I am speaking to no one. However, I find that I must trust in he whom I have just met, he who refers to himself as the Commander. And so I will assume that such an interaction is going on, that someone is apparently hearing as I am speaking.

For me, receiving you is subtle. I was told by the Commander that it would be thus; yet I am not sure that the interaction is taking place. Yet again, I will trust and assume, as I have been told to do, that the message is getting through.

I have been told things which are strange to me, yet I have chosen to be party to this idea. Therefore, I must assume reliability upon the information I have received, in that the information does come from what I have come to recognize as a source that is inexplicable within the system with which I am familiar. And the being does represent the idea of something from a time closer to your own, I will assume—you being the ones who are supposed to be receiving this communication.

I have been told that I will be communicating to those I have known, though I have been told things I do not understand—such as in the life you are in at this time you are not the individuals I have known, as I have known them. Nor are you supposed to remember who you are. Thus, even for you this contact, if it is indeed taking place— I will still assume that there is some content within the conversation you have been having with the Commander that perhaps will enlighten you to a certain extent. And perhaps even more than I have been enlightened.

I will therefore make the assumption, once again, that this is occurring as I have been told, across the span of 175,000 years of time. And I will assume that the idea of this communication, although it be going on in what I consider to be my present, is reaching 175,000 years ahead of time—as you count. Something similar to this is happening, I assume. The message is being delivered and received, not in my present time, since you are not here, but in a time where you *are*—regardless of the idea of where I should be now, and where you should be now.

Should this truly be occurring —for it brings me joy to think it might be— allow me, then, to say once again that what I send you is greetings and dearest wishes—in the hopes that your endeavor has been successful as you have created it. For I have been told that you refer to the idea of where I find myself, and where I know you once existed, as something called Orion.

You will know that much has transpired since your leaving here, and only a few here recognize at this time that you have left. Though again, not to be confusing, I will assume that much time has passed by your reckoning, and that there will be many more individuals who will be aware of what I am speaking of now— though I find myself to be quite alone in this understanding with all whom I talk to where I am.

I have been told that there are several among you in your society, as you call yourselves —whatever society that is in your time— who are now recognizing and remembering the idea of connections to many places, here among them. And what I used to refer to as my colleagues shall no longer be those who even remember themselves. But I will still entrust that you are the same colleagues who left, and I will talk to you as such—for that is the only way, surely, that I can make sense of the conversation.

Therefore, let me now begin after this preamble. As I said, I send you greetings, and you may refer to me by reckoning as Neamon. I am told that you would understand best in your present reckoning the idea of what I am by referring to something akin to a priesthood idea. I am told to clarify that this is not literally the case in your terms, but it will do.

I am told I may share with you the idea of the sending of this information now, to express that the idea of your leaving the Orion systems will be representative of your willingness to continue the idea of reaching beyond what you have recognized as a great deal of suppression within the systems. And again, I can only hope that you are successful: that you have arrived where you have deemed yourselves to be, and that it will do you the most good in the completion of your journey, wherever that journey should be.

Although I am not unfamiliar with the ideas that are referred to by this Commander as afterlife, some of the ideas of reincarnation that he has described to me are in terms I do not understand. However, I will assume, once again, that you have lived many lives by the time you receive this message. And that according to the understanding I have, in the living of these many lives you have worked through the ideas that you tended to work through by relocating yourselves at least enough to a point to receive this communication—should this communication be any measure of anything at all. I am not certain, but perhaps it will make more sense to you.

I have been told that the position I shared with you all at that time will have some bearing on the idea of forming connections for yourselves. And so, I willingly grant, in my hopes and my desires for your success, that what small part I may play may reach you across the span of ages, and bolster and support your cause. For again, many of you were colleagues—either whom I may have known as contemporaries, or the idea of individuals who are known to me.

It seems that there will be certain individuals to whom this may relegate more sense, but to all of you it does apply—all who are supposedly present and listening to this communication. What I have been instructed to share at this time is a reminder of your heritage; that there is within the Orion systems, and from our point of view within the idea of the present, what will be your recognition of creation now of what is referred to as three primes. I have been told that in your vernacular it will translate into the terms Shadrach, Meshach, and Abednego. It will represent something that is referred to as sorcery. It is recognized as the action of the three primes of the fundamental triad consciousness, as we recognize all symbols within the Orion system to be representative of our heritage within this fundamental understanding of what you would call religion.

I have been told that you have taken much of this baggage with you, but you have applied it in ways that are more in reference to the system within which you now find yourselves. It has not been understood for what it was: the actual interaction of your mentality, your personality consciousness, on the primal energy exemplified in what the Commander has termed an archetypal energy flow of your subconscious stream. If I may assume I am simplifying anything, since this and some of the terminology is outside of my experience—: the formation of polarities within your system —positive, negative— when blended into a third persona that is neither and both, all three together form the interaction in mentality that will actually create an effect in the electromagnetic field of the planet on which you now reside. And in your history, I am told this effect is referred to as magic.

I am told to relate that this is the idea of the interaction of your mentality, individually, with the primal field of mentality which represents the idea of your entire civilization. It is a personification of the mass consciousness through an individual. I am told to repeat this. **Magic is the personification of the mass consciousness through an individual.**

Therefore, you will find that each individual, by blending the polarities and becoming the third identity, becomes a reservoir and a wealth of all that is possible within any particular system or universal tangent in which you now find yourselves.

In my priestly endeavors I sought to have some measure of understanding of these ideas within our home systems. I understand the idea that you have reached out to form scenarios which will allow you the recognition of not necessarily needing the suppression this time to go along with the utilization of these abilities. Therefore, you have removed yourselves from a universal time track system, and this removal has allowed you to experience the pure nature of this interaction without the idea of the burden of the mass consciousness of domination and suppression that has been within our systems for so long.

Again, I can only assume that what I am perceiving is real, in terms of the idea that you are hearing any of this, even though it is most subtle within my imagination. But I am relying upon the information from the Commander. I am instructed that I am to hold some sort of paternal image for you. Not that this is a calling that I have asked for, but that I would treat you as the friends I have known. Through my love for you and my willingness for your success, I have formed for you the idea of an anchor in the home system. This message, as it is being delivered, is something that can be allowed into your system as a reflection to allow you to know you are forming the connections you need to be forming. I can only hope that this has been of some service, and that I have played my part for you.

I have been told that I may continue to send these interactions from time to time, and that you will receive them. It is this belief, this trust, and this hope that you will receive it that gives me even the shred of willingness to act in this manner—so unlike our own society—to assume that mentality can be bridged and linked up in ways that are not the property of the mass, that are not privy to our communication. Had I not been patronized and convinced enough by your friend that such was the case, I would fear for my life at the possibility of being discovered. But my love for you will transcend this to some extent. I must trust that the idea of this love, in and of itself, is a conduit that is pure enough to remove all doubt, to remove all of what you would call eavesdropping; and that there will be for you a clearness of communication.

I am told at this time to simply extend to you my thoughts and my wishes for your well-being; and I am told that in some form I will have the opportunity to meet you all again on some other stage. I will take this to heart as I bid you my leave.

Bashar: Message received?

Yes.

We thank you for the opportunity to complete a cycle, and the beginning of many new interactions and doorways that shall be opening to allow there to be the further acceleration, so that you may blend the idea of the past you are creating in the present, *with the present*, and create the future you desire in the now. We thank you for your release. We thank you for your willingness to allow there to be the reflections in your life that you have all chosen to place within you.

How are you able to be in communication with that beingness? How do you communicate with him?

In much the same way I communicate with you, but it took a little more. There was the allowance in this case of a physical visit.

You physically manifested before him?

Yes.

I see. Was that a surprise to him?

Oh, yes!

He said that he would fear for his life if anybody knew what he was doing. His life would be in jeopardy.

Yes. However, that did not occur.

Good. I found the experience fascinating and wonderful, aside from the message that was delivered, in the reflection of how some of us have uncertainty when we communicate with others. We're saying, "Gee, now I'm putting this in my imagination and I'm trusting that it's happening. But I don't even know if it's being received." This experience was us being on the opposite end of our communications when we use our imaginations to transmit. . . . So was the entity who spoke to us connected to you in a similar way that you and Darryl are connected?

A different way. A different route, different track altogether.
Not an earlier self? A past self?

Not exactly in the same way; not such a strong connection.
More of a generalized one.

*The fact that he was afraid for his life, it sounded like he was
involved still in the old energy of dominance that we all came
away from.*

Yes! He is, in your terms, still there—in terms of 175,000 years
ago from whence the message came. Not now is he still there, but
from whence came the message he is still there.

*That's right. So what we're doing, then, is being the transfor-
mation from that type of energy?*

Yes.

Does he understand what we're doing?

Not clearly; but his wishes are with you, and what you have
done has made a difference back there. At this time that individual, in the life in which that individual now lives back there, is
part and parcel of a dramatic change within those systems. For
there is now, as there was not then, light in those systems.

Oh, which planet was he from?

No particular planet, but rather the general idea of the Orion
systems. For there was travel from planet to planet. At the time
the message was delivered there was a transliteration—from an
origin point within the system that would translate into your
vibrations as Hoova.

What is the relation of Hoova to Mintaka?

Mintaka is the star close to which was the idea of the dark
crystal moon that was utilized by the resistance to the suppression.

Did we come from Mintaka?

Many of you are from the resistance, and strong connections
abound.

*The individual was there then. Has he left in the intervening
175,000 years?*

As I have said, the individual is now in a new life, still within
the system, and is partaking of the interactions of beings that are
now within the light in those systems.

So he did not leave as we did?

No, he stayed to form an anchor and a foundation in many lives paralleling your own. Then there would be someone to receive the communication that you have learned you are sending back there—so that there could be growth in the Orion systems paralleling your own growth.

In which density were those individuals in the Orion system 175,000 years ago?

Third.

And what density are they in now?

Like you, third/transitional fourth.

So they are actually paralleling what we're doing?

Yes.

What did he mean by "he'd lose his life"?

Communication outside of that which is recognized within the mass consciousness of those systems is not allowed, and is punishable by death.

When you say "no light within the system," can you give us an actual description of what you mean by that?

The idea of systems suppressing its populace. Governments of suppression. All interaction being that which dominates, seeking only to dominate others. The only authority that has any say on anything within those systems is within the hierarchy that is set up. There is not even a remote idea of assuming that working together will achieve anything. The idea is that there are a few under which all shall work, and they work only for the gratification of those few. The majority of those being suppressed do not even have within them the belief that they are being suppressed for any particular reason that is going to benefit them.

Since Neamon was third density, and he was speaking as a priest, was he conscious of what he was doing or was he in a dream state?

Conscious. Again: allowed and assisted to be put into a trance-like state, a daydream state, but still very aware of what was going on.

So he had somebody with him.

Yes. . . . Me. I am the one to whom he was referring as the Commander.

Oh, I know that. But I thought you had gone there and left, and he then transmitted the message.

I would not do that to him.

A Message to Yourselves

Would it endanger Neamon's current existence, that which parallels our existence right now, for any of us to communicate with him at this time?

No, for he is within the light, and this is now an opportunity that is open.

If he's existing in present time, why or how, or for what purpose was there communication from 175,000 years ago?

It is not clear because you are not connected to that series of events as some other individuals here are.

Okay. Then perhaps you could explain, or just put into some kind of understandable framework for me, why this came through at this time.

Because now is the timing for the recognition and the opening of areas and doorways within certain individuals. It is the timing for receiving the message many of you sent to yourselves so very long ago.

I see. Then I would like to communicate gratitude and an understanding of the profundity of his love to agree to do what you said.

I have already done so.

I did not have any conscious recognition of this message, but I had a sense that on other levels this was really powerful. I'm not certain, though. How would I know?

You have recognized it according to whatever level you are functioning within for now. The way in which you have recognized it at this point is as much recognition as you need for now. For we do not want it to interfere in the path you have chosen to be, nor to stop you from what you are more natural at doing. Recognize that that being turned out just fine. Your willingness to be who and what you are, and where and when you are, has been what has assisted him, and now he knows that.

The Religious Connection

Bashar, would you trace with me the experience I had with the Ward Gospel Singers at Disneyland—the phrase they sang, "Lord come down and he say to Noah, Meshach, Shadrach and Abednego . . ." This is a point of integration there where many factors came together. What was the historical origin of that phrase— connected to that group?

A strong exemplification of the remembrance, although only subconsciously, of Orion understandings, Orion connections in your Middle East. But it is very ancient.

Why did they pick it up biblically? What's the traceline that came through this culture on that phrase, "The Lord come down and he said—"?

Again, connections, to some degree, with the original Orion energy. A direct connection, and a recognition in whatever way was translatable. Do recognize that there is, even within your Commandments, some Orion influence. You see, to speak pragmatically in your terms, what you call God does not contain the phrase "Thou shalt *not*" in Its vocabulary. The ideas that were being communicated —from higher consciousness to your level of consciousness— were understood but interpreted through the Orion framework. That was one of the things your early society was all about—the fresh inclusion of the Orion energy so that it could be balanced in your society now, thus allowing everyone to recognize the balance of energy within themselves. And then you would all know that the power is within you, and not within another individual outside of you.

The whole Orion idea was all about domination, control, servitude, slavery—the old Orion idea. Many systems were instituted on your planet, such as some of the religious organizations, that were created **by** Orions **for** Orions, in order for them to continue experiencing —and then to finally understand and integrate— the polarities of the Earth systems and the polarities of their earlier home systems. This is allowing them to assimilate the idea of the Earth's vibration in ways that were similar to how they assimilated and understood the original Orion vibrations to be.

This does not mean that other organizations, and indeed individuals, have not also used these early Orion ideas to institute ideas and practices of various sorts. For instance, much of the idea of analysis on your planet stems from the original Orion filtering of ideas. Therefore, to some degree the very way in which many individuals perceive the concept of science in and of itself stems as a trickle-down effect from an original Orion vibration. Particularly is this true for the high focus of your awareness on analytical methods and practices.

Orion Involvement

Bashar, if I understand you, Orions are involved a great deal in what's going on here at this time.

To some degree, yes. There has been the ability for the blending of light in the Orion systems for quite some time, so there is *your* involvement with many of them there as well.

So if I've gotten this right, then the Orion energy has a strong orientation toward growth through negativity?

That was the old Orion idea, yes. Recognize that many Orions incarnated on your Earth plane to begin with to set up real time scenarios that would allow themselves to get in touch with the old momentum, and explore phases of it that would allow them to begin to blend it.

I don't quite follow that.

The idea of the older systems —basically represented in the old Orion methodologies— was to explore the realms of negativity that had been paramount in those systems long ago. The idea now, in being born within your Earth system, is to, let us say, regurgitate all of that and bring it up to the surface. You can now balance it with the understanding that all of it no longer need apply—since many changes have occurred within the original Orion system. Now you can recognize that you have sent that energy to them through all the reincarnational cycles you have

228 Δ BASHAR: BLUEPRINT FOR CHANGE

experienced on this planet as Orion consciousness, and you can also receive from them what you have allowed them to become in *their* blended polarity idea.

Individuals who are connected to that energy in specific ways can now know that within themselves is all the opportunity for all the balance and all the acceleration they desire from this point forward. For you can now know that "the road is clear." That energy is now completely and utterly connected back to the original system—to create a balance within that system, and to crystallize into a positive reality.

The Dark Side

Bashar, my understanding is that some of those space beings, such as those connected to the dark side of Orion, are hostile to Earth and Earthlings.

We will discuss this idea with you if you will first understand that the idea of any consciousness which could be said to be negatively oriented can only form connections with individuals who believe that those supposedly negative individuals have the power to force connections of that nature upon them. In other words, only your fear and concern that they may have that type of power will actually give them the power necessary to form a link with anyone in your civilization. Otherwise just recognize that there are many so-called negative individuals and negative consciousnesses in many other worlds, just as there are many negatively-oriented individuals on your own planet.

It does not mean that they *must* interact with you. And if you are willing to be the vibration, the frequency, and the attitude of the perspective of the reality you choose to be, then they will not be able to intercept your reality. Recognize that the primary idea of negativity is not specifically isolated to the constellation you refer to as Orion; it does involve many other systems throughout the local galaxy.

As we have said, many of the individuals on your planet now are literally reincarnated Orions, and they have formed a connection to that origin point, so to speak, reincarnating upon Earth

to allow themselves to learn the balance of the positive and negative polarities so that they can create only positive manifestation
in their lives. They can switch themselves to a frequency that is
out of reach of the former negativity that was inherent in the original parent systems of the Orion area.

You will find that time and space being what they are, and all
things being simultaneous, some of these original Orion negative
consciousnesses still have the ability to be picked up on by whichever individuals on your planet may still choose to function along
the same old style frequency—time and space not being a barrier
to the idea of telepathic contact on any level.

However, it is also important to recognize that many of the
individuals of the Orion influence, or "persuasion," have been,
and are now, allowing themselves to crystallize into a very balanced idea of polarity. In the original home systems that energy
in turn has allowed them to now be the creation and existence of
light as well as negativity.

Therefore, it would be our advice and our suggestion to you
that you simply do not focus on the idea that there are negative
beings who exist in the universe —other than those who exist on
your own planet— that could perhaps interact with you against
your will, and focus on the reality you choose to be. Then, by the
fact that you will be on a different frequency, this will place you
completely beyond the reach of anyone who is not on the same
loving frequency.

Finding the Balance

We would like you to realize that there is a particularity within
the agreement we have made to be of service to your planet at this
time—to reflect and represent some of the original choices and
agreements that were made specifically within the Orion system.
For we are geared to allowing that original Orion energy, some
of which has been steeped in negativity, to find its fulcrum, to find
its balance, within the understanding of the triad structure of all
creation—the polarity and the third point of balance that allows
there to be transformation and change. The whole idea, in this

blending and balancing, is to always truly understand that as soon as you do with integrity the thing that excites you the most, that is when you will be allowing for the strongest blending of the polarities to take place within you.

The idea that we wish to share, and that our service automatically attracts, is the opportunity to reflect back to each and every individual who is dealing with that particular connection that the control is always within you, as to some degree you have already discovered for yourselves. The attraction and the drawing together functions as a reflection of various things, many of which you have already begun to integrate. This is just so that we can function as a marker for individuals—to allow them to know they are keeping the agreements they have made and can continue to accelerate those agreements by doing those things which excite them.

Again we thank you for your willingness to allow us to reflect to you the idea of the reality you are choosing to create upon your Earth in this transformational age. Now you know there is no longer any reason to have to feel you must struggle and create conflict in order to create the realities and the harmonies you desire in your world. We rejoice greatly in seeing that *you are now creating light on your world, and that light has reflected all the way to Orion.*

CHAPTER THIRTEEN

Friends and Neighbors

Who is the Alien?

Let us begin by speaking about the concepts you have held on your planet regarding what you colloquially call extraterrestrials. Even before that, however, from another point of view allow us to delineate a time when we first discovered a civilization, one that had a life form upon it that was, to use our term, Essassani-ish. But instead of our average height of 5 feet, they ranged on an average from 5 to 6-1/2 feet. Whereas we exhibit generally overall white/whitish-gray skin color, this civilization exhibited a wide range of colors. . . . Well, are you all catching on so far?

(Yes!)

All right. This is to give you the perspective that, considered from other points of view, you yourselves are the aliens. Your world to many other civilizations is unknown, different, unusual, unique in many ways. There really is no need when considering us, or any other civilization, to think any more highly of us than you are willing to think of yourselves—for you are unique and different in your own way. You are just as valid an expression of a form of life as any other form of life that has chosen to express itself—in physical reality or in any other level of consciousness.

You are an alien civilization to us; we are an alien civilization to you. But on other levels we are the same. The way we choose to express that sameness is what creates the different societies; and it is that sameness that allows us the opportunity to create different expressions. It is because we all draw from the same source of Infinite Creation; it is because we are all the same type of soul, if you will, that we allow ourselves the opportunity to express our-selves in such a broad, diversified range of experience and life.

Many of your years ago, any time your culture even thought of the idea of an extraterrestrial, you usually designed your aware-ness regarding what these extraterrestrials looked like to be some-thing quite different from your own human physical form. And from what we have observed, since you imbued in these non-human physical forms typically a certain degree of malevolence toward your society, you thus created these extraterrestrial forms to be terrorizing things. Now that you are beginning to change your attitudes and ideas about how other life forms can be experi-enced and possibly be encountered by you, you are beginning to think more in terms of your own human form. You have discov-ered that many of the interactions and contacts that have taken place more often than not seem to involve extraterrestrials who are human-ish, or humanoid in form.

There may be many individuals who say, "Well, why should this be so? Just because we might now think that extraterrestri-als may be friendly, as opposed to possessing a desire to consume us, does not necessarily mean that they must appear in humanoid form." And this is so. The reason basically why you are coming closer and closer to the reality wherein you can interact with ex-traterrestrial consciousness; the reason why you are now seeing many of these contacts take place between your form and forms that are not truly very dissimilar to your own, is because of the nature of reality, the nature of the universe.

As we have discussed, everything is the product of different rates of frequency, and it is those different frequencies that deter-mine the material constructs designed and created out of the pri-mal energy. Therefore recognize that when any other civilizations —at least among the majority we have encountered— first begin to venture into space, first begin to realize that they may in fact encounter other forms of life, they usually at first encounter and attract those forms operating closest to their own frequency. And thus by definition those attracted usually reflect a similar physi-cal structure.

This is not to say that there are not life forms throughout the galaxies and the multiverses that are very different from you and me in physiological form. It is simply that at first you allow yourselves to encounter that with which you are most familiar, so you can "get your feet wet" without startling yourselves too much. If you were to encounter something extremely different from you, many of you could, out of the old habits, recoil back into the idea that it might want to eat you. Or vice versa.

But recognize that if you *are* open to interaction, and the more open you become and the more you use your heart as a sensor, you will realize that there are many different ways consciousness can express itself as a physiological form and still radiate deep love and integrity. The more open you become and the more you explore all the different ranges of frequencies in which life can exist, the more you will begin to encounter many of these other variations upon your theme. There will be life forms that in no way are based upon any ideas you are familiar with at all—so much so that you may not even recognize them for what they are when you see them. But encounter them eventually you will, as you expand your sphere of understanding and your sphere of consciousness.

Do not forget there are many civilizations that are expanding in a similar manner; you will not be the last to "arrive." There are civilizations that will take many thousands of your years to arrive at places you were at thousands of your years ago. Perhaps if you are willing, you will be *their* UFOs; you will be the ones who bring them the understanding that no matter in what way their consciousness has chosen to express itself, that consciousness, being a part of the Infinite Creation, always has the opportunity to create whatever realities they are creating in whatever way they wish them to be.

Barnard

Now, it is our perception that when you begin to explore and interact with other worlds, much in the same way we are interacting with you now, one of the first civilizations you will begin to interact with —in fact, you have already begun to interact with them in your dream levels— is a civilization that is in the Barnard star cluster, as you name it.

On one of those worlds is a civilization not unlike your own, evolutionarily speaking, that is approximately where you were in your Renaissance period—as far as your technology is concerned. They are already aware of some of the communications you have had as a society with them on the dream level. You will find that some of you are actually channeling through some of the members of that society at times. In their civilization they do not label the different names, or different channels, as different things; they see it all as one phenomenon. They do not segregate it out into different entities; it is all the same level to them.

In time then, as you expand you will begin to interact with them in ways similar to how we have interacted with you. Thus if you become their UFOs, in time you can blend and assist them in their transformations somewhat as we have been assisting you up until now.

Brief Encounters

Another civilization, unlike yours in certain ways, goes by the label of *Irax*. These Irax have placed on themselves a very fascinating limitation. Their facial structures are almost completely bony, and they are incapable of expressing any emotionality on those faces whatsoever. Their feelings must be expressed in completely different ways. They are of a creamy whitish-yellow coloration, with waxy-textured skin.

Also there is a civilization very unlike yours that operates on a completely different dimensional plane, one that would best translate into the idea of the *Dilla.* Now, the Dilla beings operate in a completely non-physical sense, and yet in your perception they do have a physicality. In a sense they are extremely classic in their nature. Having no real discernible features, they can take almost any form they wish, as they are of a completely primal dimensional state—not really physical as you understand it. But one of their prime "exports" is a sense of humor.

They are of a very, very light vibration, and their world is very simplified. You would likely perceive it as a smooth sphere, with no surface features. These do not need to exist until they are required; then they are literally drawn from the surface to form many different things. The Dilla themselves can merge with the very substance of their world, being of a very plastic, molten state. The way you would perceive them physically would be through almost nothing but primary colors, as you would actually be seeing them as having a plastic-like physical nature. They can mimic your form, but that would not be their natural form. In a sense, they do not really have a form, except perhaps what you could define as a very flattened oblate spheroid shape in a state of rest. . . . However, they do not really rest.

Closer at hand, a civilization that has been interacting with your society of late is that of the Pleiadians. They are very much like you—in other words, humanish, primarily because many of you are from the same offshoots. They are literally your brothers, sisters, and cousins, and you are now rejoining many of them—literally rejoining members of your family. The Pleiadians, along with the Orions, are offshoots from an earlier system called Lyra, these having split from Lyra long ago as you count physical time. They formed into polarity systems, Orion exploring the negative existence, and the Pleiadians the positive.

Another society is that from the star system you call Zeta Reticulum. These Reticuli are very short beings with large black eyes, very pale skin and enlarged heads. They are most representative of the interactions you have labeled the abduction phenomena. These beings will be discussed more later on.

Dal Universe

Bashar, I'd like to ask you about the Dal Universe. I've been having some exchanges of energy with them, and I'm finding that they're quite different from what I've experienced before. Could you tell me more about that universe?

Yes. We cannot necessarily go much into other universal realities at this time, however. Let us just say that they function as an automatic on and off switch to regulate some of the functions taking place in terms of exchange of energy in your physiological universe. They are like a monitoring energy.

I do notice that when they show up, the Pleiadians, who are pretty headstrong, get quiet real fast.

No need to look at it that way. You are putting it back into a melodramatic framework. That is an Earth interpretation of what is going on in terms of the exchange of energy, and is not necessarily literally representative of what is actually taking place.

Okay. Are they physical like us?

They can represent themselves that way. But ultimately not really.

They're like this gaseous energy cloud?

Well, in a sense—energy beings, yes. You might interpret the idea as gaseous in your reality, but that also would only be an interpretation. It might be more easily understood as etheric.

Is the etheric fragile? Can it be broken into parts?

Well, in a sense, we "break it" all the time in order to interact with you, because in many ways we are also etheric. However, in our reality, according to our thoughts and beliefs, it re-physicalizes and goes back together.

All right. So are the Dals just totally from another reality?

To some degree, another dimensional plane altogether. Ninety degrees of a vector to those dimensional planes that you and I would call physiologically real. They are a vector universe.

How did they get here?

Through the idea of phase shifting—just as *we* come into your universe. The idea of changing your vibratory frequency to match that of the universe in question of visitation, and to project a portion of their consciousness in whatever way seems to be most necessary to represent their presence. Their presence, as you perceive it, is not even the totality of their beingness. It is in a sense but a finger—to use an analogy.

Do they have ships?

Not as you understand it, no. They do have cohesive electromagnetic consciousness that sometimes you may perceive as ships.

Or more often then not, you would choose to perceive them as merely spheres of light in your reality.

Arcturus

Arcturus represents the gate of energy through which communication from other dimensions of experience is funneled into your dimension of experience. They are the regulating gate. It doesn't mean that things are being regulated in a very structured sense, but only that they are the translators of energy from other dimensions into your dimension, into symbols you can understand. Much of the emanation of energy, of the dissemination of energy, and the regulation of the transformational rate going on on your planet, and many other planets within your galactic system, is under the auspices of the Arcturus gate.

They are also responsible for creating a particular type of energy alignment through which many of your children now being born are passing before birth—so they will forget less of who they are once they are born into your society. In that sense, they have connections into what you call the angelic realm, and therefore are represented by a lot of non-physiological consciousness as well. Some of this is an aspect of Pleiadian energy, but a lot of it represents aspects of extra-dimensional energy as it is symbolized in your material reality.

I recently channeled an energy, Bashar, that seemed to be coming through Boötes, through Arcturus. They talked about the children with a tremendous amount of emotionality.

Yes, that is the core vibration that allows you to know that you are linking with that energy, specifically within your reality at this time—the emotional core vibration. For it is an opening and a crystallization at the same time of certain doorways within you that are connected to that heart energy, and to the energy of the chakra of your intention in the solar plexus. It will create the heaving and the releasing, the assimilation and blending of energy simultaneously. For it is that atmosphere into which the children are being born. *Do recognize that the children arriving at present are not just another generation; they are another culture.*

I feel as though I am going to be a bridge and I will channel that energy through. But what was really fascinating to me was that the energy seemed to be the consciousness of the planet.

Yes! It is a collective.

And it was as though it was being relayed through that constellation area, through the Arcturean energy, before it got to me. I was wondering why that was. The only reason I could think of was that it was so intense, I may not have been able to handle it.

Yes, on many different levels. In order for you to be able to assimilate it comfortably beyond the experience of your physiological universe, it must come through a physiological valve, or representational symbol to which you can relate —to which you have already formed a degree of relationship— so it will also carry with it a degree of familiarity by the time you receive it.

Yes, that's true. I know I felt like there was more emotionality there than I could handle for very long at that time. But I did see a vision, or in my mind I guess, a brilliant, brilliant star—which was behind this being who I think was a teacher.

This is a representation of the other levels we are speaking about. Arcturus represents the *combined* triad of Earth, Essassani and Sirius on another level altogether.

Does the star —the brilliance or the consciousness of it— seem to be what we're going to be, what this civilization, or this planet's consciousness, is going to be?

In a sense, yes. You will be dealing with it in that way, and you will become immersed in the association of that nurturing, supporting vibration, that loving vibration.

Arcturean Symbol

From my perspective there is a lot of attention on the Arcturean people, the experience. Just to help me spark additional things, would you describe Arcturus and its experiences and such?

In regard to the level with which we are dealing at this time, the only description we can share with you is what has already been shared—that they are a collective energy consciousness. There is nothing that would allow us to differentiate them in the sense of individuals, as you would understand it. We can give you a symbol, however. It is only a symbol, and not something to get attached to, but it may function as a focal point. It is a twelve-pointed white star on an orange-background circle on a background of black. That symbol can represent their energy and act as a communicative link, or an identifying link, to the vibration of their energy, on whatever level you need to identify with them.

Is Arcturus physically perceived as a star, but on a different level?

Yes. There is consciousness associated with that energy phenomenon in your physiological reality. It is the energy and the consciousness associated with that particular star to which we are referring as Arcturus energy, Arcturus consciousness.

I met the Arctureans personally, and they were very familiar to me.

Yes. Do recognize that from our point of view what those individuals represent is a strong identification with that vibratory energy. On the level you are speaking of in terms of Arcturus energy, it is not so much that the energy actually, literally embodies itself, but that it forms an identification projection.

Isn't that the way it generally works anyway?

Yes. We are simply rearranging the symbols by which your society usually refers to it.

More Triads

I was wondering if you could articulate a little more on the Arcturus energy being on a different level from the triad.

We can put it briefly that your planet, our civilization, and the civilization of Sirius together combine for one consciousness, as well as, and apart from, the three distinct civilizations within it. And that one consciousness finds itself being one part of an overall triad, of which Arcturus is also one of the overall consciousnesses. The other third besides our triad is Polaris.

What's our name—the combined idea?

It can be generally referred to as any one of the names that represent the overall collective consciousness within each and

every civilization. Thus for Sirius it would be Siskeen, and for us,
Shakana. For you it is the Christ consciousness. In general any
alignment with Arcturus is simply a representation of another
threshold and a doorway that you are going through. You will
find that in your cosmology your move specifically represents
many of the ideas of your sub- and unconscious awareness now
coming to the surface. Also your Pluto alignment is generally
representative of the transformation across a threshold that you
previously would have considered to be the idea you call death—
but which now represents a transformation into a new type of life.

*I understand the concept, but could you give us an example
of the threshold?*

The threshold we are referring to is the transformation taking
place on your planet from third to fourth density. That is the
overall threshold. Every single symbol within your reality that has
any relationship to transformation is all generally a part of that.
The specifics are up to you to determine for yourselves, although
as we have said, the idea of your move does to some degree represent the idea of your subconscious and unconscious awareness
coming to the surface. The idea of Pluto is the actual *journey*
involved across the threshold itself.

In this same archetypical manner you have described the myth
you call the crossing of the River Styx. This puts you in touch
with what you previously assumed to be the darker regions of
your consciousness. It is another way of saying that you enter the
blending of your positive and negative polarities, and therefore
allow yourselves, in the crossing of that threshold, to glean only
a positive effect out of the blending of the positive and the negative. This is why you have intuitively labeled Pluto's moon with
the same name as the ferryboat driver that drives you across the
mythological river Styx . . . Charon.

*When you talk about this triad, you don't mention Spica. And
I always assumed that Spica is very connected to Arcturus.*

It is in other ways. The idea is that just as this triad is unto
itself a triad, and its *whole* energy represents one of the triads
relative to Arcturus and Polaris, then the idea you call Spica is

one of the fragments that allows Arcturus itself to also be a whole idea. In ways similar to how Sirius, our civilization, and your civilization form a collective whole, Arcturus is the combination of the idea of Spica and other consciousnesses to form *its* collective whole. Are you following me?

I'm trying to.

It is very simple. You have, let us say, Sirius, Earth and Essassani. Those three form one triangle. The energy you are perceiving from Arcturus—that is another triangle; Polaris is another one. So each one of those respectively has three components within it, and together the three triangles form another whole consciousness that is also a part of another triad yet again. And on and on and on goes the pattern.

Yah, I've heard something about how we're moving very close in the direction of Polaris.

Yes. Again, that is because like Arcturus, it is one of the major constituents of the overall consciousness triad that is represented by the main group. As Arcturus represents the emotional side, and as Earth, Essassani and Sirius represent generally a collective idea of mentality, in a certain way Polaris (by your instinctive name) represents the idea of the polarities that you are now blending together—positive energy and negative energy in and of itself.

Thus, as you are now forming an integration, and making positive and negative into one reality, so are you deriving a degree of physiological affinity in the direction of Polaris, because that is your indicator. It is the indicator of the theme in your integration—the blending of the polarities.

Moons and Planets

Around Pluto, Bashar, is that a moon or another planet?

As the definition of a moon is any body that orbits a central body, then by that definition it is a moon, and smaller than the planet of Pluto. Your society is just beginning to discover some very interesting things about that binary system, one of them being the very fine, fine atmosphere that exists upon Pluto, although it is not an atmosphere as you understand it—one that you could breathe. That fine atmosphere can extend out so far, it actually envelops Charon.

You will begin to discover something else you have not seen yet: there is an actual electrical potential between the two, and so there is a great deal of electrical arcing that goes on between the body of Pluto and the body of Charon at particular times of alignment within your solar system—when there is a build-up of ionic charge between that binary pair.

And are there any other moons around Pluto?

There is other debris, but not anything of the magnitude of Charon.

Okay. Then in our solar system, other than Earth is there any other life in the third dimension that we might discover?

Not exactly. Certain compounds will be discovered in time, remnants within certain areas of Mars, conglomerates of molecules within several of your gas giant planets—Jupiter, Saturn, Uranus and Neptune. These will be primordial forms of organic life, but they will lend you clues toward understanding what you as a mass consciousness utilized to create many of the ideas of life forms upon your Earth. In time there will be seen to be interactions with other levels of consciousness, but in your third-dimensional state, no. There is inhabitation, to use the term loosely, on every single planet in your system, but not in the third dimension.

More Cover-Up

Is there life on Mars, Bashar?

Not in your third density.

Fourth or fifth density?

Fourth, yes.

How about the moon—any life in another density?

In our perception there is life on that body in an alternate reality altogether, but that body is not in any way in your dimension at all. Only in that reality do I immediately perceive the life you are asking about; it is not barren in that dimension. However, in your third-dimensional reality, yes, it is barren on your moon. There are artificial bases, but not what you call natural life.

There are artificial bases on the moon in our density?

Yes.

Constructed by whom?

By other civilizations, not of your Earth.

And not of the moon?

No.

Inhabited? And they were not found by—?

Yes, they were.

They were found by the astronauts, and the information was suppressed?!?

Yes.

Aha! Are they inhabited now?

Some. A few. Not as many as in earlier times.

Physically, right now, there are aliens on the moon?

Physically, right now, yes.

And this information was suppressed as a result of an inability of the astronauts to comprehend what they were observing?

Oh, no, no, no, no.

They knew what they were observing?

Oh, yes.

And the information was transmitted back to space command center, NASA or whatever?

Yes.

And now authorities on Earth have prevented the information from becoming public for what purpose?

You do not know? Do you not understand the structure you have created your government to be? Have you not realized that their understanding is that unless they are controlling, they are not in power?

One of the strongest ideas of power in your civilization is information. The idea of allowing your civilization to recognize that your government does not need to rule you, that the universe is open to all to explore, would take away their power in their eyes—although in fact it would actually give them their power as individuals. But they do not understand this, because that is not what you have all created them to be.

244 △ BASHAR: BLUEPRINT FOR CHANGE

Yes, I understand that, but what I don't understand is their thought process: thinking that by keeping this information secret it increases their control.

Because, as I just said: if you are aware, as you are right now, that the ability to interact with other beings on equal levels would bring with it no more need to have your responsibility removed from you and institutionalized, then there is no purpose that they serve. They believe that power lies only in controlling others.

Now, did the astronauts have some interaction with these other beings on the moon?

Not while in space, no, nor while on your moon—not beyond photographing and visually seeing. There has been face-to-face interaction on your Earth on many occasions—with your military and your government, as we have often said.

Why did the aliens choose to have an interaction with those people, as opposed to others?

Because you have allowed them to be the ones that *have* to be met first. The idea is that by allowing that interaction to take place, then perhaps there is the ability for them to choose to realize that there is nothing to fear. And they can hang up their fear hats. You have entrusted them with power over you.

Some of us have, yes.

Some, yes. Enough of you have—and we do not differentiate. However, since not all of you have, there is some interaction with individuals within your society as well from time to time—individuals who are not of your governmental structure.

But again, the frequency with which that happens will be completely dependent upon, 1) your willingness to recognize that you *are* your governments, and 2) your willingness to take back your responsibility—not by opposing them, but by loving them, letting yourselves function on equal levels with them, and vice versa, so you can share the idea that you all run your world. They do not have to run it for you, in the sense of controlling what you know about it. They can run it *with* you. And if they choose to perform an organizational service, then they will be *serving* you, not controlling you.

Right. That was the essence, the kernel, of what the founding fathers attempted to do with the United States.

Yes, in a sense, although you were never meant to have a democracy; it was designed as a republic.

Our Defense

Does the Star Wars program have, as part of its rationale, interaction with these other civilizations?

In a sense there is a great deal of fear about what is perceived to be the loss of power. Do understand, however, that your defense program is not all it seems to be. A large portion of that idea is only for the purpose of allowing you to think you need protection, so they will stay in power.

Let us emphasize again: they already understand, in no uncertain terms, that we and other civilizations are not going to interfere. They know! In a sense they are scrambling for a foothold, because they understand that it will inevitably change. They are attempting to establish, only in ways they allow themselves to understand, that once your Earth opens up to the possibility of interaction with other civilizations, they will still want to be the representatives. They will still want to say, "Look! Look at me. I am the most powerful one here. Deal with me."

They do not understand. In all they have been offered by us, in our communications, they still do not understand—not in the way we mean it. Meaning that empowerment is the right of all. They do not believe that you can all run your own lives. They will only understand the idea of each and every one of you creating your own reality in terms of anarchy and chaos. They do not understand synchronicity and ecstatic explosion of coincidence . . . and trust. Trust in the higher consciousness, in their future selves; functioning from integrity, integration, in the idealized state.

Sirius

Another civilization, composed of both semi-physiological and completely non-physiological beings, is a civilization orbiting the star called Sirius. Sirius is at the peak of our triad and represents the further step in the evolution we are going through on Essassani and you are going through on Earth—and which both of us will accomplish in time.

The level of consciousness from Sirius that is mostly in contact with your world is the non-physical sixth-density level of consciousness that goes by the name of Siskeen. These beings have been in telepathic communication with members of your society for quite some time, and are responsible for some of the mythological manifestations in your perception of the amphibious gods —those from your Sumerian cultures, some of your African tribal cultures and your American Indian recognitions.

Although they do have a semi-physical counterpart that to some degree is physiologically amphibious, you have perceived them as amphibious beings because they exist in an energy sea. One of the reasons for this particular manifestation being very strongly connected to your planet also has to do with the fact that as we scan your Earth, we find that there is not one, but two alien civilizations on your planet: land humans and water cetaceans. Dolphins and whales are thinking, self-incarnating, self-aware souls like yourselves. They are not animals, as you classify them in that sense.

So do recognize that your planet is blessed with two civilizations that can work side by side and learn to love one another and grow in creativity. They have already begun to assist you by entering your dream states and teaching you how to play in spontaneous ecstasy. Go to them; share with them. They love you. Because of their environment, they have been in telepathic communication with many different civilizations off your planet for quite some time. They have an especially strong connection with the Sirius civilization, since they have much in common as a consciousness, and are telepathic.

Whales are to some degree the embodiment in physical terms of the higher consciousness of the dolphin. You simply do not have a physiological manifestation of your higher consciousness, because the gravity of your world would not support it. So it is up to you to be both the manifestation of the individual consciousness and the higher consciousness itself. Usually you relegate the higher consciousness into non-physical whereas the higher consciousness of the dolphin can manifest physically as the whale because of the buoyant environment of your ocean. But they are there to assist you, to love you. When you blend as one society, that will also make it easier for you to interact with other whole societies.

So now look at this sparkling opportunity you have created. You do not have to go anywhere to interact with an alien civilization; you have one in your own various oceans. Learn to communicate with them and they will teach you much about the way you will be communicating with all other civilizations you will encounter.

Three Levels

Something that we have not completely discussed before in specific detail is that Sirius has interacted with your civilization from many different levels. For in the past they have had a more physiological counterpart that to some degree interacted with some of you from time to time in your past cultures—not only telepathically, but somewhat physiologically.

We discussed with you once that as yours is the third planet from your sun, so is our world Essassani the third planet from our sun. We have also said that the planet that is represented by the Sirius consciousness is also in a sense third from their sun, but not third in the same way—not spatially, dimensionally. For there are three levels of the civilization of Sirius—one fourth density, one fifth density, and one that you may be most familiar with through these interactions, the sixth density level of Siskeen. Here they are totally non-physical beings, as you would understand physicality, and exist more or less in an energy state, an energy sea.

Their ancient fourth-density representative selves were to some degree amphibious, as perceived by many of your ancient cultures. But not exactly to the degree that they were described in the ancient American Indian, African and Sumerian lore. They were not literally half fish as these cultures have understood and represented them.

Among many other reasons, this is why there is such a strong state of identification between the Sirius civilization and the civilization on your planet you call the dolphins and the whales, and why they have been in telepathic communication for many thousands of your years. They are similar in energy format in many ways. While the physiological configuration of the old fourth-density Sirius civilization was not like your dolphin and whale civilization, their energy was sufficient to cause a camaraderie, an empathy, an identification to take place. And so their communications have been ongoing for quite some time, even while the land human civilization on your planet has been waking up from its deep sleep of forgetfulness.

Those interactions that took place here and there are to some degree responsible for some of the representations of cultural, religious, political, and economic ideas that manifested and blossomed on your planet. We do not wish to impart the impression that extraterrestrials are completely responsible for the entire idea of your cultural or sociological phenomena. No. But some interaction has taken place and has created changes in the course of how you view events as a society.

Because none of you are original to your planet anyway, you all have connections of a sort to other dimensions, other levels of existence that were established from time to time in various other modalities. As the Sirius civilization progressed and accelerated, in your terms evolution took place—while changing from their fourth-density state into the more quasi-physical, non-physical fifth-density state, and then into a completely non-physical sixth-density life, as we have said. But to some degree, because in a sense all realities exist at the same time, all interactions on all levels are still taking place, especially because in your civilization you are still awakening out of third density into your own fourth-density manifestation.

The Sirius society does somewhat represent our own higher consciousness. They are representative of the evolution our civilization is most directly headed for, as we move into the idea of fifth density from our fourth-density existence, the last stage of physicality. As you move into that last stage of fourth-density physicality, you will eventually in a sense take our place in the triad. We will then be at the peak of the triad, as Sirius moves on to another idea altogether. And then another civilization will fill your shoes in our triad. As we have said, most likely this will be the civilization in the Barnard star cluster.

The Sirius civilization is very much in an energy sea; they are in a state of complete consciousness. If you wish any kind of a representation of their world as such, we can give this physiological analogy that you can perhaps relate to: imagine a ball of clear light, clear energy on the surface. As you sink slowly into it, it becomes a white, white, white energy. As you go more toward the center, it then condenses and collapses into a bright electric blue, electromagnetic energy. And at the very center is what you could typically call a black hole gate.

This idea of their existence, existing as energy forms in an energy sea, allows them to either project themselves telepathically as individuals or as one homogenous energy, one homogenous consciousness. To some degree it can be said, technically speaking, that they do this projection and communication with other civilizations through that black hole gate at the very center of their world. It is an interdimensional gate that links to all levels, all dimensions, and through which they can communicate in either direction—with any level, any dimension. Thus this gate now has allowed them to step up their ability to communicate with many of you, now that you as a civilization have stepped up your ability to receive the idea of higher vibrations.

Let me remind you once again that biological life is the most efficient transmitter and receiver. As each one of you, in your own way, in your own time, decide to open yourselves up to more expressiveness of the consciousness you are, more recognition and expressiveness of the frequency you are, you will become more sensitized to the frequency in which they are always bathing . . . and beaming to your world from. They are always sending an unbroken radiation of unconditional love and energy, thought forms and thought patterns for you to tap into.

Let's Get Sirius

In your terms of counting, the star you call Sirius is approximately ten of your light years away. In your physical dimension it takes ten of your years, ten of your orbits, for a beam of light to reach from your star to their star, from their star to your star. But understand that the telepathic link is instantaneous, that the black hole gate circumvents physiological space, connects all dimensions in the immediate here and now. And through that gate it is as if they literally overlap you, or intertwine with you. Even in much the same way that we, and all civilizations and all dimensions, are intertwined holographically with each other.

Each and every being has that same central gate, that same central black hole through which you can receive and send any idea, any information, creating any interaction you desire. When you are in an energized, balanced, relaxed and ecstatic state, you can always be aware of all the frequencies, all the spectrum of energy and information that is always available for any of you to ride the crests of that wave—always.

Identification with their very high energy can assist in your acceleration, although it is not that they are doing it for you. You must meet them half way. In a sense, that is where we come in, for we are to some degree representative of the half-way vibration between you and them. We are the band of consciousness, of electromagnetic energy that represents what you are to some degree becoming, what you are headed for in your civilization. By allowing identification to take place between our civilizations, we are somewhat reflecting to you your own self-chosen future. Not that it will be specifically as we have chosen to express our civilization, for you will create your own version of it. But the energy, the patterns, the identification, will be very similar.

Then once again, as you move to the stars, open to the stars, you will literally be flowing, sliding on star light, using light itself for all you need —all your power, all your understanding— recognizing that light is the matrix in which all the information you need is intertwined and interlocked. When you open that light, by shining as a brilliant star yourselves, you will then match the frequency of all of Creation's life, and know everything you need to know right now, as you are.

You *are* made of light. So when you lighten up and aren't so "serious," then you too will reflect the Sirius nature—their consciousness and your own higher selves and fuller selves. We thank you for having such an interesting language to play around with.

Star Child

Bashar, you said none of us are original to this planet. Could you tell me if I am what you would call a star child?

Oh, in a sense all of you are, you know. The term *star child* that you use in your society is generally an indication of a conscious recognition of some of these connections you all have—that may, for some particular reason in this particular life, stand out more than other connections might. So in that sense, if you feel so drawn to that idea, then obviously you are choosing to express yourself in that way.

I was just saying, for lack of better words, that I believe there is some sort of a race that I belong to—

Yes, I understand. But you see, the idea is that all of you have those connections. Different connections stand out in different lives, depending on what you have created this particular life to be. In other lives you may have felt other connections, and *that* you can determine in each and every *present* in which you create yourself to exist, because you are connected to all of them. In a sense, you all come from everywhere and nowhere. As a spirit you don't really have any particular point of origin. But you can make those connections, and they can feel like true connections.

Yes. Well, how can I contact the others who are like me? I feel so different from everyone.

All right. Now, please do me a favor: take your physical form and turn it approximately 30 degrees . . . What do you see?

(Turning to look at about 200 people.) A lot of people.

Say, "Hi."

Hi.

(Audience response: HI!!)

Well? What do you think they are? They think as you do in many ways. There are many individuals who know as you do, who sense as you do. Remember, it is a very common thing, now that you are all awakening on your world, to recognize more of the other connections you have. At first, because of the way you are used to thinking of separation of space, you may get the feeling that you belong there more than you belong where you are. You have just made a recognition, and it creates within you this feeling of separation and homesickness.

But the idea is not to run away from where you chose to be so as to rejoin that energy, but to manifest that energy *here* on your planet of choice. All of you are representatives from many different civilizations, and you have chosen to be born here to assist Earth in its transformation, to transform its energy into the energy you are familiar with on other worlds that already exist in a harmonious state. So remember that even though you may have other homes, because you chose to be born on Earth, Earth is your home too—and just as equally validly your home as anywhere else.

Well, why is it that I seem so invisible to many other people, that it's almost as if I'm on my own level, so to speak?

Whatever you are not the vibration of, and whatever is not the vibration of you, literally cannot be seen. Our suggestion is to just be the fullest *you* you can be with integrity. You will radiate at whatever pitch is necessary to attract all others who wish to interact with you, and attract yourself into circumstances where you will find others willing to interact with you on that level, because that's where they already are. You are not alone.

Now, a suggestion, if you wish to use it: in your meditative state go exploring with your imagination, and see what feelings come up within you that are strongest in terms of an association or a connection to an extraterrestrial idea. But always remember: even though you have connections to everywhere else, right now you are focused as a native of your own world; and therefore that must be the most important focus. Otherwise you would be somewhere else.

The Association

Bashar, I would like to understand better just what The Association of Worlds is, and how it functions. And what importance does it have for us?

The Association is made up of many different levels of civilizations and dimensionality, all choosing to agree to interact on levels that are mutually reinforcing in a beneficial and positive way. There is among these civilizations the realization that being of service to all is to automatically allow the all to serve them. So in this way our Association of Worlds has made itself known to you.

You are now beginning, as we perceive, to blend and balance, to harmonize with our Association of Worlds, to join that particular gathering and grouping of minds and souls and hearts. Note that it is not something you are familiar with as a governmental structure; it is highly *un*structured. In its very spontaneity are the keys to how it functions. For it gives to all the ability of every world within The Association to be fully who that world wishes to be, and trust that whoever that world wishes to be will automatically, coincidentally, synchronistically fit and harmonize with the comings and goings, the interactions and exchanges that all the other worlds need it to be.

Thus there are gatherings of a sort. Many times you will find that there are projections of consciousness, projections telepathically of mentality. There are gathering spaces; every mother ship has such a chamber wherein the interactions of the mentality telepathically, the projections of consciousness of hundreds of civilizations, meet and confer, creating that spark between themselves that allows them to put their hand on the pulse of The Association. To know the flow, the current and the direction of the agreements we are all making—altogether, all at the same time. That way we will all remain in step.

It is mostly our trust, our unconditional love, that allows us to know when it is time to come together, when it is time to go about our business exploring and assisting other worlds in recognizing their power—which is much of what we do. To increase our numbers; to expand our agreed-upon universe by giving other worlds their power and allowing them to make the choice in their own right to join us in the expansion of our ability to perceive all the different ways that Creation has of manifesting itself to be. That is what strengthens us.

Within this idea can be put forth our recognition that many of you are now choosing to make that agreement with us, choosing to synchronistically harmonize your pulse with our pulse, your dream with our dream, your reality with our reality, and beginning to physiologically experience the result of making that choice. Thus there is more synchronicity in your lives; less struggle, less suffering. More recognition of the abundance you already have and less structured definitions; fewer invalidations and judgments upon yourselves; less doubt, less fear, less guilt.

All of these are the results of the taking back of your power and choosing to function as whole beings and a whole civilization. And as such that will make it easier for your civilization to function with other whole civilizations which comprise the Association of Worlds. For your willingness to do this, we thank you.

Know that by connecting, associating, all paradox, all dichotomies and conflicts will be resolved, for they are only polarity projections from the center of your being. Since you can perceive both ends of the spectrum, they both must come from within you. Within you they are blended; they are one, and in that sense there is no paradox. So association, in and of itself, is the key, allowing yourselves to *be* all the associations you make in life. One more time: *allowing yourselves to be recognized **as** all of the associations you are making in life.* In other words, recognizing that you *are* the relationships you are having; you *are* the life you are living. **You are the association itself.**

CHAPTER FOURTEEN

UFOs Identified

Sightings

I've always wanted to be able to see a space ship, Bashar, but I never have. Have I failed to be looking where one was, or is there something deficient in my perceptions?

Not really. In fact, all of you have seen them, but for various reasons have blanked it out. The idea may not serve your immediate identification of who and what you need to be at that moment. However, understand that it is not that critical for you to see our craft. The idea is to focus on your own feelings right now. When you really need to see space ships, you'll see them; nothing will stop it—nothing at all.

To some degree, yes, it has to do with vibratory rates. Even though all of you have seen them, you do not necessarily need to retain the memory of it. In fact, in many cases it would impede allowing you to be who and what you are in the most natural and spontaneous way. Where it serves you to remember the incident, you will remember.

For now you may recognize that many of you will only allow yourselves to see these things when you soften your focus into a semi-conscious realm. As soon as you begin to blend more of the unconscious with the conscious, as we have said, you will be able to see our craft all the time. You see, we allow our vibratory frequency to be in that realm which gets you to stretch. The idea is to meet us half way. In your dream states you are on a vibratory plane where we are very perceivable in our natural environment, at our own natural level.

Then how does one raise one's vibratory level?
By doing what excites you the most.

Why the Encounters?

*Bashar, I have had three close encounters of the third kind,
and I'd like to know the significance of these encounters.*

The significance! First of all: the idea of any recognition any
one of you might have with beings you call extraterrestrials are
for several general reasons and many specific reasons. Many of
the specific reasons are entirely within you and your understanding of what you have created yourselves to be, and what it is you
desire to do in your lives.

The general reasons are for forming a reunion, a reunion that
awakens you to your own power, your own godhood. That is the
fundamental reason for any such encounter: to wake you up, to
allow you to be aware of the energy of creativity you have within
you, so that you can then put it to use in your physical world,
creating the changes that will transform the world and allow more
interaction to take place between your world and other worlds.
That is the primary, fundamental significance. Any other significance in specific terms is up to you, and will be in terms of the
agreements and contracts you have made with those beings—to
have them remind you at those specific timings of who you are.

*(Another): My wife and I saw 19 UFOs that no one else saw.
Can you tell me what was going on there?*

Sometimes our craft can be seen by individuals who are sensitive to a particular frequency, and at the same time another individual standing right next to them may not see us at all. We exist
in another type of dimensional frame, and if you are attuned to
that frame, you can see us. If you are not, you cannot. A group
of individuals will not necessarily all be in synchronous alignment,
and in your case that is what was happening: your vibration was
oriented to the appropriate frequency to be able to perceive into
a slightly different dimension of experience. Now, those individuals you perceived were giving you intuitive symbolic communication, what we call identification, which is aligning vibration

with vibration, seeing who is aligned to particular frequencies, and taking note of that.

In a sense, they were locking in to take stock of what percentage of the individuals on your planet are aligning with the vibration that would allow us to interact more with all of you. So you were noticed, and you were given the idea of recognition. You were shown ideas of symbols that translate directly into your unconscious and subconscious mind to awaken within you whatever you are willing to let be awakened. Then you can be assisted with more momentum and more energy to do the things in your life that represent the strongest part of who and what you are.

Are you saying that the sightings are coming around because of my desire to meet with space people?

It is because of the vibratory frequency you have placed yourself upon, but those sightings are indicative of the level of energy you are operating on. It is a reflection, a mirror to you, and there "should" be a reflection of exactly how much energy you have and a reflection that you can do anything you want to with it right now. You do not have to wait.

Oftentimes out in Malibu I point out different stars which I perceive are space craft.

Rarely.

Well, you've mentioned that when people can't sleep is when the ships are around, and that's when I'm pointing them out.

All right, that can be the perception of energies. However, they do not always manifest as space craft.

I often see star-like lights that rotate colors. Specifically red, green, blue. Some yellow. Orange, maybe.

Some of these are only stars aberrated by your atmosphere. Some are energy doorways, dimensional doorways. These are doorways or tunnels to other dimensions of existence. Through these doorways many of the so-called space craft emerge.

But the color is really vivid. And they do tend to move with the flow of the stars.

Yes. Again understand that when it is for the most part the idea of atmospheric aberration, your atmosphere will act like a prism, and take and bend the starlight so it will have the entire range of the spectrum. Understand that above your atmosphere the stars do not twinkle. The atmosphere is a lens that distorts.

That's what bothers me. Because there is a distinct difference in these in the twinkling. It's like a rotation.

That may appear to be the case. But again, your atmospheric aberration can also cause that. We are not saying that this is the case every time, but it is the case in the majority of times.

Okay. How would you know if you were seeing a space ship?

You would not necessarily know. Now, to be practical for a moment, let us suggest a rule of thumb that you may use, one that many individuals have found to be convenient for them: **Unless it is obviously a space craft, then it isn't one—even if it is.** For what purpose does it serve if you have to guess? Therefore, if you see something, and you are not sure, go on about your business. When you are sure, you will be sure. There will be no mistake.

All right. One night about six weeks ago this same thing happened. We saw a star-like object moving away from us specifically. It felt as if it were a shuttle leaving a mother ship.

This is what I will share with you at this time. Understand that you were witnessing the idea of a motion as you describe it, but not in your dimension. This leads to many other areas, and depends upon your willingness to extend your senses further. What you see many times is not physical sight, although you do not know it. Go with that for now.

Here is a suggestion: when you see something in your sky, extend your imagination and your senses to that point in space and see what you pick up. You will always pick up some form of consciousness, for everything is conscious. But see what you get. That is one of the reasons you are being lured into extending your senses into what you are seeing. You have not yet begun to extend yourself in the manner of the invitation being offered, and so we cannot yet discuss what you yourself will create yourself to find. When you begin to interact a little more, there will be the co-creation of the delineation of some of that interaction.

Thank you.

Going for a Ride

(Another): In contacting ships, in some certain contexts people have gone aboard and gone on flights, hanging out physically with ETs. In what context can I do that?

In the context of the fullness of the agreement of your timing. Go and do what excites you.

As I do that, and am running around the desert in search of—

Do not wait for it.

I don't. I'm wondering if there is some shift necessary, some timing? Or is there some agreement that can be made? Can I just check on when is the next available flight—?

You have already made the agreement. You will fulfill the appropriate timing by continuing to do what represents who you are. That is what will take you most quickly into any timed agreement: be the person you need to be. That agreement will be met.

Is there some way I can get an advanced glimpse of the schedule?

Certain areas on your planet that attract you—do you physically go there?

Not as often as I'd like. There are a couple places—

Bye-bye. . . . In other words, if that is what you are all about, then act upon the impulse. Place yourself in the locations carrying the highest degree of conductivity for those types of blendings. There are many, many places around your planet that we have visited, and visit all the time. You may simply go to where you are attracted. But again, recognize that you do not necessarily have to go very far. Generally speaking, however, it is usually more conducive to see our ships if you are not in a large city.

What we are saying is that we recognize many of you have ascribed to us abilities that in many ways we do not have—in the sense of being able to just pop in, pop out, anywhere any time. We also follow the natural lines of flow of timing and the electromagnetic field of the universal reality. And therefore sometimes even when you might be ready, the timing on our side does not match the fullness of the agreement.

Is there some way to find out what that timing would be that does work in conjunction with your agreement?

Sometimes in meditation it can come to you. But always in the exploration of the things that mean the most to you in physical life, and in the action on those endeavors you will have whatever type of recognition of the timing you need. But do realize that usually you think you're ready when you really are not. Trust that when you really are ready, nothing in the universe will stop it.

Great. Thank you.

(And another): Bashar, I wouldn't mind being abducted and temporarily detained on a space ship. What do you think would be the best way to do that?

By not giving it a second thought. By going about your business, living your life to the fullest, and being the person you really desire to be. By not *needing* to do that. Many of the ideas of these so-called interactions— it is not that they cannot occur, but only that many times they will not occur *because* you are requesting it in the context that you will not be complete unless it happens. And therefore we will not show up and reinforce your sense of incompleteness.

Not that we will guarantee anything, for the timing is always going to be dependent upon the individual, but if you still have a penchant for a contact, simply be somewhere alone. Then your chances are greatly increased. But do also understand: all of you have been aboard ships in your dream states. All of you.

Yah, I remember dreams of doing that, but I want to do it in my physical body.

As soon as the dream state and the physical body are not considered different, you will be. Do not need it to be different; do not need it out of desperation. Live your life; all things are happening according to perfect timing, and according to agreements that serve the best of all concerned. And relax. Many times —and this may surprise some of you who are so very eager to meet us, as you say, in the flesh— we have heard many of you express the same desire: "I'm really ready; I'm really ready to meet you now— really. I'll meet you down at the corner in, oh, half an hour."

We are very aware of all the levels of your consciousness that are involved in the need to focus on us, and to focus on yourselves. But when you have expressed the idea of your readiness, finding yourselves in a remote location, and finding the energy changing and you are very aware of exactly what is happening —that we are coming closer to you in vibration, and are in many ways about to literally appear to you— boy, do you run! When it comes right down to it, many times you are not as ready as you think you are. "Not yet; not yet," you say. . . . We will know when you are ready.

I don't think I'd run, though.

I know you don't think you'd run. And in a sense, many of you may not. But also understand this: one of the reasons for the timing of everything is because, as we pointed out earlier, being exposed to a higher vibration will often bring things up with you that you are not ready to face about yourselves. And in fact, ***most of the running you do is not from us. It is from yourselves!***

We will trust the timing that is best for all concerned. Do not give it a second thought; just live your lives. And as we have said, you can open the lines of communication in loving ways with your government, and allow them to share the information of our existence. Make it not such a surprising thing that your civilization and ours should interact, thus laying the groundwork for that interaction.

My Own Ship

I've been focusing in on what excites me, Bashar, and what really seems exciting to me is having an interplanetary space ship.

We understand that it excites many of you as you form different connections, and we are not saying this is by any means impossible. Recognize you do have the technology on your own planet to create this, and many of you are beginning to do so. The idea also to remember about what excites you the most is that at any given moment if you act on what excites you that you are capable of acting on, it will lead you to anything else that excites you that you may not immediately be able to act on because of the way you have set circumstances up, or the way the timing actually is. You may find that having the idea of space craft will represent your willingness to utilize the technology that exists on your planet, creating the space craft you can create.

Well, I wouldn't mind if I could have one that already exists, one that was not necessarily manufactured here.

Yes, I know you wouldn't mind, and this is even possible. But again, the idea is to utilize the timing for what it is, and it is not quite the timing for that yet. But you can bring it closer by creating your own craft and meeting us half-way. There are many things for you to understand about the principles, the nature of that level of technology. If you are willing to explore that on your own terms, in your own understanding, then by the time you are able to access a space craft whose origin does not come from your world, you will understand how to use it.

I'm willing to take lessons now.

These *are* your lessons. Do you not understand? Using what you have access to on your own planet *are* your lessons. . . . We understand that this does not sit well with many of you who are anxious for the endeavor and the experience to which you can relate. Nevertheless, it is representative of the timing. And again, it is not outside the realm of probability at all. The timing being what it is allows you to be aware that actions on your world must be turned in the direction of using what you already have access to. That is what brings any other probability closer.

In your dream realities you are now in a sense being taught, and you already know how. When you apply this in the reality in which you have chosen to exist, you will then be acting in the direction of showing that you know how. You have chosen to be where you are, and you have chosen to be in this type of society, at the technological level in which the society exists right now. That is for a reason. Tap into that reason.

UFO Crash

Bashar, I have a new book here, and I'm very proud of this book because I had a hand in it. Do you remember 7-7-47?

Absolutely!

This book is called **UFO Crash at Aztec**, *and it tells the complete story of that investigation and what was found, complete with illustrations, photographs, some of the original texts from magazines, and some information released under the "Freedom of Information Act." I feel that injustice was done to those entities, being brought down in the manner that they were, and the dissections and the things that followed. . . . I'm glad that the truth is finally coming out now, because it's true—*

It is part of the leakage of information that has been long suppressed.

Yes. There's one part of it in the back that I found disturbing, some writings by a Paul M——, who says that in the state of New Mexico the government has given over certain labs to alien beings who are responsible for cattle mutilations and the abduction of women and things of that sort. That was upsetting because I don't fully understand all of the ramifications.

We understand what you are saying. For now we will say there is some exaggeration to that idea, but we are not allowed to comment. I do not mean to seem mysterious about this, but it is simply not allowed. All we can suggest is that the idea serves your population in a beneficial way, and is not exactly as it has been described.

Some other information has come up through a writer named George, who said it was channeled to him by some entities who were engaged in an ongoing conflict with other beings, and that Sirius was also involved. This had been going on for some time.

This is not a conflict as you understand the term, but only the idea of the created pressure of intersecting dimensional realities. It is something that does not translate very well into your physiological terminology.

So there's no war conflict?

Not as you understand it, no.

There are a few legendary stories about our government having in fact shot down some space craft—such as the story about Hangar 18.

264 △ BASHAR: BLUEPRINT FOR CHANGE

Now, it was not literally shot down, although there have been attempts of such nature. Of those that do exist, the one specifically referred to as the Hangar 18 scenario was a craft of Zeta Reticulum origin, exploring an area of your planet during a storm with high electrical activity. Your radar installation at that time had the ability to interfere with navigational guidance systems of those craft—although this is no longer true now. In interfering with the guidance systems, in altering the shape of the protective field around the craft, it created portions of the metallic hull of the craft to be vulnerable to the electrical storm; it was struck and knocked out, then recovered and retrieved by your government. That was in July of your year 1947.

There have been several similar incidents, and some attempts have been made to utilize the same radar effect upon other craft, so in that sense you can say "shot down." But not with the idea of missiles, bullets, or anything of that nature. There have been a couple of rare occurrences where certain utilizations of your more typical weaponry have caused malfunction, but not to any great degree. But yes, your government has possession of several craft and remnants thereof. That particular craft is still in pieces under surveillance in many different areas of your country—but primarily near the area of Virginia.

Were there beings aboard?

Yes.

Were they alive?

No, not in that first crash.

And what was the value they got out of creating that reality in their lives?

You have now been initiated on the 40-year cycle that allows you to begin to be brought into the association of civilizations. Whether they were conscious of what they were doing or not, the incident began a series of events in your civilization that has brought you now to the understanding you have, and the ability to join the association. Many circumstances will occur that may seem on the surface to be accidental.

What did those beings look like?

They were the type of Zeta Reticuli we mentioned earlier—about 3 to 3-1/2 feet tall, enlarged heads, no hair, very large black eyes. They have very thin bodies, almost no mouth, almost no nose, almost no ears, very long and slender, pastyish-white skin. Other types from that civilization have beige or tan skin, or sometimes very dark grey-green skin.

Let me remind each and every one of you that regardless of the scenario —I'm not saying it had to be that way— still there is a timing for everything. *Those beings, in their own highest understanding, know that they have served a purpose by allowing themselves to interact with your society, even at the cause of their own physical death.* For they have accelerated your awareness on many levels, and made it very possible for us to be speaking with you today—simply because of that interaction.

Billy Meier

In this past month I visited a Swiss citizen, Billy Meier, who has had an eleven-year ongoing encounter with UFO contacts—with the Pleiadians.

To some degree; not as much lately as you might think.

His last encounter was in August of this year. His original mission was to make all the UFO contacts and information known to the world.

Yes. And it was done.

It was done. However, he has had nothing but regrets for doing this.

Yes, because of the reactions of your society.

They've been very bad. He's had another attempt on his life, and is in seclusion. But I did get to see him.

All right. That is why to some degree —not in a very strongly accelerated manner, but to some degree— some of the Pleiadians are also contacting other individuals as well.

But do understand that Billy chose to be one of the vanguards, one of the forerunners who would take the brunt of the ridicule. Many things have become twisted; much of the information is now no longer reliable, because it has been interspersed with false information. But the ice has been broken. The job has been done to some degree, and in a very real way Billy can relax a lot more than he thinks.

Now information is being spread to other individuals. He is not bearing the brunt alone. Although he may have created for himself a little bit of a rut where he thinks he is burdened by the entire weight, he is not. Some of the things he is experiencing now are due to his own reactions of becoming caught up in the idea of the intrigue—which he did to some degree bring out in other people. But it does not necessarily have to be quite so strongly focused in that area at this time, for he is no longer bearing the brunt of the entire dispersal of the information.

Yes. But very recently there was a two-hour broadcast which was on national television in this country. While the program seemed to be very informative on UFOs, the announcer did make a statement that of course the Billy Meier story was a hoax.

We understand, yes. That statement was made based on certain information that they did not research thoroughly. It was based on information that has come to light, to some degree, to discredit that particular idea. Understand that they could say no more than that because they had no more information than that. The purpose of the program was to focus on the idea of the interactions between your society and the society that is called Zeta Reticuli, anyway. Those were comments that were made because they felt they were necessary to add into the idea. But there really was no information or research that was done.

That statement in a sense was quite off-handed. While this does not take into account all of the facts, the statement was based on the idea that at one point in the contact of the Pleiadians with Billy, when some of the photographs were taken, Billy constructed a model so that photographs of it could be taken to see if there was any difference between photographs of the model and photographs of the real ships. The idea was that it could be proven that photographs of the model could be detected as such, by knowing that those photographs were photographs of the real ship because of the difference in quality between the two.

That's absolutely correct.

The model was found and taken to be proof that Billy Meier had faked all of the photographs. The statement made on that program was based on that and other assumptions. That is why they could not really go much into it—they had not really done their research. As we said, the purpose of the program was more to familiarize your society with one of the strongest contacts going on now between your society and the Zeta Reticuli, and that it did.

Space Travel

Bashar, can you travel to any space and time?
Absolutely.
So it's completely limitless?
Absolutely. Because space and time are your own definitions. You see, we understand that an object does not exist *within* time and space, but that space/time are properties of the object, and can be changed. In a sense, that's how our space craft travel. They are projected into astral material, and then they are redefined with a vibration that represents the space/time locale we wish them to be at. They are then reinserted into physical materiality at whatever locale is representative of that vibrational equation—having in a sense avoided the issue of travel altogether. Instantaneous teleportation. It is not really breaking the speed of light; it is not traveling within your dimension at all.

Have you dealt with magnetic drive at any point?
There are some forms, fluctuations of electromagnetism within some of the ideas of drive. It is not purely electromagnetic exactly, but more the idea of gravitational dynamic tensor fields.

Can the ships go into the water?
Oh yes, and very often they do. Remember, something that can travel in space where there is no air can very easily go under water. Since our ships use electromagnetic energy, we do not have to worry about the idea of rocket flames and fuel and the like. There are no openings in our craft for water to get in or air to get out. Therefore we can go where and when we wish. Our ships can

also create a particular type of vibration that puts us out of phase with solid matter so that they can go into that solid matter or through it—or into other dimensions within it.

Does your space ship relate to you in the form of thought, Bashar?

Yes, in a sense. The mind of the pilot is connected to the mind of the ship.

If I were a pilot here, and wanted to transfer from this system to your system, what thoughts or ideas would I feed into my computer?

The *feeling* that you have of us. That is the vibration. How you would recognize us is the vibration. You can always key off of any single individual such as myself, since my vibration is of my system.

In using that vibration to key off of any particular person in any particular system, could I then easily go from system to system just by signaling in on that particular entity?

Yes. It is like the tuning of your radio. You get what you switch the dial to.

I'd be running up and down the dial there.

Do understand that this is what you do when you are out of your body in your sleep state anyway. You become the vibration and there you are, instantaneously. The space craft is only an extension of the consciousness that represents the same idea in physiological symbolic terms. But it is still only an extension of the consciousness.

I was aware of that, but I didn't know how to construct one, or how I would deal with traveling.

Well, you also create the idea of the so-called self-aware mentality or consciousness of the space craft, because the space craft can also *hear* you. It is completely and totally keyed to your vibration, and thus responsive to it—and only to yours.

In that you said that the mind of the pilot is connected with the control mechanism of the ship, could you give me an example of, say, plotting from one system to another system, how the pilot would do that?

Yes. There is the creation of the isolation field around and about the craft which isolates that field from any one particular universe, thus opening up its navigational banks to all probable universes which are represented by their signature frequency vibrations. The pilot, being intuitive, and simply tapping into the internal imagination dimension, picks the frequencey he desires. This is imparted through the navigational spectrum of the ship, which then views the entire ship with that vibrational frequency. Thus when the isolation field is removed, the ship by definition must take up residence within the universe that represents the vibrational frequency.

Thank you very much.

Time Travel

You say you create your isolation field around your space craft, and redefine the space/time coordinates to relocate to another place. Can you define the space/time coordinates in such a way as to transport back to what we call our past or our future? That is, can you move to planet Earth in the 15th century?

Yes. Space/time is one thing. Traveling in space is traveling in time; traveling in time is traveling in space. It is one thing. However, recognize that everything will still fit in place, even from the apparent linear point of view. So any apparent changes that may appear to take place within any previous time track you came from will actually not be taking place in that literal time track, but in one parallel to it.

So exactly what do you experience?

The effect is basically the same. In other words, you could step into your craft and go back in time. If you are assuming that you wish to change the way something happened, then to make that change, you can go back to the exact same time track where you left off. There will be no apparent change, because that's not what happened in your current time track, but the change can be made there, forming an alternate time track by definition.

The change, so to speak, is not a change. It is part of the normal history of a parallel time track. So if you wish to see the effect of the so-called change, you must go to the future or go back to the present of the *parallel* time track, where you made the change. Is this making any sense?

Somewhat.

You have time track A, time track B. Time track A is your time track, let us say, your history. Time track B is another history altogether. Everything is occurring simultaneously. Let us say time track A and time track B are very similar. The idea, leaving this point in your time track A, is that if you go back to the supposed past, you are actually going into the idea of another time track, and being a part of its history in a natural progressive way.

Now, you cannot actually literally change your own past in the same linear coordinate system. When you "change your past," you are simply shifting gears into another time that contains that ability to change, so you will have the experience of that change in your new present.

You cannot change history.

More correctly, you alter yourself to another history that is appropriately representative of the change you desired to make.

And the same applies to moving to the future?

Yes.

Isolation Field

How exactly do you create the isolation field?

It is a microwave energy effect that is an alteration of light, stepped up many magnitudes above what you typically think of as an electrical discharge. It is dispersed through the hull of the craft, through various devices after the light is stepped up by other various devices—one of which we call the flash matrix—which incorporates many different elements.

The isolation field is a microwave effect. Microwave generation at that high rate of speed will disconnect any object within the bubble from the universe in which it existed. This is because you match the vibrational frequency of the speed of light itself in a very highly condensed way, the speed of light being the barrier limit that represents physical dimensionality.

When you create around your craft a wall or a shell made of light, the very substance of the physical universe, then within that shell you have created a bubble, a hole, in that universe. You are redirecting the light, out of which everything is made, *around* you rather than *through* you. You are now sustained by the primal template universe, which exists on a completely different frequency far above and beyond the frequency of light. Therefore, in that universe you literally are everything at once. So you can be anywhere and anywhen you want to be.

Can this be done with our technology now?

Yes.

How do you do it—have a piece of matter bombarded with microwaves?

No. Listen to your media; read your literature. Many individuals are working on this idea now, beginning to explore and experiment, and they will come out with public notification of many of these ideas. Basically, it involves the idea of counter-rotational masses that are highly magnetically charged. These will generate in a fundamental way the field of which we are speaking —fundamental enough to allow the isolation to take place. More sophisticated control will come from the generation of these fields through more highly conductive materials.

Navigation

My curiosity is: when you're traveling in interstellar space, do you navigate in other ways beside the stars? Or do you also have to take into account the magnetic—?

We do not navigate by the stars at all, except that we recognize patterns and charts of where it is we wish to go. But the idea of our navigation is primarily through tonal vibration. As we have described briefly, the idea in our understanding is that objects are, in and of themselves, vibrational equations, and location is one of the variables in that equation. Therefore we have created a grid, if you will, a holographic three-dimensional spherical map, that plots out the extrapolated vibrations of any particular distance from any particular point.

So then you're looking at your different points of reference as vibrational frequencies.

Oh, absolutely! Now, we do have a type of call-out reference; put into your language, you can consider the idea to be a sphere. If you have a circle, a plane in the middle of and intersecting that sphere, it can be referred to as the galactic ecliptic, the plane of the galaxy, if you wish—or simply "G.E." Therefore, if you bisect it with a line, that line from the center towards you through your world would be considered zero.

The one away from you is 180 degrees, either 180 degrees starboard or 180 degrees port. If you have the sphere, the top is positive, the bottom is negative. Thus you perhaps also have rings from the center, or what we call radials from the center out. So any particular distance from the center will be at such and such a radial. Then you determine the angle, either positive and/or negative. And that tells you where you are in three locations. But that is within our computers as a vibratory equation.

Therefore, as we create the isolation field around our craft that unlocks us from any particular vibratory universe, and imposes, through the harmonics of light, the new vibrational equation upon the craft, when we reinsert the craft into any particular reality, it will automatically take up residence at that location represented by the vibratory signature frequency. It has not really *traveled* the distance, but simply removed itself from that reality and redeposited itself at that particular other location.

Then as far as the magnetosphere of our planet, or any other planets, do you have to make calculations or adjustments?

To some degree, yes. Because once we are traveling within any particular reality, we then must navigate by the gravitational dynamic tensor field, the electromagnetic field, the masses of stars and planets within that particular reality, if it contains them.

And then when you get closer to our planet, for instance, you would be subject to our compass, our magnetic pull?

Not unless we removed the gravitational field from around our craft. Each and every space craft has its own gravitational bubble; that is why our craft can be completely perpendicular to your world, and yet we still feel as if we are facing "down" when we stand on our floor.

This is exciting to be asking you questions like this, because I think some other level of my intelligence is speaking here. I've never had any chemistry or engineering training at all—

Me neither. Our science, our engineering, our technology in that sense is mostly intuition.

I would like some more of the technical picture of the fluidity of your craft that was portrayed in flight—of the navigator that was in the channel's memory banks.

It is mostly the interior that is fluid, not so much the exterior.

In its constructed or molecular density, is it made of metal?

It is more of a crystalline metallic form that is grown.

Could you give me the molecular counterpart in the gradient to us creating that here?

It is a metallic crystalline state refined by a cold fusion process. You do not yet have the technology for this. It is instilled, or programmed, to act in a holographic fashion, and when certain types of current are introduced into that crystalline metallic matrix, it takes upon itself the form of the identity with which it is infused, and becomes crystallized according to that template. When the template is removed, it collapses back into its original state until another template is introduced in electrical form.

But this goes on at very deep atomic levels concerning the actual interactions between subatomic particles. As we perceive it, it will be a while before you even have the support systems necessary to create this type of effect.

How do you create the substance?

It is, once again, *grown* upon the energy templates that we create. Once we have refined the particular substance, it is then grown, molecule by molecule, atom by atom, along the lines of the energy template we lay down for it to grow upon.

Field Trip

And now let us take you on a field trip to the Solar Wind, our mother ship. . . . Close your eyes.

In your mentality have the picture of the room you have created around you, and envision each individual, all of you together, all at once, surrounded by a blue crystalline bubble of energy. This bubble is your elevator, your ship. Relax and allow yourselves now to become the devices within the ship that activate it. Leave the idea of your earthly devices and tools behind; pay attention to them no more. You are the transference point; you are the ship.

Allow yourselves to recognize that the crystalline shell is quite transparent; you can see through it and you can see the room. In whatever way works best for you, in your imagination feel and see at the same time the room around you dissolve into a gray, fog-like state. You are all now together in this ship; you are all linked and you are all breathing the same energy.

Breathe it in three times deeply and prepare yourselves. Align yourselves; assimilate yourselves; unite yourselves. Feel the connection; feel that while you are individuals, every single other individual in this craft is *you!*—an extension of you, an expression of you, a facet of you. You are all one, one master crystal. And this crystal, in allowing the white light of your consciousness to glow within its very core, within its very heart, now comes alight with life and light, energizing the entire crystalline craft and rising above the Earth—higher and higher into the upper atmosphere, into what you call space.

Rising, you look down below. You see out of the fog now everything clearing into brilliant space, black with white stars everywhere. You see the beautiful Earth below you, shining like the jewel that it is, in the velvet curtain of deepest space, and you send your love. You see and feel and taste and hear the love of the Earth that is supporting you, that is extending you on its arm, extending you on your journey out into space. You are riding on the crest of the wave of the heart of your planet.

Now as it offers to you the jewels of space, you look up. You see suspended in space before you a long cylindrical metallic object. It is approximately a mile in length. You allow yourselves now to see an opening in the side of this metallic object, wider and wider as you approach. You enter that opening, and as it closes below you, you are surrounded by a whiteness. You may sense in that whiteness, here and there, solid or nebulous, consciousness peering at you, smiling with you, loving with you, fading in and out—out of the milky whiteness. But laughing and sharing joy all around.

Allow yourselves to know that you can now begin to explore any area in any way, any aspect of this ship you so desire. There will always be someone with you in some capacity. You will also always be connected and feel the experiences of every other person you came with.

Now you are exiting the bubble and entering the milky whiteness of the ship, exploring and breathing the new atmosphere. Feel the gentle touches and caresses of the beingness all around you. Scatter and explore; enjoy and become fascinated by what you discover. Taste, touch, hear, feel, see, marvel. Recognize that you are sharing and participating in the creation of a multitude of worlds. Experience and take to heart these experiences.

Whether or not it appears to make sense to you, allow yourselves to interpret, in whatever way you so desire, the different chambers and areas of the ship. Let yourselves have the opportunity to recognize that in a very real way you are projecting astrally a portion of your consciousness. And that you are going to be funneling that information back to your idea of your earthly selves, incorporating that information into your very molecular structure. You will be feeding this information into the atmosphere around you, and when you carry this atmosphere back to your planet Earth, you will release the information and energy on your planet—to change the very air that you breathe, to change the very energy that sustains you.

Explore to your heart's content. Feel the vibrant pulse of life and light, for it is light itself which powers the vessel, and all vessels like it. It is the very heart and soul of the movement of space and time through the central core of this ship that creates the illusion of the ship's motion through all the dimensions of reality. Now be aware of the whereabouts of each other. Gather yourselves back together into your docking bay, into the milky whiteness. Feel all the caresses and the kisses that are given to you from heart to heart and soul to soul.

As you form your craft round and about you in its crystalline beauty, and the iris opens below you, allow yourselves to drift back outside the hull into space and begin your travel toward planet Earth. Recognize now, as you bid farewell, that this is not goodbye, that this experience is directly with you now and it always shall be. And as you look down through the crystalline bottom of your energy craft, you see once again the beauty of the jewel of your Earth. Recognize that it is in every way truly a new world to explore in all of its unlimited fascination and facets.

You are eager to allow the atmosphere of the new crystalline reality that you know you are participating within to burst upon contact with your Earth and allow the shards of brilliant seed-like beauty to go scattering everywhere, reflecting the beautiful light of your central star. And as you sink gently back to Earth, see your feet gently touch the ground. Send roots deep down to drink of the nourishment of the fluid of the life and light of your home world, while knowing that all worlds are your home world. Know that the life you are, the Earth you are, is the nourishment that will allow you to grow toward the light as high as you wish to go.

Know that every one of you have incorporated the information of the experience in your own way, encoded it within you, and it will release in its own fashion, after your own kind. And that much of your dream reality can become quite vivid and vibrant. There may be more release, more malleability, more recognition that life around you is but what you dream it to be. Allow yourselves to know that it was a real experience, and that you have projected a portion of yourselves aboard that craft.

In every way there is still, and always will be, a portion of yourselves aboard that craft that we will share, that you will share together with us. We thank you for your participation, and we will allow you to remember: *All reunions are simply awakenings to the union that already exists everywhere, everywhen.*

CHAPTER FIFTEEN

Zeta and the Legacy

Intruders

July, 1987 (Note: Ken, our video cameraman, often left his camera for a brief encounter with Bashar, usually starting it off with a joke.)

What's happening, dude?

Everything! All at once.

Life, right?

Yes.

Hey, Bashar, I understand that on your planet your people have white/whitish-gray skin.

Yes.

Okay. Well, if you'd be willing to share with us your space craft technology—

Now, we already have, to some degree, but as you know, it is not yet the right timing.

Well, I was going to say, in order to accelerate that timing, we would be happy to share our sun-tanning technologies with you.

No, thank you.

Okay. That's a joke, anyway.

Yes.

*I've just finished reading **Intruders**, by Bud Hopkins, which I believe you know of—a book which talks about the encounters that several people on our planet have had with extraterrestrials—abductions, where they have been taken aboard the craft—*

At this time we would suggest a replacement for that term. Rather than abductions, perhaps . . . "detainments."

Detainments, okay. Anyway, they underwent examinations of various kinds. The account in the book indicated that there was some pain and discomfort and a lot of fear created on the part of the detainees.

Yes. Generally the fear is what creates the pain and discomfort. There usually is no real inherent pain or discomfort in the interaction—except what is caused by the fear. Part of the reasons for those interactions is to release those fears, so there will no longer be any form of fear, pain or discomfort in your lives. That is one of the reasons for those interactions. They are all being made by agreement, even though your conscious minds may not remember those agreements.

Some of the pain has been physical pain, in that there have been probes placed up into the nostrils.

Yes. Some of this is physical, and some of it is not. Some of it is such a strong telepathic idea that you think it is physical.

Knowing that these people have agreed to have these interactions, then since they have agreed, why are they still creating the fear? And then corollary to that: one of the detainees said, "We wouldn't really mind it if the aliens would just come out and say, 'Hey, would you be willing to do this?' And we would be. They don't have to abduct us." . . . That made a lot of sense to me.

Yes. Understand, of course, that the agreements are usually unconscious; that is part of the reason. Many times, as long as the agreements are unconscious, an individual may consciously say, "Oh well, wouldn't it be nice if it were to happen this way?" But when it comes right down to it, the fear comes up anyway.

Well, if the agreements are unconscious, can they not also be done consciously?

Obviously on your behalf, not yet. Otherwise there would be no fear—for the fear is an indication that it cannot yet be done consciously.

Yet there is this request on the part of at least one of the interviewed detainees that the aliens come out and make a conscious request.

Yes, but that is after the fact.

True. Well, what I'm also doing here is suggesting that these agreements start being made on a conscious level—and perhaps you can be our ambassador—

They are doing so more and more. Do understand one very important thing: all the individuals who have been chosen —even those who seem to go through abject terror— are actually quite close to integrating the last remnants of their fears. We are choosing all those who are very close indeed to the end of having fear. So you may realize that when you see them having that much fear, if that's an indication of a small part of the total fear that your society has, just imagine if someone were to be chosen who had more fears than that!

So the individuals we are choosing *are* the ones, many times, who are the closest to integration, the closest to conscious recognition. And yet they still have that amount of fear.

I see. Are these individuals also helping to drain off the fears of the rest of us through themselves?

Yes! They have agreed to do this for all of you. That is why they are now sharing their experiences—so you can "vicariously" go through their "ordeal" with them, get in touch with the fear left within *you* and integrate it. Then the next series of interactions can become more and more conscious.

Okay. I am contemplating sending a copy of this tape to the guy who wrote the book.

By all means.

Do you have any final comments that you'd like to communicate to him and to his people in the book?

Only that we appreciate that he is doing what he agreed to do. And he is making a difference in the ability of your entire planet to allow your society and our respective societies to live in harmony with each other.

Communion

Bashar, I've been under this dark cloud after reading a couple of books recently. One of them is a brand new book called Communion, by Whitley Strieber.

That initial reaction is not unusual for your society. But no need to fear. All the fear that you may experience in the idea of those interactions basically stems from that individual experiencing those interactions and allowing himself to release the fears that have been planted in his life. And also, nothing has happened in those interactions that the individual did not agree to at some point in his life—although granted it is on an unconscious level. Everything is done by agreement—*everything!*

Those extraterrestrials were assisting that individual in releasing much of that fear. Thus at this time he is very much aware of what the purpose of that idea was. I'm not saying he has come to terms with all of his fears, but he understands that the fear he felt was basically from himself, not from them.

Now, those beings have interacted with many beings on your world. One of their primary functions, per the agreements they have made with many of you, is to assist you in releasing your fear. It may be a very fearful process while you go through it, but you agreed to experience it. You know what you are doing. All you need to do, if you find yourself in that interaction, is to trust that you know what you are doing. The more trust and love you have, the less you will feel the interaction in a format of fear. That's all it takes.

Remember, a higher vibratory state exposing itself to a lower vibratory state will raise the vibration of the lower being to force it to face many things it has not been willing to face within itself, and that is what the being is terrified of. But that being is dealing with it, integrating the fear and transforming it into positive understanding. That has been one of the purposes for those interactions, because it was understood that that being, that author, would communicate his experiences, allowing other individuals to come to terms with their own fears, so that by the next wave of interactions there would be less fear to integrate.

I understand that, but my reaction was that the book might be scaring more people than it is uplifting.

That's all right, because it will still allow them to face certain ideas, to come to terms with them. And again, these things are done with agreements, do not forget. Your entire planet on one level is agreeing to this particular type of teaching. It doesn't have to happen that way; it's completely up to your world as to whether or not it will wake up or be shaken awake.

Well, I think that that book has perhaps disadvanced the progression, because it's sort of creating the opposite effect of, for instance, your teachings.

No. I understand what you are saying, but there are many individuals who cannot relate to the idea in any other way. Therefore, they have been given the tools that will work best for them. True, it isn't for everyone, but it will hit those who need it. And do not necessarily view it as a disvalue, because then you will reinforce the inability of certain people to absorb it. Know that it will evolve where it needs to. It has already awakened many.

How does it serve the extraterrestrials to contact us in what appears to be frightening ways—at least to our conscious minds?

Understand that different individuals in different cultures have different methods; different cultures think and perceive in different ways. The intention is always there to be felt for what it is, and the Zeta's intentions can always be sensed to be loving in an overall way. The methodology through which those intentions are expressed, however, can and do seem alien to you. Their thought patterns are alien to yours, and so there is that fear, that dichotomy, that often crops up in your society when you see something that is extremely different from you.

It is not so much that they have an absolute desire to approach you in specific methods that will generate fear. It is just that because of your methods, their natural methods do in fact generate it. They are not necessarily about to alter their entire psychological structure to accommodate you beyond a certain point. They know you can handle it, and they know you have agreed to learn how to handle it. Learning to do so is one part of the agreement, a part about which many of you are not aware.

Yes, I can see that, because there's a point in the book at which he says to one of them, "You have no right." And she says, "Yes we do."

Yes. The right was granted by the agreement that was made. Many individuals on your planet *do* wish that contact with us and other civilizations. These Reticulum beings are primarily doing the job of acclimatizing many individuals on your world in ways that are buffered. Even though the individuals may experience many degrees of fear, it is actually a far smoother transition than they would have experienced had the alien beings simply come to them straight out first time full blown.

Bit by bit these individuals have been contacted over long periods of their lives, many times from when they were children. And bit by bit they are allowed to remember more and more of the interaction until they get to a point where they realize there is nothing to fear. They can handle it, and then the contact can occur more openly and more obviously.

I thought it was very significant that every person to whom Strieber talked who had had a similar experience —even though some of them were still frightened, and didn't know if they were going crazy, or if it was their imagination or what— still in spite of all that, they felt love and affection.

Yes. At this point in their lives. To put it simply: the aliens are acting within their integrity to the best of their ability, but they are not responsible for the way you have created your society to be, and the reactions that you often have. You have made the agreement; they are fulfilling the agreement. They are doing it in the way that is easiest for you.

As we have said, when you encounter those beings, for the first time in your conscious life perhaps, you will actually get a reflection on how powerful you are. Any fear that might come from that is merely a reaction to the belief that you cannot possibly contain that much power. And therefore, "It isn't coming from you, and so it might destroy you." But it can't. It is an absolute reflection of you—and that is what you are learning.

Fear's Message

So how do you stop letting fear control you and take over your life?

Know it is your friend. It is giving you messages. "Tap, tap. Look here! Here's a part of yourself you didn't know existed: I'm bringing it to your attention. Isn't that wonderful? Now that you are aware of it, you can integrate it into the rest of you and be more of who you are. Haven't I done you a wonderful service?"

"No?!? What do you mean you didn't want to see that part of yourself? I thought you wanted to see everything there was to see, experience every facet of the multidimensional existence that you are. Do you not want to integrate it in yourself so that you can accelerate? . . . You're not sure? Well, all right. I'll hang around until you are sure, until you allow me to deliver the message. Of course, as long as I hang around, you might as well feed me, pay for my meals, allow me to grow and become a live-in. I'll get stronger and stronger and nag you constantly until you allow me to deliver my message so I can get out of here."

That is the only reason fear is there—because you do not allow it to deliver the message it brings; because you attempt to reject the message, thinking it is something not worth having.

Well, if fear is delivering a message, I don't always know what the message is. I would rather have the message than the fear.

Well now, I am not saying this is something that carries any more power than you do, but many of you have put much stock in the belief of habits. And so because you believe things can happen in your lives habitually, as second nature, without even knowing you are doing it, then many times you do not even realize you are rejecting the message coming from the fear, and doing so before you can even think about it. You do not pay attention quickly enough.

Therefore, it is a matter of allowing yourselves to know that the messages are there, that you *can* hear them. Even allowing yourselves to be fascinated by the fact that the fear might be bringing a message can curtail or dull the negativity—just because you might be fascinated enough to say, "Well, what is the message?" The minute you become curious, no more fear.

Could you give me an example of what kind of message a fear would bring?

Well, one such as this: you are walking down one of your streets. Someone walks up to you, and all of a sudden you are fearful. "What do they want? What do they want? Why are they bothering me? I do not want to be accosted. Are they going to rob me? What do they want?"

"Excuse me, do you have the time?" "Oh! Well, yes." "Thank you very much. Good bye." "Why was I so fearful? Why was I so automatically fearful without knowing anything at all?" Assumptions and structures that you build. Habits that you believe in. The message is there that lets you know that reaction shows you the beliefs you have within you, structures within you that you may not prefer.

That may be the message. If you do not prefer to live that way, then you have now allowed yourselves to let the fear show you these beliefs are within you. Now you can change them. That is one way you can allow fear to deliver a message.

Yes. Of course, there is a situation where a guy does have a gun under his coat—

Yes. So?

Fear is really telling you to get out of there!

All right now, once again: understand that that situation can occur that way, but it also does not have to. The idea of knowing your reality, and knowing it without fear, can give you the cognition that the event is there. But you know it will not affect you in any negative way. Cognition of a situation does not have to create fear.

True. But what I'm saying is that sometimes the sensation of a fear comes up, and I go, "Well, look at that. That's neat." And I find that I'm able not to feel fearful because I'm in the moment, and I know that there will be a positive outcome. So, if that does occur, then what is the message? Or have I just made the message unnecessary?

Yes. The minute you begin to become curious, you have gotten the message. The idea of many of the fears is to simply spur your curiosity to begin exploring that facet of yourself. That is all. It is a gentle reminder. And the more you are willing to explore, the gentler the nudges become, until you just do not experience that fear anymore. Again, it is simply the idea of little bits and pieces of beliefs and remnants. That is all. Little twinges of old habits. But as soon as you acknowledge that it is something worth exploring . . . no more habit.

So in the case where the guy does come up and he's got a gun, and his initial intention was to rob you or whatever, you will experience the fear and say, "Okay, I can just view this as a positive thing." That will flip us into the dimension where we co-create—

It can happen that way. It can also allow you to not come anywhere near that individual, and vice versa.

Well, I'm saying he's two feet in front of me—

But understand: you are missing the point. Not that it cannot switch in the middle of the idea. But generally speaking, you do not usually need to have that particular type of scenario to know that if you create your reality in a certain vibration, you will never meet that robber at all. He will take one street, and you will take another. You will not have to come down to the idea of the confrontation at all . . . although that may be one way individuals may find an exciting way to come to terms with what they believe in the moment. It is certainly valid if they create it, and it has happened.

Well, it sounds like what you're saying is that in the case of my going down a street other than the one he goes down, I've already dealt with my fears.

Yes, that is the point. If you are using the situation to allow the fear to be there in order to deal with it, then yes, you can transform the situation right in the middle. Therefore recognize that if that is what you are willing to do, then the individual you have attracted is someone willing to change with you. And so in a sense it has already been changed.

The Facilitators

April, 1987: *(With Bashar's facilitation the following was channeled through Darryl, later being identified as "The Facilitators" from the Zeta Reticulum.)*

The fear within you can be a tangible thing at times. We extend in whatever way you will perceive it our thanks for allowing us to evoke this fear from you. For in evoking this fear, you give yourselves the opportunity to experience that which you have locked within yourselves, that which creates a vibration which is not conducive to our interaction with you in an easy manner. We thank you for allowing us to unlock this fear from you. For the temporary time you feel this fear, there will be a greater time of joy in your futures.

We are *The Facilitators*, and we thank you for allowing us the opportunity to function in this modality with you. We are your friends. You may not know us well yet, but you are beginning to. It is true that you have the capability —as do all beings within creation— of recognizing your own godhood. We choose to recognize our godhood in our own way—collectively, and you choose to recognize your godhood in your own way—individually. Not that we are not individuals; not that you are not a collective, but we are mirror expressions in many ways of the things that are feared within each other—or have been feared until now.

In allowing us to participate in the release of your fear, you give us the opportunity to give to all things past, within our civilization, and all the ideas of the fears of our own individuality that we have faced. You give us the opportunity to realize how that fear can be expressed in the individuals you are. As you look into our eyes, you will recognize only the mirror of your own soul and the potential of your own godhood. There is nothing in this to fear. But we thank you for allowing yourselves to feel that fear— even temporarily. For as you feel it, you will own it, and as you own it, you will transform it. For you have been told by many beings in various ways that you cannot transform what you do not own.

In realizing the mirrors of your own souls that you see in our eyes, allow yourselves the opportunity to accept and acknowledge your willingness to own the very idea, the very core, the vibration, that you call fear. Recognize it as those things you have shunted from yourselves in the many years you have lived on your planet, and for the various years and centuries we have been observing you.

We thank you for your release; we thank you for your blending. We thank you for your agreements above and beyond all that allow us to participate in the modality we are used to. We thank you for allowing us to be part of the exploration and the awakening of your world. We thank you for allowing us to help lift your eyelids to a new dawn and a new day. We thank you for allowing that new dawn and that new day to be something in which we will also participate with many other worlds—in our own good timing.

We thank you for allowing us to present to you the calling card of membership within The Association of Worlds. You will find it an exhilarating experience, we guarantee you. Recognize that all you may be passing through now, what you call fear, is a passing thing—truly a passing thing. Surely it will become the stuff of your legends; surely it will be something you will not be able to fathom as having been able to experience—in a very short time on your world. It will be the stuff of nightmares, and it will be as if you have truly awakened from a dream—and into another dream you prefer to dream.

We thank you for allowing us to be the windows of the eyes into your own souls, for you are only looking into that which is your own godhood, your own potential. We thank you for allowing us to open your eyes as widely. We meet upon the plane of understanding.

The Zeta Mirror

December, 1988: *Bashar, I recently had a real interesting meditation, where I found myself apparently hovering over a planet—*

All right. Describe; define.

The people looked similar to Essassanians, but I got the feeling they were not. They were a much paler white, although about Essassanian size. But they were sickly. Something was happening to the planet. It was being destroyed and they were having to leave, or something of that nature. And it was very intense for me, because I felt very much like it was my people, or I had been there, and my heart was aching.

All right, let us say this: more than the idea that they are your people, you have very strongly tapped into certain things that are happening on your planet, certain reasons for why these things are going on. You are very tuned into the transformation that is taking place; you know the part those people are playing in interacting with your society. To some degree what you are perceiving is the Zeta society. You are perceiving, from your point of view, a sickliness—because the idea is that they do, in fact, require something from your civilization, even as your civilization needs something from theirs.

The blending that is going on is going on for many reasons, but one of the most important ones is that in very many ways you do need each other to be what you are becoming. You see, they represent one side, the unified mind, which you do not understand, and you represent the other side, the individual conviction, which *they* do not understand.

They have something like a hive mentality, wherein all the bodies are representations of a unified linked mind. They are more of a mass mind, something many of you fear greatly. You are far more individualistic, which is something *they* fear greatly. The sickliness is because they know that to some degree they are dying without you. And that is why the interaction is going on. From their point of view —were you to look at it the other way— you might see your planet as harboring the same kind of sickliness.

Does this mean this type of interaction will continue?

It will continue. And there will be more blending, as we perceive that idea. More and more information will come out, making it that much more easy for more blending to take place, until you allow yourselves to become whole within your own beings. And then you can allow each other to be reflections of the wholeness that you have become.

So in a sense they're mirroring us?

Oh, yes! They are polar to you, but they are mirroring you. It is very profound—all these different levels on which your first official encounter with extraterrestrial consciousness is taking place.

For you, then, I will simply suggest pleasant dreams, for you are being of assistance in the dream level in ways that you may not yet be aware of, but which you may become aware of very strongly within the next three years.

Thank you, Bashar.

Thank you very much for being the teacher that you have chosen to be.

The Legacy

Bashar, you say you're Darryl's future self—

'Tis one way of looking at it, yes.

But it seems like you would be a definition in Darryl's consciousness of his higher self. And then you, as Bashar, are created as Darryl's symbols.

In many ways that is so. As we have said, the reality that your world has always called real —the physical reality— is a particular vibratory wave length. The vibratory wave length that your reality has always considered to be unreal is actually the level we exist in. The level of dream, the level of etheric energy, is our solid reality. Therefore we are very intertwined with your imagination, your archetypal energy.

You therefore have already unveiled a portion of the legacy. We are very much representative of your archetypal stream of consciousness. Now, that does not mean we do not have our own existence. It is only that your society is beginning to truly understand that what for you has been a fantasy realm is our real substantial dimension of existence. Now you are accelerating to meet that dimension of existence, where you will in a sense become someone else's dream, someone else's fantasy to their reality, respectively.

Yes, I am concocted out of all the ideas of the symbology of the channel's mind. That is how you experience me in your world. At the same time I have my own existence. Although it doesn't exactly parallel the way it happens for you, in very many ways

I could say that I know you and your civilization are concocted out of *my* symbology.

* * *

And now let us express the idea to you that we have termed, "The Legacy." Listen to us with all the different types of ears you have. Take us on one level literally, and yet take us not literally at all. For we are now entering a true phase of the construction of dream time.

As we have mentioned before, the understanding is that you exist on an energy level, just as we do. All things are made of the same energy, but there are different frequencies. Our frequency of reality to you is the idea of dream reality, etheric reality. Many individuals on your planet have referred to extraterrestrial consciousness as etherean consciousness. This is to some degree quite accurate. It is why it is basically easier for us to communicate with you in this manner than it is to use your physiological radio devices. For we operate on that frequency not at all!

Biological senders and receivers are far more efficient and usable, once they are trained to identify with the energy of love and acceptance. The energy of light links all mentality, as you are linked not only to every member in your own civilization, but to all other civilizations as well—sometimes in very specific ways to play out very specific ideas.

We have been allowed at times to briefly discuss with you some of the notions for some of the interactions taking place on your planet that you have called abductions—which we have chosen to call, as we said, temporary detainments. We have also reminded you that these interactions between your species and the alien species we have referred to as the Zeta Reticuli are all done through absolute agreement, even though on your part many of these agreements may be done unconsciously. And they are only brought to the surface reluctantly through the idea of the release of your fear.

But you are serving each other in many ways. We have briefly discussed the understanding, as many of you yourselves are now beginning to realize, that your species operates on a very highly individualistic level, that their species operates on a very highly developed mass consciousness level. And that to each other you are extremely alien.

Just as much difficulty as you have had understanding the idea of how it is to operate as one consciousness, they have difficulty understanding what it is to operate as a single individual cut off from the whole. And although they do not express it in exactly the same way, in many ways they have just as much fear and uncertainty about you as you do about them.

You are learning to understand each other; and in understanding and blending with each other, you are performing services for each other. You are boosting and supporting each other's society, aiding in each other's transformation. You are giving them what they need; they are giving you what you need—to mature as a species, even as you allow them to also mature as a species.

They have come from an evolution that is completely different from the one you have taken. You are true polarities on many different levels. But now, through these interactions, through these sharings —whether they are understandable on the surface or not— you have begun the true blending in many ways that will allow you both to mature and interact. To become fast friends, side by side in your expansion and exploration of the universe—in many ways you cannot yet understand, but ways you will understand in the time to come.

We have shared with you the arbitrary nomenclature . . . that in various ways we have the existence of our evolution approximately 150 to 300 years beyond you. We have told you that this is an arbitrary nomenclature; and we will now endeavor to define and precisely explain the relative frequency of the time span of your reality and our reality. For there will be a seeming time, a temporal paradox, in what we are about to explain about your connection to us. It has already occurred to some of you; it has not occurred, quite surprisingly, to a lot of you.

Once again, what we are about to say you can take in many ways and on many levels very literally. But understand it is also archetypal energy, the substream consciousness of your realm—of your realm and of their realm, the Zeta Reticuli.

We have told you that we are the representation of your own future selves, and in many ways that is allegorical. And it is also largely quite literal, reincarnationally speaking. It is at the same time a representation of the parallel type of civilization you yourselves will create upon Earth.

But there is one other way that we also mean it, that we have not really shared with you, and that is this: even as we have endeavored to describe our physical reality, we have not brought you fully to the understanding that *we are an exact cross between the idea of your human form and that of the Zeta Reticuli.*

We are the children of the blending; we are the hybrids that you are creating. We are your future selves, and have come back to remind you that there is a marriage going on that gives us reality, that supports us. You are in many ways our fathers and our mothers. And we are your children.

We send you our love across the ages. The idea to understand is that this blending is taking place in your time frame. And that an evolution does occur where there is the population of our world and another dimension by the cross-breeding of the Reticuli and the Earth human. We are that population. And that is why we have remained in that other dimension: so that we would not interfere with the marriage that is taking place, so that we would not interfere with the consummation of that marriage. And we would not interfere with your right to experience our birth from your point of view.

But now, because of the timing, and because of the sharing, we can be allowed at this time, with great joy, to share with you that we greet you as your children. And we thank you for allowing us to reflect back to you the brilliant trust you have placed in us, the brilliant future you have given yourselves and the brilliant present you have bequeathed unto us.

There are many more levels to this idea, and we will share those in time as well. But understand that there is a distinct purpose in the creation of our species by the blending of yours and the Reticuli. To a very large degree you are creating the future you desire.

And do remember one other thing, another thing that many of you sometimes do not stop to realize. In our present time, we are also side by side with your future Earth. And we interact together in joy, in harmony, in love. You are our legacy, as much as we are yours.

Our love to you. We thank you for your blessing. We thank you for your strength! We thank you for your love. And our life. And our joy. We only give you back what you have given us in allowing us to exist as we do.

Infinite Creation dreams you into ecstatic creations of reality—forever and ever.

Session Source Materials

PART I

CHAPTER ONE: *Theology Class*, 17 Nov 87; *TV Interview*, 6 Jan 87; *Foreign Relations*, 12 Nov 87; *Avatar Group*, 11 Dec 87; *Golden Gate*, 15 Jan 87; *Summation III*, 6 Dec 88; *Integrity and Opportunity*, 18 Jun 87; *The Peace Clock*, 3 Dec 87; and *Confict/Association*, 25 Jun 87.

CHAPTER TWO: *Summation I*, 4 Oct 88; *Summation II: God Seeds*, 1 Nov 88; *Feedback*, 23 Jul 87; *TV Interview*, 6 Jan 87; *Essassani*, 9 Jan 87; *Ecstatic Transformation*, 10 Sep 86; *Theology Class II*, 10 May 88; *Friends and Neighbors*, 28 Jan 87; *Turning on the Lights*, 19 Feb 87; *Miracles*, 22 Jan 87; *Yardsticks*, 2 Jul 87; *Energy Gate*, 9 Jul 86; *Foreign Relations*, 12 Nov 87; *Ignition*, 27 Aug 87; and *Autumn*, 1 Oct 87.

CHAPTER THREE: *Harmonic Wave*, 13 Aug 87; and *Convergence*, 4 Jun 87.

CHAPTER FOUR: *TV Interview*, 6 Jan 87; *Autumn*, 1 Oct 87; *Friends and Neighbors*, 28 Jan 87; *Ecstatic Transformation*, 10 Sep 86; *Turning on the Lights*, 19 Feb 87; and *What You Are*, 12 Mar 86.

CHAPTER FIVE: *Jesus Said*, 13 Jan 86; *Overcoming Inertia*, 28 Jan 88; and *Theology Class*, 17 Nov 87.

PART II

CHAPTER SIX: *Made of Ecstasy*, 30 Jan 88; *Pure of Tone*, 14 Mar 87; *TV Interview*, 6 Jan 87; *Essassani*, 9 Jan 87; *Conviction*, 2 Apr 86; *Autumn*, 1 Oct 87; and *Systems of Belief*, 12 Nov 86.

CHAPTER SEVEN: *Synchronicity II*, 18 Jun 86; and *The Limbo State*, 6 Sep 88.

CHAPTER EIGHT: *Welcome to the Fourth Density*, 12 Feb 86; *Essassani*, 9 Jan 87; *Christmas Bells*, 24 Dec 87; *Connections*, 4 Jun 86; *Theology Class*, 17 Nov 87; *Ignition*, 27 Aug 87; *Old Friends and New Friends*, 16 Apr 87; and *Convergence*, 4 Jun 87.

CHAPTER NINE: *Theology Class*, 17 Nov 87; *Theology Class II*, 10 May 88; *Feedback*, 23 Jul 87; *Pure of Tone*, 14 Mar 87; *Golden Gate*, 15 Jan 87; and *Body and Soul*, 24 Sep 87.

CHAPTER TEN: *The Agenda*, 19 Nov 89.

PART III

CHAPTER ELEVEN: *Essassani*, 9 Jan 87; *Theology Class II*, 10 May 88; *Heaven and Hell*, 12 Mar 87; *Ecstatic Transformation*, 10 Sep 86; *Consensus Reality*, 8 Oct 87; *Om Circle*, 4 Jan 87; *Conviction*, 2 Apr 86; *Systems of Belief*, 12 Nov 86; and *Foreign Relations*, 12 Nov 87.

CHAPTER TWELVE: *Connections*, 4 Jun 86; *Orion Light*, 22 Oct 86; *Om Circle*, 4 Jan 87; *Energy Gate*, 9 Jul 86; and *Happy Anniversary*, 17 Sep 86.

CHAPTER THIRTEEN: *Friends and Neighbors*, 28 Jan 87; *Theology Class*, 17 Nov 87; *The Peace Clock*, 3 Dec 87; *Let's Get Sirius*, 19 Nov 87; *Made of Ecstasy*, 30 Jan 88; and *Trust*, 27 Aug 86.

CHAPTER FOURTEEN: *Miracles*, 22 Jan 87; *Conflict/Association*, 25 Jun 87; *What You Are*, 12 Mar 86; *Summation II: God Seeds*, 1 Nov 88; *Convergence*, 4 Jun 87; *Old Friends and New Friends*, 16 Apr 87; *Golden Gate*, 15 Jan 87; *Communication*, 5 Nov 87; *Yardsticks*, 2 Jul 87; and *Summation I*, 4 Oct 88.

CHAPTER FIFTEEN: *The Legacy*, 18 Feb 88; *Feedback*, 23 Jul 87; *Miracles*, 22 Jan 87; *Energy Gate*, 9 Jul 86; *Old Friends and New Friends*, 16 Apr 87; and *Summation III*, 6 Dec 88.

Wishcraft, by Barbara Sher (Ballantine Books: New York), 1979.

SPECIAL NOTE: Suggested for a concise history of our galactic family is a recently published book by Lyssa Royal and Keith Priest: *The Prism of Lyra*, $11.95. In metaphysical bookstores or from: Royal Priest Research, P. O. Box 12626, Scottsdale, AZ 85267-2626.

Glossary of Terms

All That Is: God; the Creator; Infinite Creation. Using the term *All That Is* points out that *nothing* is outside of The Creator, including you.

Association of Worlds, The: This is made up of many different levels of civilizations and dimensionalities, all choosing to interact on levels that are mutually reinforcing in a beneficial and positive way. It is a networking body, a serving body, rather than a government—or even exactly a federation.

Atlantis: An early Earth culture, technologically advanced, covering roughly today's Atlantic Ocean area. When Atlantis sank the last time— about 11,000 years ago—"The Flood" resulted.

Belief systems: A series of ideas, observations or perceptions which you use to give yourself the type of approach to life that has a seeming continuity and cohesion. Along with emotion and thought, belief systems create your artificial construct personality. These create your physical reality and reflect that reality through your physical senses back to your mentality.

Cetaceans: Marine mammals, such as dolphins and whales, who have the same type of consciousness as humans.

Channel: The receiving and relaying of communication from any number of dimensional realities. It can be in verbal or written form; it can be the expression of art or music or anything creative. Also the physical vehicle through which any of this is expressed is a channel. We all channel.

Confusion: Fusing with; co-fusing. Removing yourself from one oriented reality and scanning other possible realities that you could be. It is a natural process of reorienting yourself to the new idea you wish to become.

Density: A relative term referring to the amount of vibrational awareness you have of yourself. *Or:* different frequencies of existence or dimensions of experience. A higher density is a more accelerated and less material frequency.

Fourth density: A higher frequency existence characterized by a more positive consciousness and a greater responsibility for your actions— because you *know* you create your reality. There is a greater desire for expressing unity, peace and unconditional love.

Frequency/vibration: The rate at which matter (energy) vibrates; the rate at which molecules and consciousness vibrate.

Holographic: The nature of the energy of the universe, in the sense that every point in the universe has the potential to contain the totality of the universe. As in cloning, where every cell in the body contains information for a whole body, so can any point of view exist equally everywhere within Creation—and all points of view are relevant and true.

Integration: Creating a unified oneness. Pulling together and blending all the different formerly segregated aspects of your consciousness into one unified whole.

Integrity: Integral; integrated. Blended. One. Whole. Acting with integrity, in a positive attitude, maintains the connection to All That Is.

Legacy: Something valuable handed down from the past/future.

Lemuria: A culture predating and overlapping Atlantis. The continent was located in the Pacific region, and is said to have been populated with a blue-tinged race of people.

Limbo: A floating or coasting, disconnected, seemingly standstill state where you are waiting for things to happen. Viewed more positively, you are accelerated to a point of perfect equilibrium with the rate at which you are creating your reality. A balanced state, with no inertia to overcome, it is your point of power. You are living in the now.

Lyra: A constellation from which came the earliest humanoid race, the descendants of which are the Pleiadians, Orions, Sirians, Earth humans, and others.

Maldek: A nearby planet that destroyed itself a long time ago, leaving behind the asteroid belt in Earth's vicinity. Beings from Maldek mainly migrated to Earth after blowing up their planet.

Orion: A constellation often identified as the hunter. Its ancient energy was very negative and oppressive, but now it is integrating their polarities, just as Earth is doing.

Personality construct: The personality or person you are. Not the essence of you, but an artificial tool or representative of the higher consciousness or oversoul—a tool used for interacting in physical reality.

Pleiadians: Beings from an open star cluster in the constellation Taurus —about 500 light years from Earth. They are the most like Earth humans, being our closest relatives—our brothers, sisters and cousins.

Polarity: The presence or manifestation of two opposite (or contrasting) principles or tendencies. *Or:* The energy that represents the ability or the symbology to recognize positive and negative energies within the physical universe.

Reincarnation: Living and being many lives, many physiological personality constructs in a linear time track.

Second density: The expression in linear terms of the idea of consciousness that does not need to think about itself, but acts from an ingrained instinct.

Self-empowerment: The recognition of the self as All That Is and acting upon that principle. Knowing that you create it all.

Sirius: A member of the constellation Canis Major (Dog Star), 8.7 light years from Earth.

Synchronicity: A representation—through the idea of coincidence and through your conscious perception—of the way linear reality best represents the simultaneousness in manifesting All That Is.

Telepathy/telempathy: Linking or identifying with the electromagnetic pattern of another being, thus sensing and sharing similar thought forms and *seemingly* reading the other's mind. This identifying so closely with another—with empathy—can be more accurately termed tele*m*pathy.

Template: A pattern or blueprint that represents a foundational expression upon which a particular reality derives its existence, and from which it derives its shape.

Tetrahedron: A four-sided solid figure with four triangular faces. It is the simplest possible volumetric idea that can exist in our dimension.

Third density: A frequency existence where you can look back on yourself with a removed point of view. You are in volumetric awareness in this density.

Trust: A mechanism and principle that reflects the expression of your willingness to know that you know what you are.

Unconditional love: The expression of the energy that is the supporting foundation of the reality in which you exist. The vibration that gives rise to the validity of all that has been created within creation.

Zeta Reticuli: Beings from the binary star group in the Reticulum constellation (seen from Earth's southern hemisphere). They average 3-1/2 feet with large craniums and extremely large dark eyes, and are mainly the ones responsible for the "abductions" on this planet.

Index